BRITAIN
REVISITED

BRITAIN
REVISITED

One man's journeys in the steps of the travellers

ANTHONY BURTON

Oxford   New York

OXFORD UNIVERSITY PRESS

1986

Oxford University Press, Walton Street, Oxford OX2 6DP

Oxford New York Toronto
Delhi Bombay Calcutta Madras Karachi
Petaling Jaya Singapore Hong Kong Tokyo
Nairobi Dar es Salaam Cape Town
Melbourne Auckland

and associated companies in
Beirut Berlin Ibadan Nicosia

Oxford is a trade mark of Oxford University Press

British Library Cataloguing in Publication Data
Burton, Anthony
Britain revisited: one man's journeys
in the steps of the travellers.
1. Great Britain – Description and travel – 1971-
I. Title
914.1'04858   DA632
ISBN 0-19-211659-2

Library of Congress Cataloging-in-Publication Data
Burton, Anthony.
Britain revisited.
Bibliography: p.
Includes index.
1. Great Britain – Description and travel – 1971-
2. Travellers – Great Britain.
3. Authors, English – Journeys – Great Britain.
4. Burton, Anthony – Journeys – Great Britain.
I. Title.
DA632.B915 1986   914.1'0485   86-2491
ISBN 0-19-211659-2

Produced for Oxford University Press by
Curtis Garratt Limited, The Old Vicarage, Horton cum Studley, Oxford OX9 1BT
Filmset by SX Composing Ltd
Printed in Hong Kong

To those who shared my travels: Sarah, Mike, John, Penny,
Sheila, Neil and, as always, Pip.

Contents

Introduction

Wilkie Collins, in the introduction to his book, *Rambles Beyond Railways,* spoke for all travel writers when he commended his own work as a friend to accompany others on their journeyings:

> He is neither so bulky nor so distinguished a person as some of the predecessors of his race, who may have sought your attention in years gone by, under the name of "Quarto," and in magnificent clothing of Morocco and Gold. All that I can say for his outside is, that I have made it as neat as I can – having had him properly thumped into wearing his present coat of decent cloth, by the most competent book-tailor I could find. As for his intrinsic claims to your kindness, he has only two that I shall venture to advocate. In the first place he is able to tell you something about a part of your own country which is still too rarely visited and too little known ... You will inquire, can we believe him in all that he says? This brings me at once to his second qualification – he invariably speaks the truth. If he describes scenery to you, it is scenery that he saw and noted on the spot; and if he adds some little sketches of character, I answer for him, on my own responsibility, that they are sketches drawn from the life.

A first glance at this volume will, I hope, convince even the most casual of browsers that it too is a fit and respectable companion for a journey. And, with Wilkie Collins, I can honestly say, with my hand on my heart, that I have tried to tell the truth as I see it. Unlike Collins, however, I have not ventured into 'unknown' lands but have deliberately set out to follow in the footsteps of others. This is not mere idleness on my part, but rather a reflection of my personal view of the British landscape. For me, this landscape has a richness that derives, in good measure, from the many centuries during which man has used, and at times abused, the land. To think of the landscape principally in terms of its long history is not to indulge in some sort of arid, academic exercise, but rather to use the imagination to people it with past generations, each of whom was once as alive as we are, and each of whom left his or her own special mark on the land. To travel along the paths trodden by Defoe or Johnson or any of the other writers who will appear on these pages, is to give each journey a unique historical perspective. It is also to give it something extra – not just an historical context, but a very personal context as well.

In choosing the writers to follow, I obeyed one very simple rule. The original writings had to excite me. I had to feel that stirring in the blood that said – I want to go there, I want to see what they saw, or to see what changes have been wrought over the years. Each journey described in this book has been a journey of love – a homage, if you like, to those who have given a uniquely vivid portrait of Britain at one particular time in the past. I have enjoyed the accounts of each and every writer and, without exception, have had equal pleasure in following them along the routes of their journeys. If this book persuades others to turn back to the originals or, better still, get out to see the land for themselves, then I shall certainly be quite content.

JOHN TAYLOR (1580-1653)

The Working Thames

The Description of the Two Famous Rivers of Thame and Isis 1632

Travels begin from home and, if this journey does not quite begin on my own doorstep, it does at least go past the door. On summer Sundays I will often wander down to the little Anchor pub beside the Thames in Abingdon. Once there, I collect my pint, stroll across the road and lean on the rails to watch the river and its busy traffic of boats. There they go, the pleasure seekers of all ages and all kinds: the day boats put-putting along, the hired cruisers of every shape and size, and lording it over all the big sea-going vessels with more bridges than the *QE2* and enough radar and aerials to communicate with other galaxies. The crews are as different as their boats: one will be all holiday fun, Radio One, and bikinis on the foredeck; the next blue blazer, yachting cap, and cravat straight out of the Royal Yacht Squadron; and between those extremes the ordinary boaters, ordinarily dressed. But all have this in common – they are on the river for pleasure. And that has been true of the river's users for a very long time.

Run an opinion poll up and down the river and ask which book best epitomizes its appeal, and I would wager a fair sum of money that the answer would be Jerome K Jerome's *Three Men in a Boat*. The mere mention of the name produces a kaleidoscope of images: striped blazers at Boulter's Lock, parasols and claret cups in a lazily drifting skiff, the splendour of a steam launch despised by all true rowing men until their arms grow tired and the prospect of a tow appears. It is a book redolent of a specially English, faintly self-mocking sense of humour, though behind that mockery is the assurance of the Englishman living in the heyday of empire who can afford to laugh at himself because he knows deep down that he is only laughing at the foibles that offset his solid, indestructible worth and virtue. Today, when sun sets the water bouncing with light, it is hard not to think of Jerome's beautifully cosy, untroubled world where disaster means little more than wet feet or an unopened can. It is a world viewed in a perpetual hazy glow, like a shampoo advert filmed through gauze.

Jerome was as concerned to tell of the past as he was to speak of the present, but the past, too, has a special Victorian flavour. Here is 'slippery John' deciding not to fight at Runnymede:

> But the heart of King John sinks before the stern faces of the English fighting men, and the arm of King John drops back on to his rein, and he dismounts and takes his seat in the foremost barge. And the Barons follow in, with each mailed hand upon the sword-hilt, and the word is given to let go.
>
> Slowly the heavy, bright-decked barges leave the shore of Runnymede. Slowly against the swift current they work their ponderous way, till, with a low grumble, they grate against the bank of the little island that from this day will bear the name of Magna Charta Island. And King John has stepped upon the shore, and we wait in breathless silence till a great shout cleaves the air and the great cornerstone in England's temple of liberty has, now we know, been firmly laid.

Jerome introduces this little section as 'Historical retrospect, specially inserted for the use of schools'. And it is text-book history; it is also four-star tourist attraction, pomp and circumstance history. It is History of the Nation. It is only, almost accidentally, river history.

John Taylor, in 1655; artist unknown.

Magna Carta could have been signed just as easily at almost any other spot. Yet we still invest the place with a special aura, and set it high in the order of sites of secular worship. It is a shrine to democracy, that seems as appropriate to the memory of a long-dead king, who was never as black as painted – a far more wholesome character than bully-boy Richard, his brother – as it is to that of a more recently deceased democrat, John F Kennedy, whose modern Camelot was a good deal less chivalrous than portrayed. Runnymede may be of national, even international, importance; the historical events conducted here more than seven centuries ago may even have been just as Jerome described. But it is not river history. Yet the river does have its own story, perhaps not as gaudy as that told by Jerome, but a story which I find far more intriguing and appealing.

I cannot remember when I first fell in love with the world of working boats, but it was a very long time ago. It began with the canals and later moved on to those most stately of Thames denizens, the sailing barges. Today, narrow boat and barge are seldom used for anything

but pleasure, and those of us who take a delight in these vessels no doubt invest them with as much spurious glamour as did Jerome K Jerome when describing the world of courtiers and kings. But whatever the life led by those who made their way in these craft, at least we still have the vessels themselves, real and solid before us. Nothing can diminish the pleasure of seeing the ingenuity of shipwrights who produced, in the Thames barge, one of the most economical sailing vessels the world has ever seen. And nothing can stop me dreaming of the days when these vessels traded up the Thames as far as Abingdon and on to Oxford and beyond. It is a world that has gone, that will not return, and one which we can only glimpse in writings of the past. But barge men and lightermen were rarely great men of letters: if they had the education, they lacked the time, and seldom had either. Dry, dull accounts survive of goods sold and cargoes carried and I never expected to get nearer to the heart of the old working river than such semi-official documents. Then I came across the writings of John Taylor, the Waterman Poet.

Taylor was born in Gloucester in 1580, but moved to London to be apprenticed as a waterman, the sixteenth- and seventeenth-century equivalent of a modern cabby. In his day, the river was London's great thoroughfare and, if you wanted to go between the city and Westminster, then you went by river. The watermen and lightermen also moved cargo so that, like a modern main road, the river was full of traffic of all kinds. This was the world Taylor knew and the world he recorded in verse – practical verse mostly, with fact to recount or an argument to express, and something of that character comes across in the introduction to his most important work, his description of a trip down the Thames by rowing boat.

> But ancient Isis current chrystall Spring
> Inspires my braine, and I her praises sing,
> And Tame with Isis joynes his pearly
>   streames,
> Whose combination are my ample
>   theames:
> Though (for the most part) in the tracks I
>   tread,
> Of learned Camden, Speed and
>   Hollinshead,
> And Draytons painfull Polyolbyon,

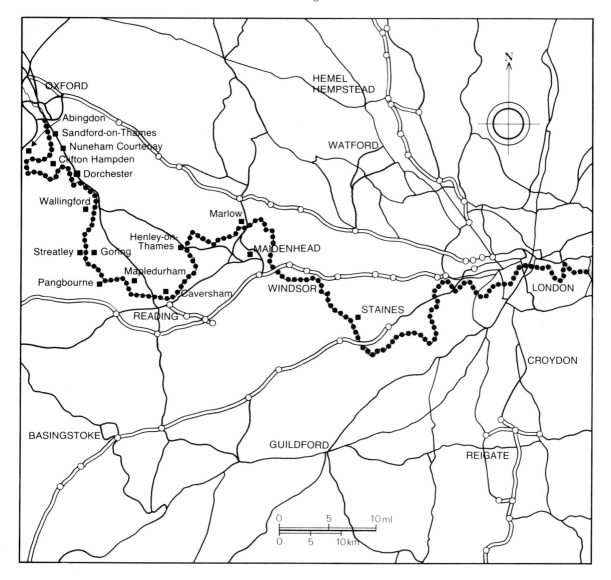

Whose fame shall live, despight oblivion,
these are the guides I follow, with pretence
T'abbreviate and extract their
    Quint-essence;
Nor can it be to them disparagement,
That I came after in the ways they went,
For they of former writers followers be,
I follow them, and some may follow me;
And man to man a Precident is made
In Art or Science, mysterie or Trade,
As they before these Rivers bounds did
    show
Here I come after with my Pen and row.

Three-and-a-half centuries later the precedents have multiplied, but there is still only one way to come to any sort of understanding of the river, and that is to get into a boat and travel, even if it is no longer necessary to use muscle power for propulsion. Or, in the Taylor idiom:

In his wake come I, a modern boater
Not moved by oars, but powered by diesel
    motor.

I was, in fact, to be powered by more than one diesel motor, for the journey was to be done in stages. I felt that I wanted to make the

trip itself have some sort of Taylorian connection. He was both a poet, a man who used his art to tell the river's story, and a practical, working boatman. So I separated off the two sides: for part of the journey I travelled with modern equivalents of the waterway poet, Mike and Sarah Lucas and their Mikron Theatre Company. They travel the rivers and canals in a former working narrow boat, *Tyseley,* and put on shows along the way, shows of which I felt John Taylor would have heartily approved for, like him, they sing the river's praises and condemn its ills. The other part of the journey was made in the company of John Walters, a Senior Navigation Inspector with Thames Water, the body which has responsibility for the non-tidal river above Teddington.

Taylor described the entire river in some detail, beginning very properly with the rain that falls on the hills, though he shows something of the partiality of a Gloucestershire man in describing the source.

> No place in *England* could a treasure
>   keepe,
> *Thames* to maintain, but *Cotewould*
>   (queene of sheepe.)

Having got the river started on its way to the sea, he lists all the tributaries that go to swell the main river, a catalogue by no means lacking in charm.

> From Banbury desirous to adde
>   knowledge
> To zeale, and to be taught in Magdalen
>   College,
> The River Charwell doth to Isis runne,
> And beares her company to Abington,
> Whilst very neare that towne on Barkshire
>   side,
> The River Ock doth into Isis glide;
> These fountaines and fish-breeding
>   Rivolets,
> (The Countries nurses, nourishes, and
>   teats.)
> Attend Dame Isis downe to Dorchester,
> Neare which her lovely Tame doth meet
>   with her.

All this, however, is no more than a prelude to his main theme – the working river, how it is used, and, more importantly as far as he is concerned, how it is abused. It is worth quoting him at length here because he shows the diversity and richness of river life as it was when he was writing in the seventeenth century.

> I have brought Isis and her partner Tame
> With twenty seven helpers losing each
>   their name,

The North Prospect
of Winsor Castle By
Mr Knife

Who spend themselves to make the
   Thames grow great,
Till (below Lee) it lose both name and seat,
Through many Countries as these waters
   passe,
They make the Pastures fructifie in grasse:
Cattell grow fat, and cheese and butter
   cheape
Hey in abundance, Corne by stricke and
   heape,

Beasts breed, and fish increase, fowles
   multiply,
It brings wood, Cole, and Timber
   plenteously:
It beares the lame and weake, makes fat
   the leane,
And keepes whole towns and countries
   sweet and cleane;
Wer't not for Thames (as heavens high
   hand doth blesse it,)

We neither could have fish, or fire to dresse
    it,
The very Brewers would be at fault
And buy their water dearer than their
    mault,
And had they malt and water at desire,
What shift (a Gods name) would they
    make for fire?
There's many a Seaman, many a
    Navigator,
Watermen, fishers, bargemen on this
    water,
Themselves and families beyond compare,
In number more than hundred thousand
    are,
Who doe their Prince and Country often
    serve,
And wer't not for this river might goe
    sterve;
And for the good to England it hath done,
Shall it to spoyle and ruine be let runne?
Shall private persons for their gainfull use,
Ingrosse the water and the land abuse,
Shall that which God and nature gives us
    free,

For use and profit in community,
Be barr'd from men, and damb'd up as in
    Thames,
(A shameless avarice surpassing shames;)
    Much has changed since his day. The river's
old importance as a trading route has ended,
but its role in the land is still essentially the
same, watering the valley, providing home to
fish and fowl. And the abuses have not yet
ended, even if their character has changed.
This account of my river trip is not intended to
be a complete description – a book rather than a
chapter would be needed for that. Instead, I
have tried to pick out the main themes as I saw
them at the time, and looking back through my
notes, it was interesting to see how far I had
been influenced by Taylor and his preoccupa-
tions. I found myself often looking to see what
had gone wrong with the river, and musing
over what might be as well as what is.

But I (from Oxford) down to Stanes will
    slide,
    And tell the rivers wrongs which I espide.
That was Taylor's route and it was to be mine as
well, so it was in Oxford that I began my

journey. One advantage – or disadvantage one might think – of travelling with professionals such as Mikron is that you are left with no choices over what has to be done. They were in Oxford and needed to be in Abingdon for the next performance, and the fact that the rain was hurtling down made no difference whatsoever to that situation. The show must go on, an old theatrical cliché but no less true for being well worn. Our journey began, in fact, on the Oxford Canal and we joined the river at Isis Lock.

I am rather fond of the waterways through Oxford, if only because they provide a corrective to the popular notion of a city entirely populated by dreaming spires, under which one will presumably find equally somnolent dons. The canal takes you past factories and the old coaling wharfs, and even the river tends to slide round the outside of the city, for it was the two rivers, Isis and Cherwell, which formed the first city boundaries. There is a glimpse of grandeur, of Christ Church meadows, cathedral and college, but down at the riverside itself you keep company with a much more impish creation, a lovely little folly of a house, extravagantly gothic with a fine array of figures peering out from niches.

Perhaps the first picturesque, truly romantic spot you reach is Iffley Lock. This is somewhat ironical because, when Taylor came here, it represented the first intrusion of 'modern' technology on to the river since medieval times.

> From Oxford two miles Iffley distant is,
> And there a new turne pike doth stand amisse,
> Another stands at Stanford, below that,
> Weeds, shelves, and shoales all waterless and flat;

These lines can strike a modern reader as enigmatic, and certainly do not seem to suggest any startling innovation. In fact, the 'turne pike' was what we go through now, without

LEFT *A modern weir, but one which gives an impression of what the navigation weirs or flash locks of Taylor's time were like.*

BELOW *One of the last remaining examples of the old style of weir known to Taylor. The vertical 'rimers' stand above the water. Each one can be lifted with its attached paddle to release water over the weir.*

question or worry, a lock. A pound lock to be exact and technical. If there was no lock, how would you ever get down the river? The answer in Taylor's time can be found in the next couplet:

> At Newnham locke there's placed a fishing
> weare,
>
> A gravell hill too high, fearce waters there;

It is time perhaps for a short explanation. A river left to its own devices will find its own way down hill, sometimes forming shallows, sometimes deep pools; cascading over rocks at one point, running sluggishly between its banks at another. This does not make the natural river an ideal transport route. You need to control it, by only allowing it to drop its level at points that you decide upon. If you build a barrier across the river the water will accumu-

late behind it until it reaches the top of the barrier and then it will pour over like a waterfall. So you have your deep water for boating, but how do you get down the giant step? We can see one answer at Iffley: the lock. You build your barrier or weir and the water tumbles over, but you also dig a short canal and in that you have a chamber with watertight gates. Fill the chamber with water, let a boat in, close the gates and let the water out through sluices, and the boat will slowly fall with the water in the chamber to the lower river level. At that point the lower gates can be opened and the journey continues. This is Taylor's turnpike, now a familiar part of river travel but still a device which intrigues the spectator and boater alike. Go to any lock in summer and you are likely to

find a crowd of watchers. For the boater it has a quite special appeal – or at least it does for this boater. It punctuates the journey, breaks it up into manageable chunks, and it also produces a sense of excitement. For the lock temporarily closes the view. You go into a narrow cutting, leaving the wide river behind and, when you emerge at the other end, the scene is not quite that which you left behind. So each lock introduces a sense of anticipation.

This, then, is the lock with which we are all familiar, but which was a novelty in Taylor's day. So what was the system he faced? If you turn away from the modern river lock, you will find the modern river weir. Sometimes the weir will be no more than a series of steps down which the water tumbles; at other times it will

be a single drop where the flow of water is controlled by sluices. Now, you must imagine one of the latter where the water is being held back, and then imagine that water being suddenly released 'in a flash': over the weir it pours, a cascade that joins the upper level of the river to the lower. Such was the navigation weir or flash lock. Boats would ride the flood of water downstream or, when the first power of the flash was abated, be winched upstream against the torrent. When Taylor described locks and weirs, this is what he had in mind. Some were built to improve navigation, but others were placed to trap fish, as at Newnham, or, more commonly, to build up a head of water to drive a mill. It was the latter which earned Taylor's fiercest condemnation. A conflict had developed between those who saw the river as a source of power to serve their land-based interest and those who saw it primarily as a trading route. Taylor was never in any doubt as to where he stood in the controversy:

> Haules Weare doth almost crosse the river all,
> Making the passage straight and very small.
> How can that man be counted a good liver
> That for his private use will stop a river?

The old system has long since ended, and now we have to play detective to hunt out its remains, but the old arguments are not yet over. Who owns the river? Who has what rights? How can the conflicting interests of riverside landlord and river user be resolved? There are no simple answers, and we shall meet examples of conflict on our journey just as Taylor did on his.

At least we can go on our way, spared the hazards of riding the flash of water down over the weirs that dotted the route. The greatest anxiety most Thames travellers experience these days is whether the day will prove fine or miserable. That argument had been resolved from the moment we set off. It was to be misery, misery all the way. The day grew darker, the rain fell ever more insistently, and only the most immediate surroundings made any impact at all. And even here a certain sadness

The Monk's Map of Abingdon, which probably dates from the late sixteenth century and which shows a flash lock to the right of the bridge.

crept in. Sandford boasted the last real working mill on the river. It was a nineteenth-century paper mill, but it stood on a spot where water had powered all kinds of mills, starting with a grain mill established by the Knights Templar in the thirteenth century. This will be a recurring theme of the journey: the ending of the working life of the river. We no longer want to use the Thames, but are prepared to pay a great deal of money for the privilege of looking at it from our windows, so new houses replace the old mill. Taylor hated the mills, for the owners built their weirs to hold back the water and held back the watermen who traded on the river at the same time. But would he have been any happier with the new generation of riverside dwellers who make no impediment to navigation but who add nothing to the river either? They bring no trade, no work, nothing it seems but a rash of notices: no mooring, no landing, no fishing, this is mine, keep off! Perhaps it was a feeling compounded by the gloom of the weather, but there was a sense of loss, of forlornness at the thought that the last reminders of the old Thames, the working Thames, were sliding inexorably away.

Bits of the past still do, however, slip through into the present. Nuneham Park reaches down to the river's edge and up on the hill you can catch a glimpse of Carfax conduit, an elaborate stone monument that once covered the water system that gushed forth to serve the citizens of Oxford. That is a prelude to Abingdon and I do not think it is either resident's pride or enthusiasm brought on by the knowledge that it represented the end of the day and an opportunity in Robert Benchley's immortal lines to slip out of wet clothes and into a dry martini, that leads me to declare that no town presents a more interesting or attractive face to the river than this. You pass through the lock and travel on – one bank bare and unoccupied, for the meadows are liable to flood, the other marking the site of the ancient abbey. And it is the old town that calls for your attention: the tall spire of St Helen's Church, the squat, solid, yet never grim, face of the old gaol, now a leisure centre, and the ancient town bridge. It all works together, all harmonizes, and the best is still to come. Before the bridge, the town had kept its distance; beyond, it edges cautiously up to the bank, dips in a tentative toe and then deciding

that all is well turns its happiest face to the water. St Helen's Wharf is, for me, an almost perfect river frontage. The slipway acknowledges a connection between town and waterway; the old almshouses and the Anchor pub seem all of a piece and smile benignly out over the water. Even the incessant rain did not diminish the appeal. The very worst thing that could happen to Abingdon would be for someone in authority to recognize what a gem the riverside is. For then, they might want to 'improve' it, make people aware of it, open it out. The old sense of a working wharf which still lingers here would be lost; the atmosphere of an old boatman's pub that still pervades the Anchor would be gone. For you cannot manufacture the elements that meet and cohere at the wharf, only accept them for what they are and give thanks.

Moving on after the rain was entering a different world. No-one else had ventured out into the deluge, but a bright, sunny morning was sure to bring crowds of boats on to the river. But not yet: the early morning was all ours, as we cautiously edged away from the wharf, cautiously because the river here is not altogether free of the hazards recorded by Taylor:

At Abington the shoales are worse and worse

That Swift ditch seeme to be the better course.

Now that is the sort of thing that brings me up short. Swift ditch – an alternative channel, a mill stream, or what? You have to look not on the ground but at old maps and documents to find that Swift ditch marks the original line of the river across the water meadows, but is now no more than a narrow land drain. It is a happy reminder that the river is not a dead thing, but alive, eating new paths for itself, constantly changing, forming new lines. Change is an essential part of its nature and of its fascination.

If you are travelling the river in summer, then the early morning is by far the best part of the day. The light is still soft and the calm water has a slight haziness like the scarcely discernible fluffiness on a young girl's arm. There is a wonderful stillness about the river which it seems almost indecent to break, so that even an engine as gentle as *Tyseley*'s is a noisy intrusion. We divide the river: ahead is the stretched silk of water; behind a spangled, busy wake. It is a pleasure, however, for which you have to pay. Locks on the Thames are manned by lock keepers and operated by electricity. A lever is pulled, paddles are raised and lowered, lock gates opened and closed. That is during working hours. The early morning does not qualify as working hours and the locks become do-it-yourself. So when we reached the first lock, everything had to be done manually, and it is decidedly hard work. But at least the locks are well maintained and, once through, you can be reasonably certain that the river will be well dredged and the navigation channel clearly marked. It is very different from Taylor's day, when there was a navigation weir at this same place. So it is worth taking a moment to look at the present weir and lock. There is a drop of 8 feet (2.4 metres) here. It seems unlikely that it was quite so fierce in his day, but just imagine the effect of the water held back behind such a weir and then released in a sudden flow, down which you and boat had to pass. And the prospect was none too good for travel once you were down:

> Then Sutton locks are great impediments,
> The waters fall with such great violence,
> Thence downe to Cullom, streame runs
>   quicke and quicker,
> Yet we rub'd twice a ground for want of
>   liquor.

Things did not get very much better as he went on:

> At Clifton there are rocks, and sands, and
>   flats,
> Which made us wade, and wet like
>   drowned rats.

Life is easier now, and Clifton simply registers as a place of delights. The bridge is Victorian but manages its fake medievalism with a great deal of success, not surprising as it is the work of one of the masters of the gothic, Gilbert Scott. There is a scattering of thatched cottages, a tiny church on a cliff and one of the most famous pubs on the river, the Barley Mow. It is thatched, so low beamed as to threaten concussion, was there in Taylor's day, and was dubbed by Jerome K Jerome 'a fairy tale inn'. He stopped there for a good long while to work on his book. A later writer on the Thames, Eric de Maré, described stopping here on a hot summer evening to enjoy 'a long and wonderful drink recommended by the host – "sparkling ice-cold cider laced with gin".' It sounds lethal. All has changed: the charm has gone, though not, one hopes, irretrievably. The Barley Mow itself is still there, but surrounded by caravans which seem almost to obliterate it from view. The caravan park reminds me of a scientific theory first expounded by a gentleman named Heisenberg which said, in effect, that measurements can never be wholly accurate for the act of measuring changes the thing measured. So the caravan enables people to get to lovely countryside, but changes the countryside to make it lovely no longer. So I turned from that view to the other bank, which is dominated by a very grand house which proclaims its presence through rows of statues peering out over the river. Once a stately home, it now belongs to the Gas Board, presumably where the Gas Board board gas.

The Thames is a great river for viewing the past; not surprising really, given its importance as one of the country's premier trading routes; and there are few places on the river which better repay a little historical meandering than the area around Dorchester. And it has a special place in the story of the river itself:

> There Tame and Isis doth embrace and
>   kisse,
> Both joyn'd in one, cal'd Tame or Tame
>   Isis.

And Tame Isis became Thames. On the Berkshire side, the view is dominated by the twin Sinodun hills with their crown of trees, the Wittenham clumps. Giant earthworks ring the hilltop and mark the Iron Age fort while, in the fields on the Oxfordshire side, you can just make out the rampart and ditches of Dyke Hills, a promontory fort. The promontory itself is formed by the rivers: the Thames bends through ninety degrees and the Thame comes in from the north to join it, forming a watery barrier for three sides of the fort, with the ramparts completing the square. The Romans came and settled here, and after them came the ecclesiastics who built the great abbey church. It is a place to linger, but theatre companies with performances to give have little time for sightseeing. It was a working day for Mikron and, as the morning sun rose, so more and more craft began to appear on the water. Locks

'There Tame and Isis doth embrace and kisse.' Cruising past the Sinodun Hills near the confluence of the two rivers.

which we had had to ourselves now became crowded; delays became inevitable. The river was beginning to bustle, but with an activity very different from that of Taylor's day. This is where his world and ours diverge.

Taylor lived at a time when the Thames was a major commercial thoroughfare. The Speaker of the House of Commons in 1655 described rivers as 'Veins in the National Body which convey the Blood into all the Parts, whereby the whole is nourished and made useful'. The Thames is still a commercial highway but not in quite the same sense, for the cargo is now

human, families out for boating holidays. This is a genuinely busy commercial trade. It provides employment for boat builders and repairers, for hire companies with their office staff, engineers and cleaners; it brings trade to shops, pubs, and restaurants along the river bank. And, as we shall be seeing later, there is a work force employed to make sure the river remains navigable and properly maintained for the holidaymakers to enjoy. The river must, in fact, be just about as busy as it has ever been. This is the trade that has quite taken over from the old carrying days. The balance has shifted. Once the waterway provided the most efficient way of moving goods – all you needed was a barge and a few hearty men on the towrope.

In common reason, all men must agree
That if the river were made cleane and free,
One Barge, with eight poores and
   industrious paines,
Would carry more than forty carts or
   waines,
And every waine to draw them horses five,
And each two men or boyes to guide or
   drive,
Charge of an hundred horse and 8o men
With eight mens labour would be served
   then,
Thus men would be employed, and horse
   preserv'd,
And all the Countrey at cheape rates be
   serv'd.

Then came the railways and, more importantly, the motor lorry. Door to door service is now the order of the day.

Is there nothing that could be carried by river, for Taylor's old argument still applies in its essential? You need far less fuel to move a boat on the water than you do to move a truck on the road or even a train on the rails. The rivers of Europe are still busy with cargo, and money is being spent on major, and often dramatic, improvements in navigation. Not so very long ago, the gravel workings you can see all down the Thames provided cargo, and anyone who has ever driven behind a heavily laden gravel truck grinding up a long hill will probably wish the stuff was still moved by water. But that trade too has ended, and truth to tell, it is hard to imagine gravel barges queueing up with the holiday boats at locks in the summer. Schedules for cargo boats would be as difficult to keep as those for floating theatre companies. So, it is the world of pleasure boats and marinas that we shall be looking at, our working realities, just as the barge and the watermill were the main features in Taylor's landscape.

The river's wrongs of today have a special character which derives less from the river environment and more from the river's users. Tastes change, but I do find many of the present generation of hire boats to be screamingly ugly, simply because they are not being designed as boats at all: they are designed to satisfy first-time hirers who want reassurance. So you have a squared-off object like a floating caravan to provide maximum space, a driving wheel at the front just like the family car and all mod cons. It is literally home from home, even if it is afloat. One result is that the idea of the river as being essentially different from a road gets lost, and the old habits are carried over. The motorist waiting impatiently in a traffic jam simply becomes the boater fuming at the lock. Finally, he gets into the lock and, when he is released again, charges off at full speed to the next. There he has to wait while his slower brethren catch up and you can see the anger and frustration in his face. Families snap at one another, tempers rise, and you wonder what on earth they can be enjoying on such a trip. Happily, such behaviour still only affects a minority, but it is a very obtrusive, clamorous minority. One solution would be to make the locks far bigger, but then you would lose a vital element of the river's character – the charm of its rich diversity. For me, the whole point of a river holiday is to leave the stressful, ulcer-forming habits of a working life behind for a while, to slow down, relax, give myself time to see the world. After all, if you do want to get from Oxford to London in a hurry, the river is scarcely the ideal route to choose.

I am pleased to say that there seems to be a movement back towards sanity. Camping skiffs are making a comeback: three men (and the dog) can again hire a boat and row up river. Individuals are doing their bit to restore graciousness. Peter Freebody restores wooden boats of all kinds, from sleek slipper launches to a magnificent tender for a J-class yacht – and he must be the only boat owner on the river with a Chinese junk. Swan Cruisers are introducing electric boats for daytrippers – no noise, no pollution, what a splendid notion – and they have added their own touch of daftness. They run a trip boat decked out to look like a Mississippi steamer. It has paddle wheels and two tall chimneys that have to be taken down for bridges. It is absurd but what a dull, dreary place the world would be without absurdity. So there is hope yet.

What are the features that appeal most to the Thames lover? Often they are scarcely definable, accidental meetings where the elements combine to produce a truly memorable effect. During the second part of my journey, the launch was nosed into the bank, the engine switched off, and we were alone on

agrees as to what they are. They are unlikely to include the one attraction over which Taylor enthused at some length, a spa near Wallingford.

> A Bath, a Spring, a Fountaine, or a Rill,
> That issues from the bowels of a hill,
> A hill it may be tearm'd or demie
>   mountaine,
> From out whose entralls springs this
>   new-found fountaine
> Whose waters (cleare as Chrystall, sweet
>   as hony,)
> Cures all diseases (except want of mony,)
> It helps the Palsey, Cramp, or Apoplexie,
> Scab, scurfe, or scald, or dropsie if it
>   vex yee,
> The Plurisie, the Lethargie, Strangury,
> It cures the Cataracke, and the Stone
>   assure yee;
> The head-ach, Megrim, Canker, or the
>   Mumps,
> Mange, Murrians, Meazles, Melancholy
>   dumps.

He adds as an afterthought that it can also cure a broken head, and offers this advice to sceptics:

> If any man imagine I doe lie,
> Let him go thither, breake his pate and
>   trie.

No one travelling downstream from Wallingford could be unaware of the steadily nearing range of the Chiltern hills which threaten to block the way ahead. Then the gap appears, the break that allows the river through and beyond that gap sit the twin towns of Goring and Streatley, one on each bank, joined by a great complex of weirs. It was here in 1634 that the river was the scene of a tragedy. A passenger boat with about sixty men, women and children on board went down the flash lock, but the force of water was too great, the boat overturned, and all were drowned. This was just two years after Taylor had sounded his warning of their dangers.

The area around Pangbourne has a special appeal, for the road joins the river and brings with it a row of fantastical houses, turretted, parapetted and verandahed in a style strongly reminiscent of the house lived in by Charles Addams' strange cartoon family. Not far beyond that is the very last of the Thames water mills, and even that is worked principally as a

a river quite devoid of other boats. The sun was low behind a tree which filtered its rays so that small dancing patches of light patterned the water and, through these, a family of swans made their majestic way. I was going to reach for my camera but decided against it. There are things you simply cannot record, that are better left to memory. These are the best of the river moments and often they seem to involve the wildlife of the river – a grebe making its solitary way, with its slightly comical head wagging, and then vanishing like a torpedo below the water. There are giant flocks of Canada geese that will never see Canada again, for they have settled down very nicely as a major immigrant community. You cannot plan memorable moments, though there are the major river attractions to anticipate, even if not everyone

museum rather than as a commercial grain mill. All those mills listed by Taylor, all those weirs that blocked navigation have now gone, leaving this lone survivor with its waterwheel still turning. Once the watermill was a part of everyday life; now it is a thing of romance. The functional has become the picturesque. And certainly there are few more picturesque spots than Mapledurham with gothic church, alms-houses, and grand Mapledurham House. Taylor says nothing about such places, but then 'old' for him usually meant ramshackle, and the picturesque cottage was probably his brand new, modern development.

You need to make the most of Mapledurham, for Reading lurks round the corner. It is not that

The Olde Leathern Bottle at Goring. The figure on the roof is not an inebriated customer, but the pub sign.

which I regard as an unwarranted slur on a harmless sweet. And who occupies this edifice? Thames Water, the body responsible for the river. I feel that, as a conservation body, they could make a good start by demolishing their own offices. It was here that we turned off the Thames into the Kennet and I left *Tyseley*, the theatre company, and summer, to resume my journey in winter, travelling with the river professionals.

Thames Water look after all the non-tidal river; below Teddington they hand over to the Port of London Authority. Up river they may be, but there is a distinctly nautical air about the personnel; navy blue uniforms, white peaked caps, and a great profusion of whiskers. Many of the lock keepers and inspectors have a naval background, either Royal or Merchant. The proportion used to be higher but, these days, applicants for lock-keeping jobs are as likely to be bank managers as ex-petty officers. You can see why. You get a lovely spot to live, an open-air life, and a pace that is very different from that of the more hectic world of commerce. If the fountain pen ever dries up, I can think of worse ways of earning a living. The inspector's life is superficially even more appealing for you normally only see him when he is out on the river, chugging along in a rather handsome launch. But a glance at the files on the desks at headquarters suggested that there were other less attractive aspects of the job. I was, however, to see only the best of it – the river journey, carried out in style.

The winter river is quite different from the summer river; even the water takes on a quite different character. Summer memories are of lightness and sparkle – memory being notoriously selective, the rain is erased from the scene. In winter, the river has a dark, almost oily sheen to it but the real difference is in the traffic, or rather the lack of it. The hire fleets are being checked out and overhauled and only the occasional private boat is seen on the move. There are, however, rather more working boats to be seen, for winter is the season for river repairs as well as boat repairs. Locks need regular maintenance and often quite major

Reading is an unpleasant place, but it has managed to present its worst face to the river. Modern blocks loom over the bridge, buildings of no discernible architectural merit, though at least the latest addition between the bridge and Caversham lock has style. But those other monsters are just appalling; one, a great striped block is known locally as the liquorice allsort,

PREVIOUS PAGE *The approach to Sonning lock.*

overhauls, including replacement of the massive timber gates. And they need cleaning. Algae build up on the walls and have to be removed. We met a cleaning gang, working with divers, who were trying out a new bio-degradable detergent. The old cleansing fluid had been caustic soda, which did not do a great deal for the local fish population. The new wonder fluid would, it was said, disintegrate into a harmless substance which actually made quite a good fish food. The man in charge was very enthusiastic, a dedicated conservationist who, in his spare time, dived for Greenpeace, testing outflow from nuclear power plants. If you want to know why there are no longer Morecambe Bay shrimps in Morecambe Bay, ask Greenpeace. Don't bother asking the Government. They won't tell you, and they are doing their level best to make sure no-one else tells you, for this diver had already been arrested twice and had his diving gear confiscated each time. But let us get back to the river.

One of the attractions of a lock keeper's life would seem to be the winter when there is nothing to do. That is not quite the case. You soon learn that the river is something more than a broad highway for boats. It is the great drain for all the surrounding lands and for all those tributary streams and rivers assiduously listed by Taylor. I had never before, I think, been really conscious of the complexity of the Thames weirs. They are the river's regulators, controlling the flow and the water levels, and what an immense variety of mechanisms there are. There are the straightforward 'flight-of-steps' variety we all know, over which the water tumbles uncontrolled; but there are also many types of sluices which can be opened and closed. There are the modern ones operated by electricity, and other splendidly Heath-Robinson affairs. I particularly enjoyed the workings of one set with vertically lifting paddles – a buck is the proper name for this type of weir. A railed track runs over the top of the weir and on this is a carriage which is positioned over the paddle to be lifted. The paddle is hooked on and, with much grunting from lock keeper and much groaning from winch, slowly raised up. And as it rises so the

water roars. If you ever doubted the sheer force of the water held back by the weirs then this would dispel your doubts. One lock even took me right back to Taylor's day; from one of the backwaters I saw the old style of paddles and rimers that were used to control the navigation weirs, and lurking in the bushes above the lock was the old winch that was used to haul vessels up against the flow. All those weirs I had gone past without a thought, and now they were revealed as interesting, complex, and far more vital to the control of the river than the locks to which I had previously devoted my attention.

The obvious advantage of travelling with a professional is that you see the river and the river's use in quite a different way. What is the chief of the river's ills today? The speeding boater. There is no legal speed limit as such on the Thames, just a law that says you must not make an excessive wash. Now it is pretty well known that sending a wash crashing into moored boats damages the boats and, if there are no boats there, it will damage the banks. But I thought it probably depended to a large extent on the design of the boat. It doesn't, or at least not very much. I also thought that the main culprits were probably first-time hirers unused to river law. They are not: the prime offenders are private boat owners, who have no excuse. They can be and are being prosecuted. And they have to be, because the damage is considerable and has to be made good. And when it is made good, it needs to be done well. I was very impressed by the care taken by Thames Water to try to keep the appearance of the river as natural as possible by, for example, facing the metal pilings with wood.

The trip was not all technicalities. John Walters is a true river man, with a wide knowledge of all its aspects. He knows the wildlife and the human life of the river: that exotic house at the approach to Hambleden lock was, he can tell you, built out of the profit of W H Smith; Wargrave Manor is now home to the Sultan of Oman. There is a fair bit of cash floating around the Thames Valley as well as water. He can tell you about the farming land and the latest official idiocies – my phrase, I should say, not his. Once the fields bordering the river were rough grass, grazing land for cattle which would wander down to the water's edge and stare at you as you went by, and a

The straggling wooden horse bridge at Marsh Lock.

very pleasant addition to the scene they were too. Now the big farmer applies for an EEC grant so that he can drain the old water meadows, plough them up, and plant grain. And where does the grain go? Back to the EEC for storage, to add to the mountain that is already there. The insecticides and pesticides and the herbicides are sprayed on to the new crops that nobody wants and make their way down with everything else into the poor old river. Idiocy is scarcely the word: lunacy seems more appropriate.

We left Reading on a morning that was so perfectly, crisply wintry, the air so clear and blue, that no-one could dwell for ever on the river's ills. It is rarely the places beside the river that make the deepest impression and, when I think back, and even when I take to notes to jog the memory, it is the river itself and the succession of small pleasures it affords that dominate. The approach to Marsh Lock is superb. You pass a folly of a bridge, the 'ragged arch' of Park Place, and then comes a cottage orné, an extravagantly rustic building designed to grace the grounds of the big house. But best of all is the lock, and it is back in time again. The towpath is carried right across the river on a straggling wooden footbridge above lock and weir, and all the way back again below the lock. Because you have to stop here, you have time to enjoy it, whereas we went straight past Henley taking in not much more than the fact that Brakespear's Brewery, enveloped in steam, was clearly hard at work. John Taylor stopped off for a free snack at Judge Whitlock's. From the following description I imagine people hesitated before asking him back again.

> We landed neare the noble Judges
>   harbour,
> (With stomacks sharpe as razour of a
>   Barber)
> The time was short, we neither tryd nor
>   trifled
> The Cellar and the Buttery both we
>   forrag'd,

Sacke and good Claret drawne from Tierce
  and Punchion,
That serv'd one whole day, and Two
  evenings Nunchion;
Our bread as good as ever baker sifted,
Our wine (rare wine) as ere to mouth was
  lifted,
And in our businesse (though we were all
  hasty)
We did surprise an excellent Venson
  pastry,
We there did save the labour of inviters;
Whole joints of mutton proved us good
  sheepe-biters,
Our beer was bravely boyl'd and strongly
  malted,
Our Pigeon Pie was pepper'd well and
  salted,
Most tender Chickins, Pullet, and a Capon,
We (in our fury) did commit a rape on;
A mighty scarlet Lobster last we seased,
And so with these Acchats our minds were
  eased.

I should dearly like to know a friendly judge in these parts, especially after my last attempt to buy lunch in a local pub. I did not want much, just a pint and a snack, and all I can say is that the local agricultural worker must be remarkably well paid, for the ploughman's lunch was way beyond my means. This time, however, we were not stopping and continued on down the famous regatta reach, past Temple Island with temple duly in place to what must be the most famous mill on the river, Hambleden. It looks magnificent from a distance at the end of a long series of weirs, and it is only when you get closer you see that it has been converted into homes, and I must say it still looks very fine. So too does Medmenham Abbey, a suitably gothicky house with genuine monastic bits built in. It is best known for the antics of Sir Francis Dashwood and his friends of the Hellfire Club. A certain amount of romance is thought to surround their black magic rituals

Hambleden Mill standing above the tumbling weir.

The 'sounding arch' of Brunel's railway bridge at Maidenhead.

and debaucheries, but it seems more likely that they were little more than highly coloured thugs, using power and influence to get away with behaviour that would have landed anyone else in gaol.

Marlow is more appealing with its fine suspension bridge, handsome river frontage and spectacular weir. This is a prelude to what must be the most beautiful stretch of the whole river, Clivedon Reach. Steep wooded hills hem the river, trees reach down to trail their branches in the water, and, even in early December, enough leaves remain to burnish the banks. It was so perfect a peace that even the arrival of our sleek launch seemed an unhappy intrusion. After that, what can you possibly find to match it for pure pleasure? It is not quite the same thing, but I am very fond of the railway bridge at Maidenhead. Not everyone shares my enthusiasm for Victorian engineering, but this is not only shapely, accoustically remark-

able, producing a volume of sound when you shout beneath the arch that would topple the walls of Jericho, but has a good story attached as well. The engineer who designed it was Isambard Kingdom Brunel, and he planned it to stand on two flat brick arches, wider than any brick arch had ever before been built. The sceptics prophesied doom and, when the wooden centring that held it all in place during construction was removed, their prophecies seemed justified. One of the arches shifted. In fact, the contractor had not obeyed the instructions and had to redo the work at his own expense. When completed, the centring was this time kept in place, or so it seemed. The critics had much fun over the fact that Brunel was afraid to move it for he knew the arch would fall. Brunel had even more fun from the

The busy trade of the Thames at Chiswick; painted by Jacob Knyff in the 1670s.

private knowledge that the woodwork had in fact been eased away just a few inches and the arch had stayed firm. Brunel's secret remained until the useless woodwork was all blown away in a gale.

After Maidenhead come the well-publicized charms of Windsor and Eaton, and here at last Taylor ran out of things to complain about, and set out his case for river improvement.

> That's the last fault that I found that
>   merits note
> And downe from thence we merrily did
>   flote,
> Thus have I shew'd Thames wrongs in
>   generall,

> And wish they may be mov'd, or mended
>   all;
> And who can but with pity here behold
> These multitudes of mischiefes manifold?
> Shall Thames be barr'd its course with
>   stops and locks,
> With Mils, and Hils, with gravell beds,
>   and rocks;
> With weares, and weeds, and forced
>   Ilands made,
> To spoile a publicke for a private Trade?

The same arguments are still being pursued, the same principles debated. Which will eventually win on the river – public good or private trade? The answer is no more obvious now than it was then. But, although we have reached the end of Taylor's journey down to Staines, I want to look a little further ahead. For

To make a Thiefe of every Water-man!
And as it were in one consent they joyne,
To trot by land i'th dirt, and save their
  Coyne.
Carroches, Coaches, Jades and Flanders
  Mares,
Doe rob us of our shares, our wares, our
  Fares
Against the ground we stand & knocke
  our heeles,
Whilst all our profit runnes away on
  wheels.

Taylor was ready to accept coaches for the mighty, but prophesied only the most dire circumstances if the trend was left to go unchecked.

For though the King, the Councell, and
  such States,
As are of high Superior rankes, and rates,
For port or pleasure, may their Coaches
  have,
Yet tis not fit that every Whore or Knave,

Journey's end, as the winter sun sets behind the trees.

the Thames is something more than a route for pleasure boats, it is the principal river of England and its waters flow through the capital city. Taylor's working life was spent as a London waterman, ferrying to and fro between the banks. He was inordinately proud of his trade.

And sure all men, of whatsoever degree,
Of Science, Art or Trade or mysterie,
Or occupation, whatsoere they are,
For truth cannot with Watermen compare.

Although the whole of London's river was full of boats, carrying the people of the capital from one side to the other, an unwelcome competitor was already appearing on the scene to threaten the waterman's livelihood:

All sorts of men worke all the means they
  can,

And fullsome Madam and new scurvy
  Squires,
Should jolt the streets in pompe, at their
  desires:
Like great triumphant Tamberlaines, each
  day,
Drawn with the pamper'd Jades of Belgia.
That almost all the streets are choak'd
  out-right,
Where men can hardly passe from morne
  till night.
Whilst Watermen want worke, and are at
  ease
To carie one another, if they please,
Or else sit still, and poorely starve and
  die,
For all their livings on foure Wheeles doe
  fly.

The waterman's trade did die, and the streets of London did become clogged with traffic and remain so today. There has been another unhappy result; London has been divided between north bank, bustle, crowds, activity and south bank, dead and dull. There have been attempts to revive the south bank by building the arts complex of theatres, concert halls, gallery, and cinema, but the style of the new has done little more than deepen the sense of gloom. You cannot help thinking that if only the river were alive, then the banks would come to life again, be as exciting as they were in Taylor's day. You need only look across the channel to Paris to see what a wonderfully uplifting effect a genuinely alive river has on the life of the city.

Trade has died away, too, so that trucks take through the streets goods that could be carried at no inconvenience to anyone on the waters of the Thames. Attempts are made from time to time, goods are carried, but in pathetically small quantities. So the Thames seems only to have a minor role in the life of the city to which it gave birth, and that is sad. The future of the upper Thames, the non-tidal river, seems set. It will, as far as one can see, remain a tremendously popular route with holidaymakers. The problem here seems to be how to cope with the

London's river near Lambeth Palace, with the horse ferry nearing the north bank. After Jan Griffier the Elder, c1710.

*Barges and coasters by the Tower of London;
by Wenceslaus Hollar.*

numbers without destroying the pleasures of the river that they come to enjoy. London's river needs the numbers to bring back life to the heart of the city.

John Taylor wrote of the river's wrongs, and I seem to have joined him in a little complaining myself. He was a special kind of traveller. He travelled the Thames because the river gave him his living. He wrote to persuade, to com-mend a course of action. Our next traveller could not be more different: not a working man, but a rich woman who travelled simply because she wished to do so – though needed to do so might be a more accurate description, for she was a lady who required to satisfy an infinite curiosity about her native land.

CELIA FIENNES (1662-1741)

A Sovereign Remedy for the Vapours

Through England on a Side Saddle in the Time of William and Mary
(edited Emily Griffiths), 1888

'If all persons, both Ladies, much more Gentlemen, would spend some of their tyme in Journeys to visit their native Land, and be curious to inform themselves and make observations of the pleasant prospects, good buildings, different produces and manufactures of each place, with the variety of sports and recreations they are adapt to, would be a souveraign remedy to cure or preserve from these epidemick diseases of vapours, should I add Laziness?'

Celia Fiennes was born in 1662, the daughter of a Colonel in the Parliamentary army, who was himself second son of the Viscount Saye and Sele: born, then, of the aristocracy but wedded to dissent, born too in an age of change when anything, it seemed, was possible. Nor was change limited to the political and military drama of Civil War, for there were even wider social changes to be observed. The first stirrings of the industrial revolution were being felt, merchants and traders were extending the boundaries of the known world. It was a time of excitement and questioning when for anyone of lively intelligence there was a whole world to be seen, wondered at and understood. Celia Fiennes was just such a person. It required a special sort of lady to undertake such great journeys as she made in the years between 1682 and the end of the century – the greatest of all being the 'Journey to Newcastle and Cornwall' in 1698, and it is part of that journey we shall be following. But, although it is the easiest thing imaginable to respond enthusiastically to Celia

Fiennes' own enthusiasm and to share her sense of wonder at the immense changes she found going forward throughout the land, you have to be careful not to fall into the trap of believing that her notion of travel and travel writing was essentially modern, no different from our own. Some of the essential differences will appear once we get on the road – but a glance at Celia Fiennes' own introduction to her journals gives us an idea of her basic attitudes. For a start, she was writing, she claimed, not for the general public but to amuse the family. It is not a claim, I think, to be taken too seriously. It may have been a long time before her journals reached a wider public – I first came across them in the 1888 edition and then turned to Christopher Morris's more accurate versions of 1947 and 1949. After making her one-line disclaimer, she then goes on at length to recommend her journals to a wider readership, and tells that readership just what they were to expect.

Celia Fiennes began travelling for the good of her health but was equally insistent that, as her bodily health improved '...my mind should not appear totally unoccupied...'. That it did not. I cannot think of any traveller more avid for information nor any with so wide a taste. Everything was of interest, everything to be noted and, where possible, to be put to use. She gives her readers a terse little lecture on that point. As the quote at the beginning of this chapter noted, travel should cure laziness, not one would have thought a disease that ever afflicted Miss Fiennes. That was only the start.

'It would also form such an Idea of England, add much to its Glory and Esteem in our minds and cure the evil itch of over valueing foreign parts.' Now that strikes a modern note in the ear. The Great Foreign Travel Bore is a far-from-extinct species, marked by its endless repetition of the delights of the auberge that offered a five-course meal and a bottle of claret for a pound while neglecting to mention the subsequent mild case of food poisoning; which describes the perfect, lonely beach lapped by the blue Mediterranean, but forgets the floating globules of oil that have to be scraped off the feet afterwards. Yes, we all know the evil, and have probably all been guilty of it, and I certainly cannot plead complete innocence. But

Celia Fiennes was looking for something more than just redressing the patriotic balance. Travel should be useful – not just in a vague sort of moral way of improving the mind, but practically useful as well.

Nay the Ladies might have matter not unworthy their observation, soe subject for conversation, within their own compass in each county to which they relate; and thence studdy how to be serviceable to their neighbours specially the poor among whome they dwell, which would spare them the uneasye thoughts how to pass away tedious dayes, and tyme would not be a burthen when not at a card or dice table, and the fashions and manners of foreign parts less minded or desired. But

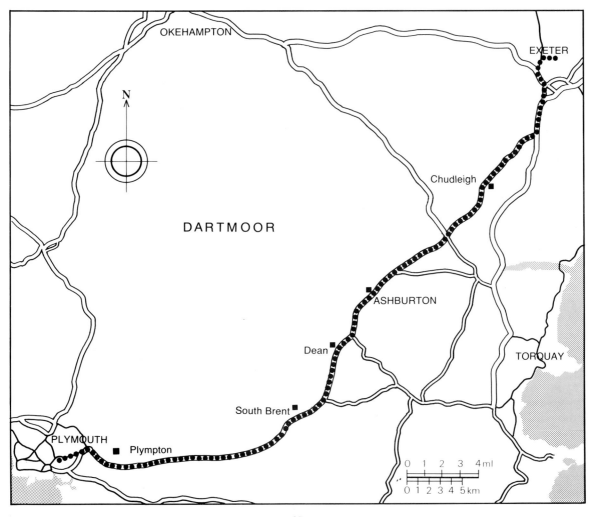

much more requisite is it for Gentlemen in general service of their country at home or abroad, in town or country, especially those that serve in parliament, to know and inform themselves the nature of Land, the Genius of the Inhabitants, so as to promote and improve Manufacture and Trade suitable to each and encourage all projects tending thereto, putting in practice all Laws made for each particular good, maintaining their priviledges, procuring more as requisite; but to their shame it must be own'd many if not most are ignorant of anything but the name of the place for which they serve in parliament; how then can they speake for or promote their Good or redress their Grievances?

Now, that is not at all our notion of what travel is about. It is, of course, a patrician view, a view of a class where men ruled and women had leisure for good works. And it is the view of someone looking at a world full of change, and change for the better, or at least so it seemed at the time. In following part of Celia Fiennes' route, I could not hope to start with the same conditions. I can claim no aristocratic background, have precious little leisure, and live in a time when change seems far from being for the good of humanity as a whole. Hers was an age of optimism: I find ours to be one of acute and growing pessimism. Yet, oddly enough, when I read Celia Fiennes, I feel as close to her as to any of the authors quoted in this book. Like her, I suffer the incurable itch of curiosity and, like her, I am perpetually intrigued by the world of trade and industry, though with one slight difference. Where she is concerned primarily with the industry of her time, my enthusiasm has been largely reserved for that of the past – but that past is, of course, her present. She brings to life that past world that I can only know through old buildings and museum reconstructions. When Celia Fiennes stops along the way to say, in effect, 'that looks interesting', I invariably find myself nodding in agreement. So in my journeys, I was constantly trying to think about what would excite and interest a Celia Fiennes of today, but found that, as often as not, I ended up looking backwards as much as forwards. She noted one current English disease, the constant praise of things foreign at the expense of things native. I,

I fear, am prone to another complaint of our day – a preoccupation with the past. At least that fits in better with the idea of travelling for pleasure as well as for information, for the present can seem almost too gloomy for contemplation.

The section of Celia Fiennes' route that I elected to follow was across Devon from Exeter to Plymouth but, as with all the journeys, I was presented with a problem: how to travel. I am not a horse rider and there would have been something quite ludicrous about attempting to follow an accurate route by trotting down the slow lane of the dual carriageway that joins the two cities. In any case, although I regard Celia Fiennes as an outstanding travel writer, the actual business of travel was of very little interest to her. She wanted to be somewhere, and clearly regarded the process of getting there as a regrettable necessity except in so far as it gave her some hearty exercise. I toyed with the notion of walking or even cycling but eventually decided to concentrate, as she had done, on the places themselves and not the bits between. So I took to the motor car, but at least tried to keep some of the flavour of the past by avoiding the main roads and staying as far as possible on minor roads – the more insignificant the better. I began by driving to Exeter for an exploration in, around, and even under the city.

Approaching a town as a tourist, what do you ask yourself? Is it attractive? Has it got any notable buildings? Are there fine walks and extensive vistas? And, most important of all, where are the old, picturesque bits? Certainly it is the latter which probably comes first into mind for, as you approach the city of Exeter, it is soon seen to be dominated by its cathedral, an obvious starting place for any modern tourist. Celia Fiennes came into the city on the Cullompton road, and here are her first thoughts:

> From thence to Exetter up hills and down as before till one attaines those uppermost ridges of all which discovers the whole valley, then you sometymes goe a mile or two on a Down till the brow of the hill begins in a descent on the other side; this

Map of Exeter by Joseph Cole, 1709. Fields full of tenter frames can be seen in the lower part of the map

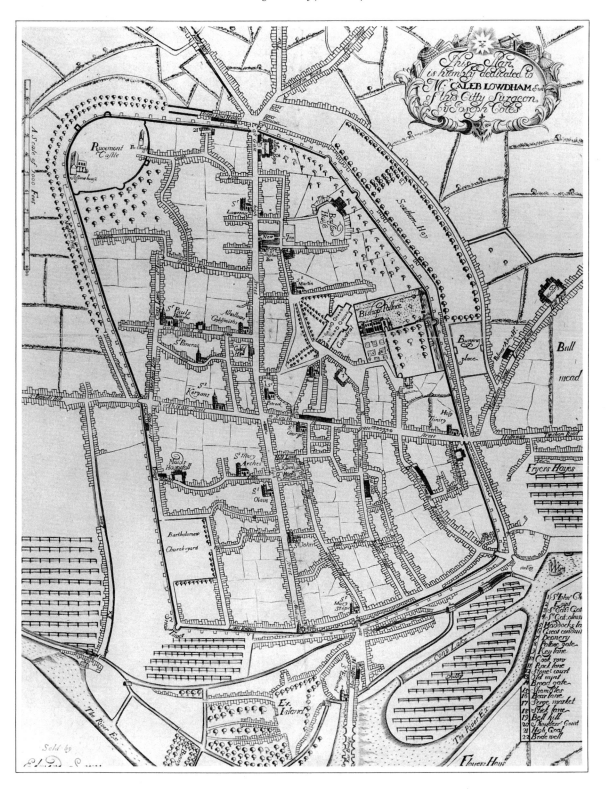

Solidity, strength, and safety: a warehouse entrance on Exeter quay.

Citty appears to view 2 mile distant from one of those heights, and also the River Ex which runs to Topshum where the shipps comes up to the barre; this is 7 mile by water, from which they are attempting to make navigeable to the town which will be of mighty advantage to have shipps come up close to the town to take in their serges, which now they are forced to send to Topshum on horses by land which is about 4 mile by land; they had just agreed with a man that was to accomplish this work for which they were to give 5 or 6000£, who had made a beginning on it.

This was to be the Exeter Canal, which was begun somewhat modestly as a river improvement scheme in 1564 but was of some historic importance, for it was here that the first pound lock, John Taylor's turnpike, was built in Britain. The canal itself was mainly constructed in the 1670s and then greatly improved and enlarged between 1698 and 1701, and this was the work that Celia Fiennes saw. Today, the area of quays and warehouses has become a tourist area, but only because it no longer has a commercial life. It is all part of the backward-

looking, searching out of the picturesque. So, in that sense, it might not seem too surprising to find a traveller making much of it. But in 1698 it was the very latest thing; it was technology on the great march forward. So if you want a true modern equivalent, you have to think of a travel book that begins by extolling the virtues of a new motorway interchange. Nowadays, however, it is a commonplace for writers to decry motorways – but use them. I certainly have reservations about a good deal that is done in the name of improving traffic flow but, as far as the approach to Exeter is concerned, God bless the new! I have awful, and all-too-vivid, memories of pre-motorway summers in Exeter, of the miles and miles of traffic jam at the approach to the dread Exeter bypass, a name that still turns strong motorists pale. Now you drive, somewhat drearily it is true, down the M5, but at least you move – and then turn off down a quite startling cutting between red banks of sandstone that mark the approach to the city centre. Where to start? I began at the area I know best, the quay, dumped the car and began walking.

I first came to Exeter to visit the maritime museum where I spent a happy day chugging backwards and forwards on a venerable steam dredger designed by Isambard Kingdom Brunel. The next visit was back to the museum again, this time to try, somewhat unsuccessfully, to sail an old Scottish fishing boat, so that I now think of Exeter as a port first and everything else second. And that is no bad way to think of the place – even the name comes from the river, from the British *Eisca*, a river full of fish. And, even if this area of the city were not of great historical importance, I would still probably start here simply because I enjoy it so much, and much of that enjoyment comes from a sense of completeness. Everything here is of a piece. It is not simply a matter of the buildings harmonizing with one another but of them belonging very much within their surroundings. The red sandstone of the cutting which provided such a colourful introduction to the city reappears here in the solid blocks of warehouse walls. And solid the blocks certainly are, great lumps of stone that provide just the right sort of assurance to any merchant who might wish to store his goods here at Exeter quay. Elegant these buildings are not, but they are enormously satisfying. It seems incredible now to realize just how recently such buildings were dismissed as simply part of the working world, with no claims to aesthetic appeal whatsoever. The continental 'form to reflect function' school of architecture changed perception for many, but my own appreciation dates back quite precisely to the day when I first looked at Eric de Maré's photographs and J M Richards' text in the book, *The Functional Tradition*. They were all there – bridges, mills, warehouses, and factories, showing a robust force lacking in so much that had previously been thought of as Architecture with a capital A. They were rough moorland to set against an urbane country park. I have always enjoyed moorland. There is a note of grace here as well. The Custom House of 1681 is an elegant structure, but not quite what it was. Celia Fiennes saw quay and Custom House when both were new.

> Just by this key is the Custome house, an open space below with rows of pillars which they lay in goods just as its unladen out of the shipps in case of wet, just by are severall little roomes for Landwaiters, etc., then you ascend up a handsome pair of staires into a large roome full of desks and little partitions for the writers and accountants.

The area where goods were stored has now been filled in, but it is still a customs house, still a reminder that Exeter has a connection to the sea. But no merchant ships arrive here now, no goods for the warehouses; just the buildings remain, and the problem of what to do with an area of undeniable character which no longer seems to have a practical role to play in the life of the city. The obvious answer would seem to be to cash in on that obvious attractiveness and turn the old commercial centre into a new centre where people come to shop, eat, and drink. Yet somehow, Exeter never seems quite to have taken to this area. There is a wonderful pub, wonderful in the sense that it is a fine building with a splendid view, but that actually had to be given away as a sweepstake prize by the *Daily Sketch*. It seems to be pros-

The Exeter Customs House.

The West Prospect of the capital city of Exeter, by Samuel and Nathaniel Buck, 1736.

pering now on a satisfactory mixture of decent food and real ale. And the warehouses, too, are coming back to life with shops and bars plus, I regret to say, an excess of recorded music. That may sound like a typical piece of old fogeyism, but I am prepared to tolerate almost any type of live music. It is the canned variety where the loudspeakers are spaced to ensure total inescapability I find repellant even when I happen to like the music being relayed. But, better that by far, than that the old buildings should decay. And there is the museum. Next to the warehouses is a series of arches behind which is a set of tunnel-like cellars. There the first set of vessels is housed. To see everything in all its glory you must take the little ferry across the water, hauled hand over hand on chains, to the canal basin where the ships ride at the quayside. What a weird mixture it is, everything from Chinese junk and Arab dhow to a steam tug. It is an international collection, gathered

on no easily discernible principle yet each vessel is different from the next and has its own materials, shape, and method of construction. I find it a visual delight, but it is undoubtedly more than a little quirky – and why not? There are quite enough formal, well-regulated museums in the world for those concerned with serious study, with arrangement and order. Here is one for all who delight in diversity.

With so much on offer, why is the whole place not bustling with life? There is a Canal and Quay Development Trust working hard at achieving that end. They have got one absolute gem of a building to work on. It does not look much at first, just another warehouse, somewhat less distinguished than the rest. That is because it has had a fake front tacked on: beyond that is a seventeenth-century building, open as an arcade at ground-floor level. You can still see the brackets, simple blacksmith jobs of bent iron, where shutters could be hung at the end of the day. Just pray like mad that whoever takes on the job of restoration respects

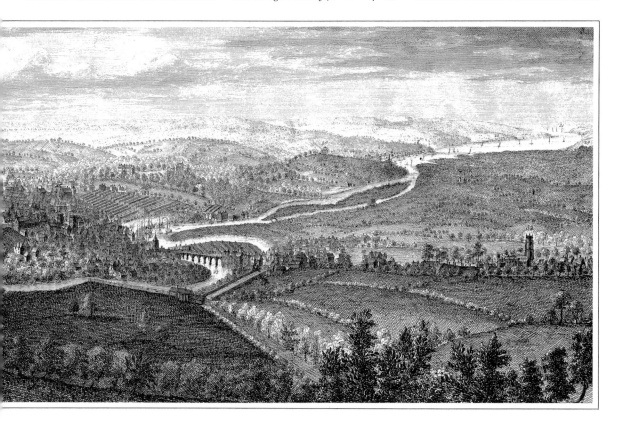

the old place. But why is the Trust having to work so hard? You find the answer soon enough as you walk up towards the city centre. At first, signs are encouraging. A new housing estate shows real effort; wood and brick and slate predominate but, somehow, the architects have contrived to clad everything in dark materials, so that the effect is distinctly gloomy. And by their insistence on having total control, they have left no room for individual expression: they did not want to see the carefully planned, show effect ruined. If I lived there I should be longing to splash about with really garish paint just to spoil the carefully planned good taste. Then, beyond that is the real villain of the piece – Western Way, an inner ring road. It shuts off the quay from the city more completely than ever the old city walls could have done. There are subways, but somehow they are less than appealing, with the perpetual aroma of stale beer and last night's Chinese throwaway. Exeter was bound to suffer from replanning if only because it has already suffered so much during World War 2. The city

had the misfortune to fall within the scope of the Baedeker raids, aimed at those centres most praised in the famous guide books. What a squalid lot we humans can be setting out with the deliberate intention of destroying history and beauty. One result is, of course, that when we do reach the city centre, it is a very different place from the Exeter of 1698.

Here, rejoining our seventeenth-century guide, we might expect that reaching the city and having disposed of the new canal and questions of trade, Celia Fiennes would now have turned to lighter matters. The start is promising. 'Exeter', she declares, 'is a town very well built, the streets are well pitch'd spacious noble streets.' But then we are off again:

> . . . and a vast trade is carryd on; as Norwitch is for coapes callamanco and damaske soe this is for Serges – there is an increadible quantety of them made and sold in the town; their market day is Fryday which supplys with all things like a faire almost; the markets for meate fowle fish garden things and the dairy produce

Sluice gates controlling the flow of water to Coldharbour woollen mill.

takes up 3 whole streetes, besides the large Market house set on stone pillars which runs a great length on which they lay their packs of serges, just by it is another walke within pillars which is for the yarne; the whole town and country is employ'd for at least 20 mile round in spinning, weaveing, dressing, and scouring, fulling and drying of the serges, it turns the most money in a weeke of anything in England, one weeke with another there is 10000 pound paid in ready money, sometymes 15000 pound; the weavers brings in their serges and must have their money which they employ to provide them yarne to goe to work againe.

Having discovered what makes the place tick did little more than whet her curiosity. She wanted to know more – and see more. The system she described now has the charm lent by distance, the interest of antiquity. But even

today, reading her account of oil and grease and cloth soaking in urine, it is very clear that she was no ordinary traveller. It is rather as if one had met a polite, upper-class lady just back from Oxford who, when asked what she saw, replied with great enthusiasm: '...it was a wonderful city! We went straight off to Cowley and spent an enchanting day watching the car assembly line'. Celia Fiennes not only went to see the equivalent of a car assembly plant, but she revelled in it. She described how the weavers first cleaned out their rooms with the cloth from the loom, even though the latter was heavy with oil and grease, which she remarked, '... by the way gives noe pleasing perfume ...'. Then the cloth was soaked in urine to rid it of grease, soaped, and sent to the fulling mill. These mills were about the closest the seventeenth century came to a major industrial unit. Here the cloth was felted by pounding with heavy wooden hammers or stocks powered by a water wheel. She went to such a mill and clearly loved it all.

> The mill does draw out and gather in the serges, its a pretty diversion to see it, a sort of huge notch'd timbers like great teeth, one would thinke it should injure the serges but it does not, the mills draws in with such a great violence that if one stands neere it, and it catch a bitt of your garments it would be ready to draw in the person even in a trice; when they are thus scour'd they drye them in racks strained out, which are as thick set one by another as will permitt the dresser to pass between, and huge large fields occupy'd this way almost all round the town which is to the river side.

These were the tenter fields where the cloth was hung on tenterhooks of proverbial fame. After that the cloth was either sent off to London as white cloth or passed to the dyers. Naturally, she went to see the dyeworks as well and watched the cloth pass through the vats of boiling liquid. It was only then, when she had satisfied herself that she had seen the whole of the manufacturing world of Exeter, that she passed on to what the rest of us might think of as conventional sightseeing.

How I would have loved to have joined Celia Fiennes on a trip to the fulling mill and the dyeworks, but the days when Exeter was a great centre of cloth manufacture have long since passed. The whole west-of-England cloth trade was to go into decline as that of the north grew: it is sometimes difficult to remember that Bradford-on-Avon was an important wool town when Bradford in Yorkshire was an insignificant hamlet. There are traces of the old ways to be found in the town, though they are by no means obvious. A leat or mill stream runs down to the quay by the customs house and, if you walk up the old cobbled path beside it, you come upon the mills. But were they fulling mills? No way of telling now – add a waterwheel to a building and you can put all sorts of things inside, for a wheel can as easily turn millstones as it can work fulling stocks. The ruins of an old wheel can be seen on the first mill, then another building appears which at first looks to be nothing more than a jumble of corrugated iron, but a closer look reveals an older structure. I went inside and there was a waterwheel and enough bits and pieces of machinery to show that, when last used, it was a grain mill. I was not a great deal nearer to Celia Fiennes' world. There was a place called Nosey Parker's which my map showed as the Bishop Blaize pub. That would have been something, for Bishop Blaize was the patron saint of wool combers, but even the name has gone now.

I made my way down to the bridge over the Exe, a less-than-enticing sight with a complex road system which pedestrians thread at their peril, unless they wish to travel the underground routes provided for them. In the middle sit the arches of the old bridge, which Celia Fiennes would have known and which now looks merely an anachronism with no proper role to play among the concrete piers. But, up Fore Street, I finally reached a true bit of the past, Tuckers Hall, home to the Guild of Weavers, Fullers and Shearmen, a body probably founded at some time in the fifteenth century but who are at least known to have acquired this site for their chapel in 1471. It does not look like a building of 1471, though it does at least carry the marks of the trade, shuttles, shears, and teazles used for raising the nap of the cloth, on the iron gateway. The exterior is, in fact, Victorian and not very impressive. So it is easy to pass by this little building without paying much attention. But it has an interior that more than compensates for the dullness outside. Fullers and shearers are part of the city's past, but the guild and the tradition live on. The old chapel was much altered in Elizabethan times when the upper part of the building was converted into a hall which remains today much as it was then. It is a sumptuous place, of rich, dark panelling, stained glass and massive furniture. You could not call it elegant, but it is undoubtedly opulent and proclaims the prosperity of the guild in its heyday. At last, I felt I had got somewhere near to the Exeter of Celia Fiennes' day, but it was really still no more than an image of the trade, not the trade itself. The woollen manufacture has gone from Exeter, but has not quite disappeared from the surrounding area. I decided to make an excursion. I went to Uffculme.

Mechanical ingenuity on display: part of a spinning mule at Coldharbour Mill.

I have to admit that this was something of an indulgence on my part, an excuse to get out on the road riding my own hobbyhorse, for I have been besotted with the remains of the industrial revolution for a very long time, and Coldharbour Mill is a prime example. It is a woollen mill, but not what Celia Fiennes would have seen as a mill for, where she saw mechanization applied to the finishing of cloth, here we have it used for the whole series of processes that turn wool into yarn and use that yarn to make cloth. I think she would have loved it, and I wish she could have joined me on the tour of the mill. She had been impressed by the fulling stocks and their incessant pounding. What would she have made of the mighty steam engine with its complex system of ropes taking the power to every floor of the mill? And would she not have been absolutely enchanted by the spinning mules, making their stately progress backwards and forwards, backwards and forwards with whirring spindles – retreat and the wool is stretched, spindles turn and the fibre is twisted, advance and the yarn is wound on and it is off again for a repeat performance. I can stand watching spinning mules for hours. Different machines for different processes, but each one comprehensible; watch it carefully and you can see what it is doing, just as clearly as you could have understood the fulling mills and the dye vat. They have been making cloth here for nearly two centuries. Before World War 2, they were employing 150 workers; by 1981 it was down to forty, and then it closed, to be brought back to life as a working museum. Some of the old workers are back, and I had an interesting discussion about the relative merits of the wool mills of the west country and those of Yorkshire; not so much a discussion really as him telling me why west country was best and me making out a case for the north. At least I could point out who made his machines. It is a really lovely place this, in every sense. Outside, mellow buildings and the mill stream with ducks and geese; inside the busy movement of old machines. I felt satisfied that, at last, I had given the wool industry its due share of attention, and I too could return to Exeter for some more conventional sightseeing.

This Citty does exceedingly resemble London for, besides these buildings I mention'd for the severall Markets, there is an Exchange full of shops like our Exchanges are, only its but one walke along as was the Exchange at Salisbury House in the Strand; there is also a very large space railed in just by the Cathedrall, with walks round it, which is called the Exchange for Merchants, that constantly meete twice a day just as they do in London; there are 17 Churches in the Citty and 4 in the subburbs; there is some remaines of the Castle walls; there is just at the market place a Guild Hall the entrance of which is a large place set on stone pillars.

Celia Fiennes has at last turned to the Baedekery of touring, and some at least of those features she observed are still to be seen. Traces of the old walls do remain and the Guildhall stands as one of the city's finest buildings. Elsewhere, the scene is notably less attractive. The spaces made by the German bombs have been filled in by a series of dull streets and offices among which we turn to the old to create relief. Behind the medieval Guildhall is the shopping precinct – a name which always leads one to expect the worst and expectations are, alas, seldom unrealized. Here, however, the church of St Pancras has been left, rather sad looking, in the middle. To go inside is to feel that here at least is a building that admirably fulfils its purpose, for a peace descends at the moment the door closes. Ecclesiastical buildings are among the most attractive features of this city. St Nicholas Priory, off Fore Street, was founded in the eleventh century and, though the priory church has gone, the priory itself remains, cool and quiet within its thick stone walls. It has, not surprisingly, changed over the centuries, but nothing that has happened has changed the essential character of a sturdy building offering comfort rather than luxury, definitely plain not gaudy.

Inevitably, at some time, you will end up outside the most prominent building in the city, the cathedral. Celia Fiennes was not unduly impressed:

. . . the Cathedral at Exettor is preserv'd in its outside adornments beyond most I have seen, there remaining more of the fine carv'd worke in stone the figures and nitches full and in proportion, tho' indeed I cannot say it has that great curiosity of work and variety as the great Church at Wells; its a lofty building in the inside the largest pair of organs I have ever seen with fine carving of wood which runs up a great height and made a magnificent appearance; the Quire is very neate but the Bishops seate or throne was exceeding, and very high, and the carving very fine . . . the tower is 167 steps up on which I had a view of the whole town which is generally well built; I saw the Bishops Pallace and Garden; there is a long walke as well as broad shady and very pleasant, which went along by the ditch and banck on which the town wall stands; there is alsoe another long walke within shady trees on the other side of the town, which leads to the grounds where the drying frames are set up for the serges.

I would not argue too much with her verdict. The west front is still the glory of the building, though something should be said of the nave with its wonderful gothic vaulting. It is, by now, not surprising to find that the serges have crept back in, and she is not quite finished with her poking around the working part of the city. Back at the guildhall, another feature caught her attention:

> Behind this building there is a vast Cistern which holds upwards of 600 hodsheads of water which supplyes by pipes the whole Citty, this Cistern is replenish'd from the river which is on purpose turned into a little channell by it self to turn the mill and fills the Engine that casts the water into the truncks which convey it to this Cistern.

This complex system was needed because Exeter, being on a hill, had no instantly available source of water, a problem which had first been dealt with back in Roman times. The cistern has long gone, but the far older system of aqueducts, water channels cut through the rock beneath the city, still exists. At the end of Longbrook Street, just outside the Horse and Groom, is a metal grille let into the pavement and, over 30 feet (9 metres) below that is part of a complex of passages. You can go on a tour starting in Princesshay. For company in this underground exploration I had a party of excited French schoolchildren who may not have understood much of the guide's really very good commentary, but still squealed with delight when they were sent off on their own down the 'children's passage' somewhat low and narrow for us bulky adults. I thoroughly enjoyed seeing this underside view of basements and foundations with traffic as only a distant rumble. It was also a pleasant way to end a city tour, for Exeter is very much a curate's egg, with some very good parts but some horribly dull bits as well.

Celia Fiennes left Exeter and headed southwestwards towards Chudleigh, travelling not on main roads, for there were none, but ' . . . all along in lanes cover'd over with the shelter of the hedges and trees . . .', and, in following her journey, I too tried to keep to the little lanes which, happily, can still be described in much the same terms as she used. First, however, she had to cross an area of marshy land just outside Exeter. This has now been drained, and is home to the new manufacturing world of the district, the industrial estate. I should, I suppose, in the best Fiennes' tradition, have gone to look at the work going on there. Conscientiously, I wrote to the local authority on the subject but, as they said, the new age of microchip technology does not provide very much to look at and enjoy. I drove around the estate, the usual collection of anonymous, all-purpose boxes you can see throughout the county, and drove on. I know I should have stayed longer but, when it came to a choice between watching microprocessor assembly and a Devonshire country lane, it proved no contest.

It is no longer easy to make your way between Exeter and Plymouth using nothing but narrow lanes. The new main road cuts ruthlessly through the older routes so that, try as you may, you keep finding yourself joining the busy main-road traffic, desperately searching for an alternative. My predecessor would not have been so concerned to search out the alternative ways, for they were not greatly to her liking.

> On these hills one can discern little besides inclosures hedges and trees, rarely can see houses unless you are just descending to them, they allwayes are placed in holes as it were, and you have a precipice to go down to come at them; the lanes are full of stones and dirt for the most part, because

they are so close the sun and wind cannot come at them, soe that in many places you travell on Causeys which are uneven also for want of a continued repaire.

And the further she went along the way, the less attractive they became.

The lanes are exceeding narrow and so cover'd up you can see little about, an army might be marching undiscover'd by any body, for when you are on those heights

A Devon lane on the road from Exeter to Plymouth.

that shews a vast country about, you cannot see one road; the wayes now became so difficult that one could scarcely pass by each other, even the single horses, and so dirty in many places and just a track for one horses feete, and the banks on either side so neer, and were they not well secured and mended with stones struck close like a drye wall every where when they discover the bancks to breake and molder down which else would be in danger of swallowing up the way quite.

The motor car makes short work of all obstacles, so that it is difficult to appreciate the problems of those who travelled on foot whether the feet were their own or those of horses. Consequently, the very difficulties that impeded progress in the seventeenth century – narrow lanes, high banks, steep hills – became attractive to the twentieth-century traveller, sated with the boom-along, zoom-along travel of the motorways. Three centuries ago, Dartmoor was a dangerous area to be avoided, now it is the chief attraction of the region. We have discovered scenery. To Celia Fiennes, it was little more than the inconvenient bit that separated the traveller from one town and the next. Even the towns were little admired. Ashburton was 'a poor little town' and 'bad was the worst inn'. Here Miss Fiennes and I part company for I find it a decidedly agreeable place: a wool town, a stannary town, a place full of interest. Up hill and down hill it goes, houses pushed tight into terraces. I met it in holiday mood, preparing for its summer fair with bunting stretched across the streets. I would have liked it anyway, as a good, honest town, buildings of granite reflecting the rocks that pushed out through the land on the distant hills of Dartmoor.

Beyond Ashburton, the moor dominates the scene, rising up steeply to the north of the road. The feeling of a wild country still pervades the area, much as it did when Celia Fiennes came this way.

> I pass'd over some stone bridges; the waters are pretty broad soe these are 4 or 5 arches most bridges, all stone; the running of the waters is with a huge rushing by reason of the stones which lye in the water some of them great rocks which gives some interruption to the current which finding another way either by its sides or mounting over part of it causes the frothing of the water and the noise, the rivers being full of stones bigger or less.

The hills are still to be reckoned with, even for those who rely on the internal combustion engine to overcome all obstacles. Dean Clapperhill is still formidable and the views are still superb. I came down into South Brent, very much my sort of place, huddled down under the lee of Brent Moor. It is a close, tight little place like a clenched fist. Last time I came here, I roamed off over the moor, now I explored the town itself, a market town, still displaying an aged scale of charges setting out the fees for practically anything that anyone might wish to sell. Like all market towns, it is liberally supplied with pubs. Names speak of a trading past. I settled on the Pack Horse on a gorgeous day of sunshine and enjoyed good ale and food – none of which prevented the customers from indulging in the favourite British pastime of grumbling, about VAT and income tax and the machinations of bureaucracy.

Celia Fiennes enjoyed the descent down to Plympton, but now it is all but indistinguishable from the rest of Plymouth, just a straggle of suburbia, best left alone. So on I went to the city itself. Like Exeter, it suffered its full share of destruction during World War 2, but here at least an attempt was made to remodel and rebuild with style. The result is a city of contrasts: wide avenues and broad vistas for the new; higgledy-piggledy confusion of narrow streets for the old. In such circumstances, the new can appear simply brash and faintly vulgar, but here it seems to work surprisingly well. It is the position of the city that makes the difference. There is no point in having wide vistas at the end of a street if that vista is no more than another street with another vista of another street and so on ad nauseam. In Plymouth, the sea puts its own end to that expanding scene, so that views do eventually open out on sea and sky and broad horizons. The sea provides that extra element that ensures that the city will never be dull, for it is to the sea that Plymouth looks for its livelihood as it has done for centuries.

> Plymouth is 2 Parishes called the old town and the new, the houses all built of this marble and the slatt at the top lookes like lead and glisters in the sun; there are noe great houses in the town; the streetes are good and clean, there is a great many tho' some are but narrow; they are mostly inhabitted with seamen and those which have affaires on the sea, for here up to the town there is a depth of water for shipps of the first rate to ride.

Even when you cannot see the water in Plymouth, you are never allowed to forget it for long. If a name from the heroic past can be squeezed into a street name, then the authorities will get it in somewhere – Armada Way, Drake Circus, Mayflower Street. I am especially fond of the Drake Cinema, where a stone ship in full sail storms out through the wall above the electric sign announcing the evening's entertainment. It was down Armada Way that I began my exploration. This is typical of post-war Plymouth, a very un-English boulevard, wide and enticing which, in Europe, would be full of market stalls and cafés. Here it is mostly full of municipal flowerbeds, neat and trim, and litter bins to try to ensure they stay that way. There is lots of building going on, behind high barriers of boards covered with graffiti, not the usual, unofficial 'Boot Boys Rule OK' variety but a sort of semi-official public art show. Local schools have obviously been brought in and encouraged to do their thing. The primary schools were best, wonderfully bold and garish, hairy giants, beaming their smiles out over the city. And there, at the end, the best-known bit of all – the Hoe, the lighthouse tower, a beacon not to warn off the rocks but to attract to the sea.

Plymouth can boast two famous moments in history: the first when Drake played bowls and took his time about beating the Spanish, the second when the Pilgrim Fathers set sail to

Drake's successors on Plymouth Hoe.

colonize America. The Hoe, the first of the historical areas, is one of the focal points of the city, an area of smooth lawns for lounging and staring at the sea. What is the one thing everyone knows about the Hoe? Drake was playing a game of bowls here when the Armada was sighted, and insisted on finishing his game. There is still a bowling green on the Hoe, announcing its presence with a pub-like sign of Sir Francis delivering the last wood to the jack before sorting out the Spaniards. No armadas in sight when I visited, no sea captains either, just a ladies' match which might have been laid on for the special benefit of one of Plymouth's most famous current residents, the painter Beryl Cook. Dressed in white, bow-fronted bowlers sailed like galleons over the green, watched by a small but appreciative audience of old gentlemen who might have been husbands or simply ageing voyeurs. One lady had a splendid action. As the bowl was delivered, one leg flew backwards in counter-balance, so that for a moment she was poised like a female Eros who had enjoyed too many cream teas. It was just the sort of scene to put one in a good mood – and to stop one feeling too bilious about the truly awful modern hotels that stand by the green. Institutional anonymous, lumpen, featureless, drab – Holiday Inn, just like every other Holiday Inn, Mayflower, a building to set modern pilgrims sailing again. Do the architects who design such places ever get a good night's sleep again? I was happy to turn to more appealing prospects.

Celia Fiennes was fortunate in her timing, for she reached Plymouth at a time of great change, and change not limited to the city but carrying out beyond the land and into the sea:

> You can just discover a light house which is building on a meer rock in the middle of the sea; this is 7 leagues off it will be of great advantage for the guide of the shipps that pass that way; from this you have a good refflection on the great care and provision the wise God makes for all persons and things in his Creation, that there should be in some places, where there is any difficulty, rocks even in the midst of the deep which can be made use of for a constant guide and mark for the passengers on their voyages; but the Earth is full of the goodness of the Lord and soe is

this Great Sea wherein are inumerable beings created and preserv'd by the same Almighty hand, whose is the Earth and all things there in, he is Lord of all.

Lighthouses do not these days usually lead to feelings of religious fervour. Our minds are more inclined to consider the magnitude of the task of building anything at all on a small rock in the middle of the sea, and to contemplate the hard life of those who man it. The first Plymouth lighthouse was designed by Henry Winstanley, an extraordinarily ornate edifice built of wood and this was the one being constructed at the time of her visit. It was soon replaced by an even more exotic and grander lighthouse but that too was to have a brief existence. In 1703 it was demolished in a severe gale and Winstanley himself and all the men in the lighthouse perished. A third lighthouse fared little better, for it was burned down in a fire started by its own lanterns. Then, in 1759, John Smeaton designed the first stone lighthouse which was to stand on the rock for 120 years. When it was taken down, the upper section was brought back to the Hoe and here it stands as a monument to Smeaton. From the top, on a clear day, you can see the successor, the fifth and grandest of the Eddystone lights.

From the Hoe, I walked to the Citadel, which roused Celia Fiennes to paeons of praise:

> The fine and only thing in Plymouth town is the Citadell, or Castle, which stands very high above the town, the walls and battlements round it with all their works and plattforms are in very good repair and lookes nobly, all marble full of towers with stone balls on the tops and gilt on the top, the entrance being by an ascent up a hill looks very noble over 2 drawbridges, and gates, which are marble, as is the whole well carv'd, the gate with armory and statues all gilt and on the top 7 gold balls.

I was less enthralled, not being a great enthusiast for military architecture, and its blank walls seemed rather more grim than attractive. I turned with considerably more pleasure to the old town.

The Barbican area must be counted as Plymouth's success story. It seems incredible now, but this was a depressed, down-at-heel,

Winstanley's first Eddystone lighthouse.

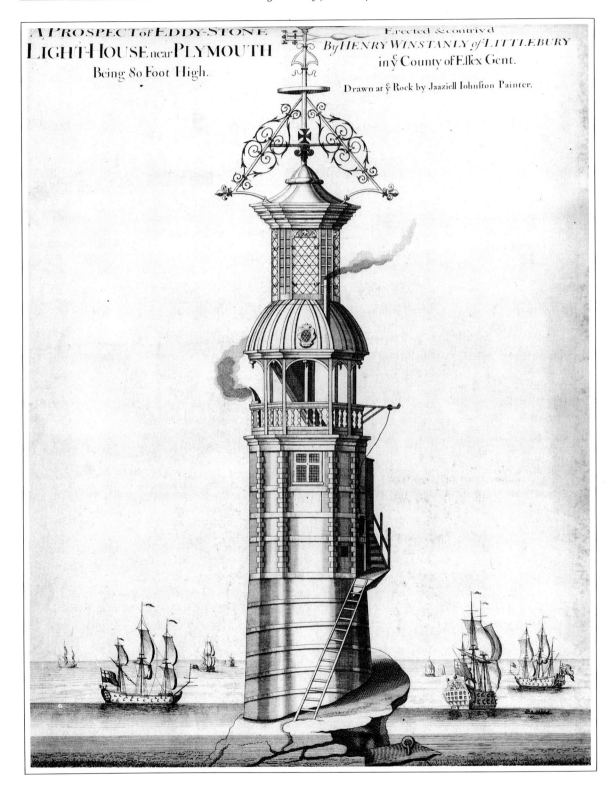

newer buildings have kept the essential character of the area intact.

And it is still a working port: fishing boats ride in the harbour, though now tourists not pilgrims use the famous steps as they go down to the trip boats. I was to join their numbers later, but there was still the Barbican to explore, the narrow streets, the funny little Elizabethan garden with odd bits of an old house left behind and carvings of ships. Best of all I like places such as New Street where the old working world and the cosier modern world meet, with cottages sitting happily down beside stern warehouses. Then there are the individual houses. Yogges House was built by a local merchant, Thomas Yogge in 1498 and is now known as the Prysten House to acknowledge its present connection with the church. It is really very splendid and it is a place which is being used for all kinds of local activities – not just a show place, there to be admired. And here patient ladies sit sewing The New World Tapestry, one of those projects which will take years to finish, for there are twenty-three panels telling the story of Plymouth and the colonization of America. How pleasant to find people prepared to take on work with such a long time scale, and to labour away year after year so slowly and painstakingly.

ABOVE *A carved doorway, now part of Plymouth's Elizabethan garden.*

RIGHT *A view of Plymouth dockyard in 1735.*

shabby, back-end sort of place. It would have been easy just to have demolished the whole lot, and much was lost before battle was joined. On the one side, the council, forward looking, wishing to build for the future: on the other, die-hard reactionaries wanting to keep a series of crumbling rat-infested buildings. That, at least, was one view of the argument. Others saw it as conservation versus destruction and, astonishingly, conservation won. Now it is the showpiece of the town, crowded with shops and restaurants, and people who have space to walk and enjoy the old streets. It is possible to argue that the restaurants are too dear, the antique shops too chi-chi, but there really is a lot more to the place than that. And, even if the criticisms were true, at least the buildings themselves survive, and use can change, while

The Merchants House is very much a museum, devoted to the social history of the city with each room having its own theme based on the cherry stone jingle – 'tinker, tailor, soldier, sailor, rich man, poor man, apothecary, thief'. I am not sure that I remember the apothecary featuring in my version of the rhyme, but perhaps beggarman was too close to poor man and, in any case, it was worth stretching a point to include the old chemist's shop. Celia Fiennes spoke of the old town as being '. . . mostly inhabitted with seamen and those which have affaires on the sea'. The Elizabethan house in New Street is the one which, more than any other, captures the feeling of Plymouth's historic past. The street was, in fact, new when the house was built to accommodate the sea captains, merchants, and pirates who came back to Plymouth with the wealth of the New World. It manages to combine rich texture with a feeling of rough honesty. There is a profusion of carving, but it is naive rather than sophisticated. If you wanted to sum up the house's air of sensible practicality, you could do worse than look at the staircase spiralling around an old ship's mast which rises right through the building. It is a tall, narrow house with a tiny garden, but must have seemed pure luxury to a man just back from a year in a ship's cabin. It is a house that helps to bring the past a little closer.

The area gets scant mention from Celia Fiennes, who found her curiosity taking her, as ever, to see what was new in the world. The latest developments were of more interest than history and, again, she was fortunate in arriving at an important time in Plymouth's development. She was soon enthusing over the new docks:

> Its one of the best in England, a great many good shipps built there, and the great depth of water which comes up to it, tho' it runs up for 2 mile between the land, which also shelters the shipps; there is a great deale of buildings on the Dock, a very good house for the Masters and severall lesser ones and house for their cordage and makeing ropes, and all sorts of things required in building or refitting ships; it lookes like a little town the buildings are so many, and all of marble with fine slate on the rooffs, and at a little distance it makes all the houses shew as if they were cover'd with snow and glisters in the sunn which adds to their beauty.

She also remarked that '. . . by boate you goe to it the nearest way'. That is still true, and so I did. Back at the Mayflower steps, the boatmen

were hawking their wares. Once it was 'Trips round the bay' or 'Twice round the lighthouse'. Today it is 'See the nuclear submarines. Come and look at the frigates.' I prefer the old, but at least our trip boat was part of a fine tradition – *Boadicea II*, proudly bearing her Dunkirk plaque. Round the headland we went and there was the fleet in for repairs, refits, repaints or simply a routine service. A big fleet-support oil tanker was in for a paint job. What colour do you fancy sir? Grey will do nicely. The buildings of the modern dock complex quite dwarf the old. Concrete and steel lord it over brick, stone, and wood. The frigate-repair docks are huge, enabling ships to be repaired under cover, and most impressive of all is the crane for lifting the nuclear reactor from a submarine. And there in the water are the subs themselves, black, menacing vessels which have no function except to hunt and, if necessary, kill. These are the predators of the seas and, among them, was the *Challenger* that sank the Argentine

The old and the new at the dockyard, dominated by the Victorian hydraulic pumping house.

Belgrano. I could hear again the harpie cry of rejoice. I served, if briefly, in the forces and was prepared, I suppose, to kill. If wars are to be fought, people will die, but it has never seemed to me to be a cause for rejoicing. I saw the *Challenger* and thought not of victory but of young men drowning.

Perversely, perhaps, I took immense pleasure in a tour of the old docks the next day, perverse because they, too, were built to serve men-of-war, just as the new docks do today. And war was no gentler then. The passage of time tends to soften the harsher aspects of history. Devonport Dockyard is so big that a day is not enough time to see it all, so I limited my visit to the old. The town of Devonport has been nibbled away by the docks and large areas have been swallowed whole. Within the perimeter wall are areas that once contained houses and shops. The old market hall has been taken in, and even Marks and Spencers has gone down the naval maw. As you go into the docks, you keep coming to different layers of history. I entered by the Granby Gate of 1688, but above it soared the Devonport Column of 1824, marking the division between old town and new, and setting a boundary to their rivalries. The great wall of 1766 had its human touch – a little niche for a lantern where men could come out to light their pipes. Everywhere there are reminders of old campaigns; bronze cannon from China, stand outside the excellent little museum that tells the dockland story. There are surprising touches of elegance in this working world. The Terrace, or what survived the bombing, is Georgian and looks it: very handsome, but I find the working areas have an even greater visual appeal. The dry docks, with their stone tiers, and the covered slipway provide an almost endless variety of shapes and forms to admire. There are parts of the docks which seem almost to have a haunted air, quite at odds with their obvious practicality. Under a later building, you can find the slipway of 1730, a dark place where divisions between water, air, and stone get lost in melting reflections and the dance of light. And anyone who does not feel a lifting of the spirit on going into No. 1 slip has no eye for beauty. It is a huge frame of timber, shaped and shapely, that calls on a tradition that belongs as much to the sea and ships as it does to the land and solidly founded

The massive frigate repair docks.

buildings. At the far end, peering out over the Sound, is King Billy, as gaudy a figurehead as one can imagine.

Everywhere in the dock there are details to enjoy. The late eighteenth-century yarn sheds have an overhead pulley system joining the buildings, so that 720-foot-long (220-metre) ropes could be moved from white yarn shed to tarred yarn shed. Lead drainpipes still carry the royal insignia, 1769 G.R. – and those with a taste for the macabre can visit the execution cell of 1793. Everywhere are the bits and pieces that make a dockland scene unique: chains with gargantuan links, bright painted buoys, enormous anchors. I specially like the sense of continuity of the place: wooden, clinker-built dinghies in the repair shop and pattern makers producing models in wood of a nuclear sub-marine just as they did for the fighting ships of three centuries ago. The ships have changed but skills are handed down. Twelve-thousand men work here, belong here, are an essential part of that continuing story. 'You've not come to bloody privatize us have you?' a workman shouted during my tour. That is one proposed future for the Royal Dockyard at Devonport – a suggestion that it should all be handed over to

private enterprise in the name of efficiency, though no-one seemed able to explain where the new efficiency would appear. Someone, however, will no doubt make a great deal of money from the change. It is unlikely to be any of the 12 000 men.

I contemplated the past and present of the city of Plymouth over a pint in one of the most unusual pubs I have ever visited. The Bank was until recently just that – and, from the outside, that is just what it is. It is another success for preservation and adaptation, a success that is repeated surprisingly often in this city. The next day I left Plymouth and Devon. I went as Celia Fiennes had done, to the Cremyll Ferry which, in her day, was a distinctly dangerous place but today offers a simple crossing of the river. On the far side was Mount Edgecumbe house and Cornwall, which we shall be visiting three chapters and two centuries later. But we are not yet ready for modern tourism. Celia Fiennes travelled to see, enquire, and learn as did our next traveller, a man who was a witness to her will, Daniel Defoe.

DANIEL DEFOE (1661-1731)

•

The Useless Hills

A Tour Through the Whole Island of Great Britain 1724-6

Daniel Defoe is unlike Celia Fiennes in that he travelled with a very definite purpose in mind, to write a book which would provide an accurate description of 'The most flourishing and opulent country in the world', Great Britain. It was to be encyclopedic in its coverage.

> If novelty pleases, here is the present state of the country describ'd, the improvement, as well in culture, as in commerce, the encrease of people, and employment for them: Also here you have an account of the encrease of buildings, as well in great cities and towns, as in the new seats and dwellings of the nobility and gentry; also the encrease of wealth, in many eminent particulars.
>
> If antiquity takes with you, tho' the looking back into remote things is studiously avoided, yet it is not wholly omitted, nor any useful observations neglected.

This could be dull stuff, but Defoe was one of the great imaginative writers of his day, author of such classic novels as *Robinson Crusoe* and *Moll Flanders* and a wickedly accurate political pamphleteer. He is a guide who can be trusted both to amuse and to instruct; a man who can be relied upon to hunt out the facts, but one far from unwilling to voice a personal opinion. He manages to be simultaneously a very personal voice and a spokesman for his times. Through his eyes we see a Britain beginning to move toward that great period of convulsion we know as the industrial revolution, so it seemed wholly appropriate to select an area where that convulsion was felt at its strongest, in the Pennine hills. I also allowed myself a little in

the way of personal nostalgia, as I followed Defoe on his journey from Littleborough in Lancashire to Ripon in Yorkshire.

Littleborough today is, at first glance, indistinguishable from any of a score of other small northern towns that crouch in the shadow of the Pennines, the buildings huddling together for protection. Almost all are built of the local gritstone, which is naturally dark, and years of

Daniel Defoe by M Van der Gucht after J Taverner, 1706.

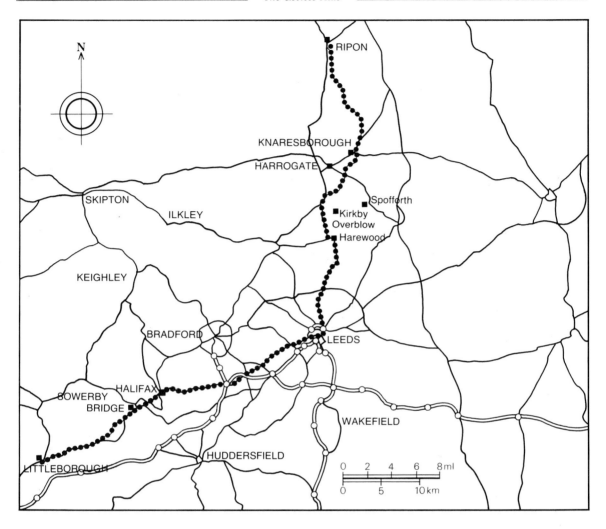

smoking chimneys have served only to make it darker still. Many back streets retain their cobbles, and seem to be waiting for the film crews and the brass band playing pianissimo on the sound track. But come here, as I have done, on a day of drooping clouds that spilled out a steady drizzle and you realize why so many regard this type of town as depressing, gloomy, and forbidding. There are few buildings of any great distinction, though the church, surrounded by its gravestone slabs that gleamed stonily in the rain, has an austere dignity. It seemed, however, no more than appropriate that a funeral procession should arrive to add to the damp despondancy of a wet day in Littleborough. Yet, somehow, I have never felt such towns to be depressing, even on

such a day. There is a rough solidity about them, an air of being prepared to withstand the worst that the weather can do. The buildings may be plain and unadorned, but they belong here. Their stone is the stone of the surrounding hills, so that they seem to have grown out of the land rather than to have been set on top of it. And always there, at the edge of the town, are the Pennine hills, offering an escape from urbanity to a place of genuine wildness.

Defoe liked towns such as Littleborough and Rochdale. He was less impressed by the delights of the hills. He wrote of the latter town that it was noted for its manufacture of '. . . a sort of coarse goods, called half-thicks and kersies, and the market for them is very great, tho' otherwise the town is situated so remote,

The Roman road climbing up the hill to Blackstone Edge.

so out of the way, and so at the very foot of the mountains, that we may suppose it would be but little frequented'. Certainly, Defoe would never have come here other than from necessity, for he almost loathed the rough upland. When he visited the Lake District and north Lancashire, he could do little other than exclaim over the 'unhospitable terror' of the hills, the 'horror' of the country, and, above all, deplore the absolute uselessness of such areas – no lead mines, no copper, no tin, no coal pits – nothing, in fact, of the slightest interest. Westmoreland, for example, was for him a country eminent only for being the '... wildest, most barren and frightful of any that I have pased over in England'. It was a great relief, then, for him to come down into Lancashire to find some 'very pleasant, populous and manufacturing towns'. Now the poor man was faced with leaving the towns and, once again, setting out across the barren, gaunt, and totally useless hills. I face the same prospect with rather more

enthusiasm. It seems so natural for us to look with pleasure at the prospect of getting away from the confines of industry or office life to enjoy the freedom of the hills, that it takes a real effort to see them as Defoe did, as no more than obstacles in the way of his journeyings.

Since Defoe's day, generations of engineers have forced routes across the Pennines. The old days of the straggling pack horse teams gave way to the age of canals and turnpike roads, to be followed by the railways and, in our own age, the motorway. Defoe, a man much in favour of progress, would, no doubt, gladly have turned away from the steep slopes of the moor and settled thankfully for the comfort, convenience, and speed of the motor car. But I was travelling as Defoe travelled, not as he would have preferred to travel, and was only too glad to be heading off towards Blackstone Edge – partly because I have always loved walking in the hills, and partly because I was going to look along the way at one of the most interesting, and certainly one of the most ancient, of the routes across these hills.

I came to begin the actual journey on a day in early November, a time when you do not normally expect to find snow covering the hills. There was mild surprise at the early covering of white, but the day was crisply cold with a sky of brilliant, cloudless blue. I could imagine Defoe's feelings on coming here in the height of summer.

> Here, for our great encouragement, though we were but at the middle of August, and in some places the harvest was hardly got in, we saw the mountains covered with snow, and felt the cold very acute and piercing; but even here we found, as in all those northern countries is the case, the people had an extraordinary way of mixing the warm and the cold very happily together; for the store of good ale which flows plentifully in the most mountainous part of this country, seems abundantly to make up for all the inclemencies of the season . . . We mounted the hills, fortified with the same precaution.

Licensing laws had not yet appeared in the land, so our party had to set off unfortified. As my companions had a good deal to do with the events of the day, I shall introduce them: Sarah and Mike Lucas, whom we have already met on the Thames, and have the good fortune to live in the Pennines and the sense to reside on the Yorkshire side, and my wife, Pip. We left the town on the lane that leads up to Lydgate, and up was certainly the key word for the hills rise steeply and there is no getting round them. There was ice at the road side, beneath which tiny rivulets could be seen like elvers in a stream, but at least the effort of climbing kept you warm. And when you raised your head to take in the view, the effort all became worth-while. A tremendous vista opened to the west. In the distance you could see the tower blocks of Rochdale, less appealing than the nearer view. This is Pennine hill farm country where fields are divided off from the moorland by drystone walls and where houses and barns are built plain and solid to keep the weather at bay. It is not, however, a peaceful country. Each farm had its share of dogs, and all the dogs felt it to be their duty to announce our arrival with a raucous chorus. Sounds of the twentieth century were also to be heard; overhead a 'plane ruled white tracks across the blue sky

and there was a distant drone of traffic that grew louder as we reached the main road to Halifax. It was just 8 miles away along the tarmac, and we could have gone that way with ease, but we were to take a more direct line from that of the modern road builders, straight over the top of Blackstone Edge.

A well-defined track heads up towards the hard rocky outline of the hill top, which is indeed an edge of black stone. It is a curious track, much too wide for an ordinary lane, and, as you climb, its true character begins to emerge. The route is paved with stone, with a well-defined groove made out of shaped stone blocks running down the middle. This is a road that has given rise to a great deal of controversy. Some have claimed that it is a pack-horse route; there are pack-horse routes in plenty in this part of the world, but none that is built to this width. Why should they be, when pack-horse trains invariably travelled in single file? Others have suggested an eighteenth-century road. But these are all documented, and there are no records of any such road being built. Tradition has it that this is a Roman road, and it is now generally felt that tradition is in the right. It certainly shows the well-known Roman tendency to pick a goal and then make straight for it, for no attempt has been made to ease the gradient by zig-zagging. That might also explain the groove down the middle. One theory is that it was filled with turf to help horses get a footing as they hauled waggons, not so much for going uphill as to help with the braking going down. I cannot speak with any

A pack-horse train, once the main transport for the woollen trade of the Pennines.

authority as to who was responsible for this road, but it is beautifully made and I raise my hat to whoever deserves the credit. We climbed up through the clear air, happy to be more fortunate than Defoe.

It is not easy to express the consternation we were in when we came up near the top of the mountain; the wind blew exceeding hard, and blew the snow so directly in our faces, and that so thick, that it was impossible to keep our eyes open to see our way. The ground also was so covered with snow, that we could see no track, or when we were in the way, or when out; except when we were shewed it by a frightful precipice on one hand, and uneven ground on the other; even our horses discovered their uneasiness at it; and a poor spaniel dog that was my fellow traveller, and usually diverted us with giving us a mark for our gun, turn'd tail to it and cry'd.

Defoe thought of going back, but they reached the top of the hill and could look down into Yorkshire even if the view of deep clefts and rocks poking through the snow was not particularly enticing. Down he went, glad at least that he had located some landmarks mentioned to him in Rochdale. If he had followed our way, he would certainly have found an unmistakable landmark for, at the top of the hill among a jumble of stone blocks, stands an upright stone carved with a cross, the Aiggin Stone. All it marks now is the crossing of the most popular long-distance walkway in the country, the Pennine Way. What an incomprehensible concept that would have been to Defoe: a route to be walked through the wildest of countryside by people who had no specific destination in mind, no trade to conduct, no information to gather but who simply wanted to walk. We did not, however, turn that way but went on down hill along the line of the Roman road which was now less easily distinguished. The going was altogether more difficult with large patches of boggy, peaty ground to be avoided. The road, however, appeared again as a broad ledge carved from the side of a deep valley cut by one of the many

Hillside farms above Sowerby Bridge.

hill streams. We had the valley to ourselves, apart from the sheep who stood steadily chewing but keeping a wary eye on the intruders. After that, the Roman road disappeared without trace and we were back at the modern main road and a choice of routes. Defoe had no such choice, and he was clearly unimpressed by the Pennine landscape.

> We thought now we were come into a Christian country again, and that our difficulties were over; but we soon found our selves mistaken in the matter; for we had not gone fifty yards beyond the brook and houses adjacent, but we found the way began to ascend again, and soon after to go up very steep, till in about half a mile we found we had another mountain to ascend, in our apprehansion as bad as the first, and before we came to the top of it, we found it began to snow too, as it had done before.

If Defoe could take a direct route on a foul day, surely we could take an equally direct route on a bright, sunny day. Ahead lay Great Manshead Hill, gleaming golden in the wintry sun, not too tall and, according to the map, once over the brow it was downhill all the way to Sowerby Bridge. 'Sorby', Defoe called it, and that is how the locals pronounce it still. Off we set, but the terrain which looked so harmless when seen from a distance, turned out to consist of huge, rough tussocks, the space between filled with snow. As you put your foot down, you had no means of telling whether you would sink up to the ankle or to the thigh. Walking became a precarious balancing act and I was first to go, but not by any means the last. Seeing that it had been my idea to come this way, I went ahead to look for the best way forward and to warn against hazards. I pointed out a stream, which Mike seemed to take as an invitation rather than a warning for he promptly stepped into it. I ploughed, almost literally, ahead. Strange shrieks of almost hysterical laughter came from behind. I turned to see Pip disappear almost to the waist while all that was visible of Sarah was a pair of legs waving in the air. It seemed wisest to march on.

A stream was marked across our way, and I found it to be surrounded by an impossibly boggy marsh. I followed it up the hill to a point where it could be crossed and turned to indicate where the route lay. No-one was in sight. I

called: answering shouts but no people. I climbed the hill a little way and saw the rest of the party approaching the boggy stream. I made my way over to explain where the easy crossing place was, but no-one wanted to know. Rebellion was absolute. No-one was going another step over those moorland tussocks, they were heading for the road and that was that. To the road we went, and it was made I thought unreasonably plain just what the others thought of my qualities of leadership and navigational abilities.

Forgiveness had to await our arrival at the Blue Ball Inn, and what a pleasure it is to be able to record hospitality far beyond the call of duty. Socks were festooned over radiators. A certain amount of acrimonious comment arose when it appeared that I, who had led the way into the moorland wilderness, was the only one to remain dryshod. However, the purchase of beer, particularly when selected from the brews of Taylor, Theakston, and Boddington did much to mollify, and a hot lunch completed the process. The landlady took pity on Mike who had paid visits to so many moorland streams and loaned him a pair of her husband's socks. After that, we retreated to Littleborough, but not across that devilish hill and I must confess to a certain sadness that we had failed where Defoe had succeeded. The following day, we came back to complete the journey into Halifax.

The land between Manshead Hill and Sowerby Bridge is a maze of lanes and minor roads, bordered by stone walls. Farms and cottages dot the land, many snuggled down into sheltering hollows. The houses are full of character, sturdy, stone built with mullioned windows – and many of the older houses have long rows of these windows on the upper floor. They are as distinctive as a brightly coloured board outside a pub, for both are marks of what went on inside. The windows lit a working space, a space filled with looms, for we have arrived at what was once the industrial heartland of Britain, the area that was to take over the great bulk of woollen manufacture from the West Country mills visited by Celia Fiennes. For when Defoe visited Yorkshire, cloth production meant work in the home: women and children at the spinning, men at the weaving and other trades, and no home without its cloth hung out on tenter frames. Defoe found a land rich in natural resources with sheep on the hills, water in the streams, and coal to be had from the collieries in the valley.

Among the manufacturers houses are likewise scattered an infinite number of cottages or small dwellings, in which dwell the workmen which are employed, the women and children of whom, are always busy carding, spinning, &c. so that no hands being unemploy'd, all can gain their bread, even from the youngest to the antient; hardly any thing above four years old, but its hands are sufficient to it self.

This is the reason also why we saw so few people without doors; but if we knock'd at the door of any of the master manufacturers, we presently saw a house full of lusty fellows, some at the dye-fat, some dressing the cloths, some in the loom, some one thing, some another, all hard at work, and full employed upon the manufacture, and all seeming to have sufficient business.

They are still there, the manufacturers' houses, the weavers' cottages, and the tight-knit settlements such as Mill Bank where the houses seem almost to fall down the hillside, piling one above the other. Names are an evocation of those days: Making Place Hall appeared, which must surely have been one of Defoe's manufacturers' houses. But for all the reminders of that busy past, nothing of the work now remains except the memory. For the trade left the home to go to factory and mill, and, in the latter part of the twentieth century, the mills too are closing at an astonishing rate. But it is that world of the first factory age that you meet as you come down to Sowerby Bridge. For Defoe it was a landscape of cloth:

The day clearing up, and the sun shining, we could see that almost at every house there was a tenter, and almost on every tenter a piece of cloth, or kersie, or shalloon, for they are the three articles of that country's labour; from which the sun glancing, and, as I may say, shining (the white reflecting its rays) to us, I thought it was the most agreeable sight that I ever saw, for the hills, as I saw, rising and falling so thick, and the vallies opening sometimes one way, sometimes another, so that sometimes we could see two or three miles

this way, sometimes as far another; sometimes like the streets near St. Giles's, called the Seven Dials; we could see through the glades almost every way round us, yet look which way we would, high to the tops, and low to the bottoms, it was all the same; innumerable houses and tenters, and a white piece upon every tenter.

For us it was a landscape of tight-packed houses and mills, through which was threaded a narrow ribbon of water, the canal, the great transport route of the first industrial age. Everything was about to change: countryside was to disappear beneath buildings and town was to merge with town and scarcely a gap between. No point – and no fun – now in walking, so it was back to the car which would take me to the main town on Defoe's itinerary. He began in Halifax, a place that made a great impression on him.

For take Hallifax, with all its dependencies, it is not to be equalled in England. First, the parish or vicaridge, for it is but a vicaridge; is, if not the largest, certainly the most populous in England; in short, it is a monster, I mean for a country parish, and a parish so far out of the way of foreign trade, Courts, or sea ports.

Halifax was a great centre for cloth trading and manufacturing and it went on in that way through the eighteenth century and on into the next. It has changed, but something of the old splendour and the old character remains. And Halifax still clings to the last of the open country. You can walk down a busy shopping street to find a grassy hillside rising before you, closing off the view. It is a place too with its share of grand buildings, and none is grander than the Piece Hall, built in 1775 for the cloth traders, a market where 'pieces' could be bought and sold. It was designed as a working market, but one very conscious of its wealth and importance. Entrance to the market square is through an arched opening that can be closed by a pair of magnificent, painted iron gates, which combine devices of the lamb as provider of wool with the lamb as a Christian symbol. The traders of Halifax had, it seemed, little difficulty in worshipping both God and

Halifax: shopping precinct, parish church, and the moorland that reaches to the town's edge.

Mammon. Inside is a cobbled square, surrounded by galleries where the merchants had their offices. You could be in a piazza of Rome for the galleries are elegantly decked out with rusticated columns on the ground floor and Tuscan columns above. It has only quite recently been restored and, to get the true feel of the place, you should come on a market day when the square is crammed with stalls. We arrived on a quiet Tuesday and found a deserted, empty, echoing place. A few tourists wandered around and two old ladies sat on a bench sharing a thermos of tea in the winter sunshine. But even at its busiest, its old trade has gone: it is just another market for fruit and veg, pots and pans, woolly jumpers and cheap jeans. Now if you want to catch a glimpse of old industrial Halifax, you have to step out of the colonnades and into the newly opened Calderdale Industrial Museum. Here steam engines puff, gently wagging their beams, and workshop reconstructions show the old life of a manufacturing area. As with so many northern towns, we have managed to salvage some of the pride of the past, even if no-one seems altogether certain where to go in the future. A fatuous politician on the radio that night said that the problems of unemployment and depression were greatly exaggerated. He spoke in London: he would have never dared to say it in Halifax.

There is, however, a lot of life left in Halifax still. There is a busy commercial area which gave birth to the famous Halifax Building Society. They are still here. You can see their rather dourly grand building of 1904 which was once the headquarters of the biggest building society in the world. Now it is just a local office, like any other High Street branch. The headquarters have moved to a new, if unexciting, building up the road. You cannot see the best bit, the vaults, three floors of them cut out of the solid rock beneath the building. There is a million cubic feet (28000 cubic metres) of storage space, full of mortgages and deeds, each one representing somebody's proudest possession. The deeds to Mr and Mrs Jones's semi and Lord and Lady Something's castle sit together beneath the streets of Halifax. But, if you want to see commercial Halifax at its best,

The classical formality of the Piece Hall, Halifax.

go and see Lloyds Bank. It was built in 1898, no expenses spared: Corinthian pillars in front, carved from Norwegian granite, and a wedding-cake interior topped by an astonishing stained-glass ceiling. It cost just over £14,000.00: the new Halifax building was nearly £10 million.

I like Halifax very much. It is a bustling sort of place, and I can never resist anywhere that has had the common sense to retain its old Market Hall. Halifax's is a rather splendid, surprisingly ornate affair, but what counts is what you can buy here – fresh vegetables, fresh meat, black pudding, local cheese. And it is crowded, that is the great thing. People like it and they use it. There is not perhaps very much of Defoe's Halifax left, but there is a lot of the same sense of small-scale enterprise to be found. In among the very elegant houses that have been taken over by doctors and lawyers, you can find little courtyards and workshops. There was a carpenter and joiner and over the road an engraver, who it seems could make anything from a rubber stamp to a memorial tablet. Inevitably there is change: no wool now in Woolshops, a street behind the Piece Hall, but the old stone cobbles have been kept, arranged in a fan pattern that is typical of the town.

I was advised to go to see the parish church, but it was locked. It was a shame for it looked interesting enough from the outside, a black, much-begrimed building but you could see it had some good carving – and in the porch I noticed a gravestone that carried the emblem of a pair of shears. It dates from 1150: wool has a long history in Halifax. But if the church was closed, the pub was open. God and Mammon do seem to have a good working relationship in Halifax, for local lore has it that there was an underground passage connecting church and inn, though whether for the benefit of the clergy or for use by the congregation when faced by an unusually dry sermon was not made clear. The friendly landlord showed me round the cellars and also told me about the pub ghost, Wally. I really cannot blame either ecclesiastics or ghosts for haunting the Ring o' Bells for it is one of those splendid northern pubs that still offer traditional fare. Black pudding and peas was on the menu and you cannot get more traditional than that.

The traditional fan pattern of stone setts in Woolshops, Halifax.

Halifax is a place with a great deal to enjoy, yet remains associated with the old rhyme:

> From Hull and Halifax and Hell
> Good Lord deliver me.

I first met the rhyme as a handloom weaver's lament, a despairing cry from a man who was being forced to leave the old style of work for the new world of factories and towns. But the rhyme was, it seemed, already current in Defoe's time and has a more macabre origin. Cloth that was hung out on tenter frames to dry was all too easy to steal so the laws of Halifax were strict. Anyone caught stealing cloth was executed, not by hanging but by a form of guillotine, from which there was only one escape:

> They tell us of a custom which prevailed here, in the case of a criminal being to be executed, (viz.) that if after his head was laid down, and the signal given to pull out the pin, he could be so nimble as to snatch out his head between the pulling out the

pin and the falling down of the ax, and could get up upon his feet, jump off the scaffold, run down a hill that lies just before it, and get through the river before the executioner could overtake him, and seize upon him, he was to escape.

Was it possible to escape? Defoe thought not, though he recounted an old tale of one man who made it. You can judge for yourself, for a replica of the old 'engine of execution' can be seen at the end of Gibbet Street. And how did Hull get into the rhyme? No-one appears to know.

The route from Halifax to Leeds has not changed all that much since Defoe's time, at least as far as the density of building is concerned.

> From hence to Leeds, and every way to the right hand and the left, the country appears busy, diligent, and even in a hurry of work, they are not scattered and dispersed as in the vicaridge of Hallifax, where the houses stand one by one; but in villages, those villages large, full of houses, and those houses thronged with people,

for the whole country is infinitely populous.

A noble scene of industry and application is spread before you here, and which, joined to the market at Leeds, where it chiefly centers, is such a surprising thing, that they who have pretended to give an account of Yorkshire, and have left this out, must betray an ignorance not to be accounted for, or excused; 'tis what is well worth the curiosity of a stranger to go on purpose to see; and many travellers and gentlemen have come over from Hamburgh, nay, even from Leipsick in Saxony, on purpose to see it.

The difference now is that far from being bustling with employment, there is the grey pall of depression hung over the area. And no-one comes from Germany to marvel at it. Leeds still has a bright air to the city centre: it is in a sense Halifax writ large, a great cloth-trading centre whose old world has largely gone and which is striving to find a place in the new.

Defoe came to Leeds in the days of its first prosperity as a market town, and he considered it of such importance that he devoted many pages to a description of the market and its working. Early in the morning tables were set out along the main street from the river bridge to the market hall, the present Briggate. At seven, the market bell was rung and the clothiers came forward to lay out their cloth on the trestles to begin trading.

As soon as the bell has done ringing, the merchants and factors, and buyers of all sorts, come down, and coming along the spaces between the rows of boards, they walk up the rows, and down as their occasions direct. Some of them have their foreign letters of orders, with patterns seal'd on them, in rows, in their hands; and with those they match colours, holding them to the cloths as they think they agree to; when they see any cloths to their colours, or that suit their occasions, they reach over to the clothier and whisper, and in the fewest words imaginable the price is stated; one asks, the other bids; and 'tis agree, or not agree, in a moment.

The role of Leeds began to change by the end of the eighteenth century. To the old role of cloth market was added a new as cloth manufacturer. Factories and mills came to the town, but they in turn were overtaken by a new trade – tailoring. Wool and the rag trade made Leeds rich and made Leeds famous. It was all here. Sheep grazed on the hills around the city. The mills turned their fleeces to woollen yarn and the wool into cloth, and in literally thousands of establishments, large and small throughout the city, skilled fingers turned the cloth into suits. No-one, they said, could do it better. Sarah Lucas's mother, Marjorie Cameron, worked in the trade and she remembers the dummies used for the special customers. There was one tubby little dummy in regular use, which represented the shape of Mr Alfred Hitchcock. He was perhaps the most famous film director in the world; he lived in Hollywood and could have gone to any tailor he fancied from Hong Kong to Savile Row. But he came back to Leeds. That was the sort of thing on which Leeds' pride was built. However bad conditions, however low the pay, you were making the best. They have not yet killed off Leeds' pride which is still expressed in the public monuments and the Victorian buildings of the city centre.

Leeds has, like all our cities, seen great changes in recent years. When I was here in the 'fifties, trams clanked up Woodhouse Lane from the city centre to the University; now the inner ring road swoops and loops and dives all over the place, and I have long since given up trying to get anywhere by using a sense of direction. But the city centre itself remains remarkably unchanged. If anything, it is better than it used to be, for a great civic clean-up has brought out the qualities of the Victorian architecture. I think that most of us who lived in this area believed that the huge town halls of Halifax, Bradford, and Leeds were all built of black stone. Then came the clean-up and lo and behold these great white confections appeared gleaming in the sun. Not everyone approved. There was something frivolous about this new creation, something that lacked the dignity of old sombre black as if mourners at a funeral had dashed off for a quick change to re-emerge as wedding guests.

There was a time when it was the done thing to pour scorn on these grandiose exercises in municipal pride, to regard buildings such as

Leeds Town Hall as over-elaborate, over-decorated. The pendulum has swung to the furthest extreme and there is now a vogue for all things Victorian with a consequent denigration of the modern. I like Leeds Town Hall, but then I would expect to, for this is what those of us brought up in the area thought civic buildings should be – proclamations of importance, fanfares played double forte. And the Town Hall was an important place for it was one of the cultural centres for the whole area as well. Here I first heard a massive choir sing the Messiah, the Yorkshire Symphony orchestra play Beethoven and Humphrey Lyttleton blow jazz. I cannot take too objective a view of the place even now, for a good deal of my personal taste was formed here – and next door where the presence of the art gallery is marked by one of Henry Moore's reclining figures. We might talk a lot about muck and brass up north, but we like a spot of culture as well.

It is the great Victorian gesture that has shaped modern Leeds, and it is not all just

LEFT *Victorian civic pride; Leeds town hall.*

BELOW *The Aire & Calder Navigation passing through Leeds; by J le Keux, 1715.*

memories. The Grand Theatre is still grand, they still put on variety at the City of Varieties, though in my day the latter used to specialize in 'naughty' shows, usually with the name Paris somewhere in the title. Bored and no doubt chilled ladies stood in motionless nude tableaux, forbidden by the Lord Chamberlain's Office from moving so much as an eyebrow. They were about as erotic as the marble statues in the gallery across the road which, indeed, they strongly resembled. Then there is the Corn Exchange where, once a week, corn is still sold but for the rest of the time is given over to all kinds of strange activities. When I arrived here from Halifax they were having a Psychic Festival. The building is a rather fine rotunda with a glass dome, quite restrained by Leeds' standards. Nothing is restrained about the shopping arcades, glass-canopied corridors, hung with ornate lights and gaudily decorated. The great thing about all these places is that they are still a living part of the city, still in everyday use, and still enjoyed by the citizens. Leeds was one of the first cities to experiment with the idea of banishing cars from certain streets. Traders prophesied disaster, but found that customers actually preferred not being mown down by traffic as they shopped. This is

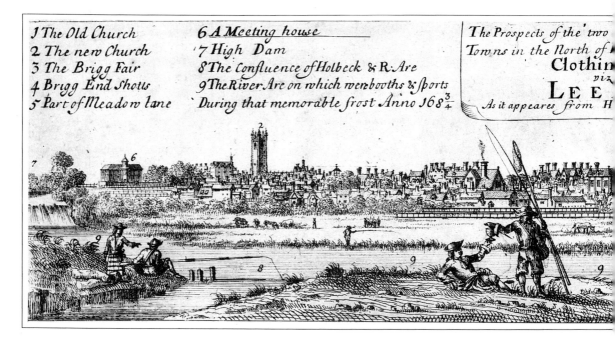

1 The Old Church
2 The new Church
3 The Brigg Fair
4 Brigg End Shotts
5 Part of Meadow lane

6 A Meeting house
7 High Dam
8 The Confluence of Holbeck & R. Are
9 The River Are on which wenbooths & sports
During that memorable frost Anno 168¾

The Prospects of the two
Towns in the North of
Clothin
viz
LEE
As it appeares from H

ABOVE *Leeds seen across the River Aire; by W Lodge, 1712.*

RIGHT *One of Leeds' splendid arcades on a quiet Sunday morning.*

a city centre that seems to work really well in the modern world, while retaining the old civic dignity of the past.

The pride and dignity were always only one side of the picture. Leeds in Defoe's time was not 'much inferiour to Hallifax in numbers of people'. It has long since overtaken it, and the people whose labour produced the wealth did not necessarily get much of a share of it. As at Halifax, you can pick up some of that story at the industrial museum, based on one of the major mill complexes, Armley Mill, beside the Leeds and Liverpool Canal. But you can still see another vital part of the Leeds story as you move out through the suburbs. Leeds is a multiracial community and has been for a long time. Defoe noted a busy international trade along the Aire and Calder Navigation, which had only recently been opened. Out went the cloth to 'Holland, Bremen, Hamburgh, and the Baltick'. In came a whole range of things: '... butter, cheese, lead, iron, salt; all sorts of grocery, as sugars, tobacco, fruit, spice, hops &c., oyl, wine, brandy, spirits, and every sort of heavy or bulky goods'. The Aire and Calder was a busy trading route, and it still is. It

helped to make Leeds into a city with connections all over Europe – and it was to Leeds that many came as refugees from the turmoils of Europe. A big Jewish community built up, and they in turn were followed by Asians. You can see it all in the people of the streets, in the names on the shops. The first wealth of Leeds was based on the labour of the spinners and weavers of the surrounding villages; in later days the prosperity depended on the work of immigrants. The symbols of modern Leeds are synagogue and Sikh temple as much as they are town hall and parish church.

I could, logically, have left the Defoe story there, as a story of wool, of the pack-horse trains criss-crossing the Pennine hills to take cloth to the markets that would grow into the great manufacturing centres of the north, but I simply could not resist following him a little further on his journey. I did warn the reader that I was to indulge in a little personal nostalgia, but I also wanted to provide something of a corrective to the view of Yorkshire as consisting entirely of grimy towns joined by empty hills constantly blasted by gales. Not that anything Defoe says does a great deal to dispel the mythology, but the modern traveller finds a landscape very different from his. He set off to head north out of Leeds, but had little to

say about the countryside until he reached Harewood, and even then it was only the bridge that attracted his attention. But he had arrived half a century too soon, when Harewood was a run-down estate with an ancient but sadly forlorn manor, a ruined castle, and a church. That all began to change in 1738 when it was bought up by a local merchant, Henry Lascelles who had made his fortune in the West Indies trade. His son decided on sweeping changes. He wanted a new house – Robert Adam did most of that – and new gardens, entrusted to up-and-coming Lancelot 'Capability' Brown. No room for the old village in this scheme, so the whole lot was pulled down and a new model village built outside the estate wall. That is what you see if you drive through Harewood: the impressive entrance to Harewood House and the rather sombre, if well-ordered, village. Then you sweep down the hill, past the ruins of old Harewood to the valley of the Wharfe.

At least the busy Wharfe attracted attention, and Defoe was quite amazed by the splendours of the bridge. It is still a good place to pause and enjoy the scenery: the stone bridge, the weir, and the distant prospect as the river flows down the narrow valley below Ilkley Moor where, as we all know, appalling fates overtake

those who venture hatless. The scene, however, does not strike one as especially desolate, and it is hard indeed to reconcile this valley with the area described by Defoe.

From the Wharfe we went directly north, over a continued waste of black, ill looking, desolate moors, over which travellers are guided, like race horses, by posts set up for fear of bogs and holes, to a town call'd Ripley, that stands upon another river called the Nud by some, by others the Nyd, smaller than the Wharfe, but furiously rapid, and very dangerous to pass in many places, especially upon sudden rains.

A glance at the modern map can make this bald statement even more puzzling, for between Harewood and Ripley sits the sizeable town of Harrogate, but not, however, in Defoe's day. Then it was no more than an insignificant appendage to the important town of Knaresborough, or Knaresborough Spaw, or even Yorkshire Spaw as it was known. The desolate moor, too, is a thing of the past. Even if you take the most minor of minor roads, it still seems a peaceful, almost tame landscape. You can see Almscliff Crag as a sandstone outcrop penetrating through the skin of the land but, compared with the rough moors of the Pennines, it is all very domesticated. It seems, in fact, to be an unchanged and unchanging land, but it is a land that is so at odds with Defoe's description of a trackless wilderness that clearly that impression is somewhat misleading. What happened between our time and Defoe's was Enclosure: the draining of the bogs, the division of the ground into neatly parcelled fields. That comfortable, timeless landscape turns out to be of comparatively modern origin but, because it retains the essential features of stone wall and stone building, there is no jarring note struck here. The villages, Kirkby Overblow and Spofforth, have a reassuring solidity. There is still something of the Pennines here, for sheep and cattle graze the rough ground between the sparse tracts of arable. Then comes the 'spaw'. Defoe was unimpressed:

The first thing recommended to me for a wonder, was that four springs, the waters of which are in themselves of so different a

The bridge over the Wharfe below Harewood.

quality, should rise in so narrow a compass of ground; but I, who was surfeited with country wonders in my passing the Peak, was not so easily surprized at the wonderful strangeness of this part; and when my landlord at Knaresborough took me short, with a But is it not a strange thing, sir? I answered him with a question, Is it not as strange, sir, said I, that in Derbyshire two springs, one hot, and another cold, should rise within a hand's breadth of one another?

He might at least have given the locals credit for introducing the word 'spa' into the English vocabulary for it was indeed a local man, William Slingsby, who tasted the waters and noted their similarity to the medicinal springs of Spa in Belgium. I have to confess that I lived most of my first twenty years in this area and only tasted the famous waters once, so I can forgive Defoe for his lack of interest. Perhaps he had read the account in his predecessor's diary, for Celia Fiennes came here to comment on the Slingsby Spaw 'not improperly term'd' and wrote at length on the 'White Scumm' that formed on the spring water. Even her recommendation was not such as to encourage emulation. 'I drank a quart in a morning for two days and hold them to be a good sort of Purge if you can hold your breath so as to drinke them down.'

Defoe declined to drink the waters and was equally dismissive of Knaresborough's most popular tourist attraction, The Dropping Well. Water drips over a limestone cliff and articles suspended in the falls gradually accumulate a stony deposit until they become set and solid for ever: stony teddy bears hang by stony boots and thousands buy tickets to see this amazing phenomenon. Red Indian chiefs have left their marks in the visitors' book, though no petrified feathers survive from their visit, and Lily Langtry left an appreciative note – but not Daniel Defoe.

The springs themselves, and indeed one of them, is nothing extraordinary, namely, that in a little cave a petrifying water drops from the roof of the cavity, which, as they say, turns wood into stone. This indeed I made light of too, because I had already been at Poole's Hole and Castleton in the Peak, and at Harwich.

The Dropping Well and Knaresborough Castle from the Lady's Magazine, undated.

Nothing else in the town made any deeper impression, and his final comments wrote the whole place off in no uncertain manner: '. . . this seems to be a most desolate out-of-the-world place, and that men would only retire to it for religious mortifications and to hate the world.' Well! I really cannot let it go at that and I must say something in Knaresborough's favour, even if I can think of little to say for the Stinking Spaw. But before I begin to rise to the town's defence, let me clear out of the way the one other major tourist attraction, Mother Shipton's Cave. Here dwelt an old lady who foretold – if you read her prophecies correctly – the French Revolution, iron ships, aeroplanes, radio, and, somewhat alarmingly, the end of the world. Her record of accuracy has, to date, been really rather good: one hopes it will not continue so, a thought that you may either contemplate or attempt to forget with a visit to the World's End pub. The Dropping Well and the prophetess's cave can both be reached by a stroll between the two road bridges over the Nidd, a pleasant wooded walk for which a

modest fee is charged. This, however, is all tourist Knaresborough. There is also a town of considerable charm with a working life of its own. This is the town I knew when I came here to the local grammar school. In fact, in an absolute welter of nostalgia, I managed to combine my visit on Defoe's trail with a school reunion. I am not a great one for looking back but this was irresistible, for the guest of honour was to be Maud who had dished out school dinners to generations of pupils. I tried very hard to remember a main course. There must have been meat and fish and veg, but no recollections came. All I could remember was puddings, steam puddings – spotted dick, ginger pudding with custard, chocolate pudding in a brown gooey sauce and, best of all, syrup sponge. Gastronomes may scoff, but we shall not see their like again. I shall not, however, linger over these delights, but take you on a little tour of the town starting at Low Bridge.

The north bank of the River Nidd is marked by a high sandstone cliff, and it is up here that the town sits. To reach it inevitably involves a climb: up steep winding hills for vehicles or by a walk up the steps to the top. I still think of those steps, for we had a games master, an honours graduate of the Maquis de Sade school of sportsmanship, who devised a cross-country route that involved running up the wretched things. We shall not be going that way, nor pausing too long at the House in the Rock which is precisely what its name suggests, a house carved into the cliff. Our route follows the river upstream. Very soon, something of the special character of the town appears. The orange sandstone crowds over the river, and there you can see the weir and old mill buildings. It comes as something of a shock to find that the spa and present tourist centre was also pulled into the industrial revolution. For this was built in 1791 as a cotton mill, but was later converted and ran as a linen mill right up to 1972. All the weir is to most people these days is an irritation, a barrier to pleasure boats for, just round the corner from the mill, popular Knaresborough takes over.

Here is the view that has graced a thousand calendars. High on the cliff stand the ruins of the castle, matched in style if not in age by the

LEFT *The railway viaduct across the Nidd at Knaresborough.*

ABOVE *Waterbag Bank, Knaresborough.*

tall railway viaduct, complete with battlements and arrow slits. This is the Knaresborough that the tourists come to see and once it represented one of the area's few direct links with the busy, industrial towns of the West Riding. Coach loads of mill girls used to come on works outings, to be rowed on the river by a sweating boatman or to row themselves to the accompaniment of shrieks of laughter. They cannot all have enjoyed it but now in memory they seem to have been always laughing and loud and boozy and fun. They were one of the things that set Knaresborough apart from refined Harrogate up the road. I miss them now when I come back. Beyond the viaduct, the town looks as if it has toppled over the edge as houses cling to the steep hillside. The chequered old manor house is a much-altered hunting lodge, where King John stayed when he was visiting the forest of Knaresborough. Close by, a narrow cobbled street leads steeply up the hillside with, rather surprisingly, for this part of the world, a thatched cottage at the foot. The path takes you up to the true town centre, and was

once a very important thoroughfare, a fact recalled in its name, Waterbag Bank. Before waterwheel and pump were installed, trains of donkeys laden with waterbags staggered up from the river. They were the town's water-supply system.

Knaresborough is a market town in the fullest sense. I always loved market days. Lunchtimes, I would come down from school to look at the sheep and cows in the cattle market behind the High Street, but the real focus of attention was the market square and the men with the patter. They were masters at chatting up a crowd. Whole dinner services would be sold by the dozen, and you could see the bemused purchasers wondering why on earth they had bought them. The salesmen were irresistible and endlessly amusing. And they offered good value, which was why people thronged in from surrounding towns and villages to transform the normally quiet town centre into a crowded, noisy – and market-day licensing laws being what they are – somewhat alcoholic place. The market is still there but things seem a little more polite these days. There have not been many changes to the square, but those that have been made have all dented the old character. There are cobbles still round the market shops, but only a token ring: the rest of the square has been tarmacked over and marked out as a carpark. There are more antique shops than before, and something of a rash of Olde Worlde. All that still gets swamped on market day, thank heavens.

For years I took Knaresborough for granted; it was just the nearby town where I went to school. It was only after years of absence, coming back with people who did not know it at all, that I really appreciated its special qualities. It is a compact town, densely packed so that, like all such places, it is full of little alleys and lanes that offer the promise of something exciting just round the corner. Sometimes the promise is fulfilled, sometimes not, but the feeling of excitement remains. It also acts as a sort of border town, differentiating one Yorkshire from another. To the west and the south is the world of industry and the hard-

edged Pennine hills. To the east and the north, the great plain with York at its centre and the gentler hills of the Dales. Knaresborough partakes of both worlds, with its rocky promontory and picturesque views, its industrial remains and its busy market. We have already come through part of the old industrial heartland, and it would be a shame to end without a short tour into that other country clearly visible from Knaresborough's hill.

Eight miles north of Knaresborough stands Ripon and Defoe, who never even mentioned Knaresborough's market square, was much impressed with the latter.

LEFT *The chequered Manor House beside the Nidd at Knaresborough.*

RIGHT *Riding between the sandstone cliffs and the old linen mill, Knaresborough.*

Rippon is a very neat, pleasant, well built town, and has not only an agreeable situation on a rising ground between two rivers, but the market place is the finest and most beautiful square that is to be seen of its kind in England.

In the middle of it stands a curious column of stone, imitating the obelisks of the antients, tho' not so high, but rather like the pillar in the middle of Covent-Garden, or that in Lincoln's Inn, with dials also upon it.

The obelisk still stands and it is here each night that the Wake Man comes to blow his horn to announce to the local citizens that they may sleep soundly in their beds for he will patrol the town throughout the night. But, of course, he will do no such thing, for night patrols have long since been taken over by the police and only the tradition remains. This is no re-assurance for the citizens, but a quaint old custom for the cameras of the town's visitors. Even the civic authorities seem less than wholly convinced of the Wake Man's ability to keep order, for the town hall carries this message across its handsome pediment in letters of gilt: 'Except ye Lord keep ye cittie ye wake man waketh in vain.'

There is a certain spaciousness about Ripon which appealed to Defoe, for he was a modernist who appreciated the new openness of towns, such a contrast to the often almost claustrophobic scene of medieval streets. Now we can stand further back and admire different periods for their own virtues. Where we differ, is in finding so much less to applaud in our own age's innovations than he did in his. We can, however, agree on Ripon's chief glory, the cathedral. This 'very handsome, antient and venerable pile of buildings' was very much to Defoe's liking. It has changed a little since his day. He described it as having three spires, one to each of its towers, though they were, he declared neither high nor handsome. They have gone now, and no doubt the building looks all the better for their absence.

Defoe was much intrigued by the history of the place. He found that in 1331 the organist was paid a paltry 14s 4d a year while the grammar school master had no more than £2 for his services, and concluded that the organist must have had a side line teaching the young ladies of Ripon to dance. He was pleased to find that things had improved and '. . . they now eat as good beef, and drink as good Yorkshire ale, as their neighbours'. Ale and roast beef – they could be said to epitomize one view of Yorkshire, but they do only tell part of the story. It is still common to think of the north of England in terms of clichés, all mills and hills, yet what a range of countryside, what variety of activities Defoe found here – and the same variety can be found today. So, just as a reminder that there is another side to the region, step inside the cathedral. Certain things you expect to find in any great and ancient church: a monumentality

Ripon in 1733; dominated, as it is today, by the great cathedral.

of high arches, an intricacy of tracery, a blaze of coloured glass. All these you find in Ripon. You will also find the Saxon crypt, which dates right back to the original monastic foundation of the seventh century. But I find the most attractive

The symbol of Ripon, the Wakeman's horn, still blown each and every night to reassure the citizens that their welfare is in good hands.

features to be among the smallest, the carvings on the choir stalls. These were done by Ripon men in the late fifteenth century, and so fine were they that William Bromflet was renamed William Carver. They are an absolute joy, full of life and vigour. These were carvings made by men who saw the church not as a Sunday place nor as a spot for visitors to wander round for five minutes to exclaim on its grandeur. For them it was central to their town and to their lives, so everything went into the carvings. There are biblical themes and angels as you might expect, but there are everyday scenes as well. An angry woman and her dog chase a fox caught stealing a goose. And there is humour here, too. So often a great cathedral can seem a remote sort of place, but here you have a sense of the people, of the ordinary men of the town, the superb craftsmen. My favourite among the carvings is a whimsical little group of two pigs dancing while a third plays the bagpipes. Inevitably, the English will have something to say about that group, for few Englishmen have ears tuned to the music of the pipes. Defoe went on up into Scotland, but found towns so few and inns still fewer that he recommended others who would follow him to travel '... with some company and carrying tents with them, and so encamping every night as if they were an army'. Half a century later, travel in Scotland was still difficult, and one visiting Englishman at least still regarded it as being very much a foreign country.

SAMUEL JOHNSON (1709-84)

•

A Foreign Land

A Journey to the Western Islands of Scotland 1775

Dr Samuel Johnson, the great lexicographer, man of letters, and wit was also renowned as a convinced urbanite. He was not over-enamoured of wild countryside, seeming to view hill country with much the same enthusiasm as did Defoe. Where the latter described the Lake District as 'the wildest, most barren and frightful' landscape he had come across and from which he turned with relief to the 'pleasant manufacturing towns', Johnson's first comments on the Scottish Highlands were even less flattering. He was 'astonished and repelled by this wide extent of hopeless sterility'. He was, notoriously, equally as harsh on the entire country which he regarded as foreign and thus, almost by definition, inferior to England. The following exchange is among the best known of all Johnsonian quotes:

> *Boswell:* I do indeed come from Scotland, but I cannot help it . . .
>
> *Johnson:* That, Sir, I find, is what a very great many of your countrymen cannot help.

The quotation is from Boswell's life of Johnson where all the quotable quotes appear, and which gives us our picture of the man. Even the trip to the west of Scotland is usually met in Boswell's description, which presents Johnson and Johnson's views through his admirer's eyes. The Johnson we meet in these pages is not the most likeable of men for he is constantly portrayed as far superior to everyone around him – which, intellectually he no doubt was – but the overall effect is one of a certain pomposity. One of the guides on their Scottish trip shouted at the goats on the hillside, to make them jump about to amuse the party. Boswell was vastly entertained – but not by the goats.

Little did he conceive what Doctor Johnson was. Here now was a common ignorant Highland clown imagining that he could divert, as one does a child, – *Dr. Samuel Johnson!* – The ludicrousness, absurdity, and extraordinary contrast between what the fellow fancied, and the reality, was truly comick.

Although this is Boswell's gloss on the event, the feeling stays in the mind that it was Johnson himself who held the low opinion of the Highlander, who had sought no more than

Dr Samuel Johnson by Sir Joshua Reynolds, 1756.

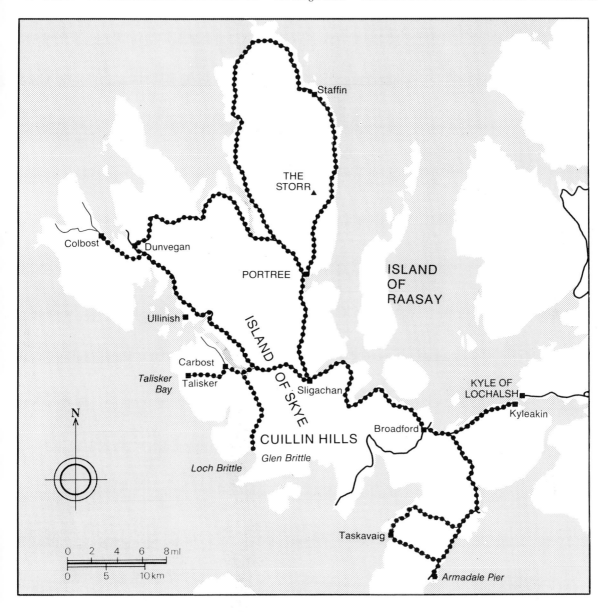

to amuse his charges. There is much in the same vein, so that by the end of the book you wonder why someone had not kicked the old gentleman smartly in the breeches. But if you turn to Johnson's own account, a very different character emerges: less witty and entertaining, more serious minded – and a good deal fairer and more agreeable. Reading the two accounts of the journey of 1773, one after the other, it was hard to remember that they were describing the same events. Boswell's was the jollier, but

left a nasty taste behind. The footsteps I wanted to follow were those of Dr Johnson, and it is his account you will find quoted here.

The section of the journey I chose was the self-contained travels round the Isle of Skye with a brief excursion to neighbouring Raasay. Why this section rather than another? The answer is that I had known Skye well in my youth, had spent three summers walking and climbing in the Cuillins, but had not been back since. It seemed the ideal opportunity to revive happy memories, though a small nagging voice kept telling me that the best way to preserve a happy memory is to keep it well clear of later reality. I stilled the voice and planned for Skye in early June. Here, at least, I was able to draw on experience and far-from-happy memories of the bane of the island summer: the Skye midge. Say 'midge' to an Englishman and he will think of a comparatively harmless, if irritating, little insect. The Skye midge stands in relation to his English counterpart much as the Bengal tiger does to the domestic tabby. No insect repellant I ever found was effective. The wretched beast seems to regard all such creams and lotions as a tasty hors d'oeuvre to whet its appetite for its favourite meal of mainland visitor. June, I hoped – and hope proved justified – was too early in the year for this monster to put in an appearance.

There is a real difficulty in attempting to follow Dr Johnson's route on Skye, not in the sense that it is physically difficult, rather the contrary. He travelled to a Skye, remote and backward, so that to journey across it was a genuine adventure.

In the Islands there are no roads, nor any marks by which a stranger may find his way. The horseman has always at his side a native of the place, who, by pursuing game, or tending cattle, or being often employed in messages or conduct, has learned where the ridge of the hill has breadth sufficient to allow a horse and his rider a passage, and where the moss or bog is hard enough to bear them. The bogs are avoided as toilsome at least, if not unsafe, and therefore the journey is made generally from precipice to precipice; from which if the eye ventures to look down, it sees below a gloomy cavity, whence the rush of water is sometimes heard.

But there seems to be in all this more alarm than danger. The Highlander walks carefully before, and the horse, accustomed to the ground, follows him with little deviation. Sometimes the hill is too steep for the horseman to keep his seat,

Kyleakin, a busy strait where the car ferries now ply; William Daniell, 1813.

and sometimes the moss is too tremulous to bear the double weight of horse and man. The rider then dismounts, and all shift as they can.

This was Johnson making his way from Armadale in the south-west corner of the island to the east coast for a trip to Raasay. Today it is 28 miles by road, and even with the wriggles and wiggles of the route, represents little more than an hour's drive by car. I wanted both to visit the spots the doctor visited, but also to try to experience some of that feeling of being on foot in a remote, wild, and possibly even threatening country. Where the road has been laid, I went by car to see the Johnsonian sites: but I also made excursions on foot to get the true feel of the country. It was to be, I decided, a week in which I would not so much follow precisely in another's steps as try to capture the essence of a time past alongside the time present. I began with a journey which seemed all present and no past, on the car ferry from Kyle of Lochalsh. Backwards and forwards they shuffle with their loads of cars, crossing and recrossing the narrow stretch of water so easily and so quickly that one magical element of the journey simply failed to materialize. There was none of that splendid sense of excitement that should always appear when you leave the mainland and head for an island. I regretted then not having done as Dr Johnson had done and as I did myself on earlier visits – taken the alternative, longer crossing to Armadale. That really is the best way to reach the island. I have vivid memories of my own first trip, steaming, literally, through the Highlands, across the wastes of Rannoch Moor and then on one of the most beautiful railways in the world, the line from Fort William to Mallaig. After that, came the crossing with a cold wind whipping spray off the wave tops. A fellow passenger, a local, with that lovely soft accent of the Western Isles, offered his hip flask. It is on days like that that you know why the Scots had the immense good sense to start making whisky. Drinking habits seem, however, to have changed a little since the eighteenth century.

A man of the Hebrides, for of the women's diet I can give no account, as soon as he appears in the morning, swallows a glass of whisky; yet they are not a drunken race,

at least I never was present at much intemperance; but no man is so abstemious as to refuse the morning dram, which they call a *skalk* . . . I never tasted it, except once for experiment at the inn in *Inverary*, when I thought it preferable to any *English* malt brandy. It was strong, but not pungent, and was free from the empyreumatick taste or smell.

Devoted as I am to the malt, I have not yet developed a taste for it as a pre-breakfast drink. No-one, alas, offered a dram on the Kyle ferry, but then there would scarcely have been time to unscrew the top of the flask before we were all over the water and off down the road which is as good as a mainland road, possibly better. There is no sense of seeing a different community here, no feeling of foreignness and there was nothing to lift the glum feeling of anticlimax as I stopped for a snack in Broadford. The café offered frozen food which reached the plate via the microwave – instant yes, but no delight. The return to Skye seemed more and more a mistake; that nagging whisper of doubt was growing in volume. This was neither my Skye nor Dr Johnson's. But then, I remembered, that this never had been my Skye. I had to find out if it was all to be a disaster, so I headed back for the parts I had known.

Along the road, I picked up a hitchhiker, rucksack on back, who was headed for Glen Brittle and the Cuillins just as I had been years before. Old landmarks began to reappear. The Sligachan Hotel, symbol of unbelievable luxury to me once, where we used to get cheap snacks at the back door, pickings from the rich man's table. Now it is just another hotel, though still with a quite magnificent view. Here the tourists stop, get out of their cars and look at the hills. We carried on along the road to Carbost and then turned south on to the very minor road to Glen Brittle. There used to be a bus service run by Mr McKay from Sligachan to Glen Brittle, though it was not noted for its reliability. On at least one occasion the scheduled bus failed to appear, so a call was put through to Mr McKay.

'How many of you are there?' he enquired.

A quick count revealed seven potential passengers.

There was a pause and a mutter of mental

The Croft Museum at Colbost.

arithmetic at the other end of the line. The profit and loss account must have worked in our favour.

    'Aye, I'll come.'

So easy now to take the car instead, but is the experience as enjoyable? The wonder of it was that, as the hills drew closer, I began to realize that little had changed. There was the youth hostel by the stream, and the barn where I had slept when the youth hostel had seemed too expensive. Glen Brittle House stood among the trees, and there was the little swing bridge that led to a cottage that was both post office and general store. It boasted a massive safe, yet stamps and postal orders were strewn over the counter: the safe was reserved for perishable food. And there were the Cuillins, the finest mountain range in Scotland. Clouds sat over the summits, flicking aside like a twitched curtain for occasional tempting views of the jagged peaks.

    The voice of doubt was quietened. I had achieved at least part of my aim – I was back in the Skye of my past. It was time to get a glimpse of part of Johnson's Skye. I drove on to Dunvegan. This is very much one of the tourist highlights. Dunvegan Castle: open 10.30 to 5 said the guidebook, which you might think means that if you arrive before 5 you will be allowed in. Not so. That's chucking out time, as I was informed by the lady at the gate who refused me admission in a voice that made it clear just what her opinion was of the half-witted tourist before her. I slunk away, suitably reproved. But if the castle turned me away, I thought I might have better luck at the croft.

    Johnson had found a 'Highland Hut' on the mainland and went inside to view it.

> To enter a habitation without leave, seems to be not considered here as rudeness or intrusion. The old laws of hospitality still give this licence to a stranger.

He found a cottage built of drystone walls with thatch for the roof and the bare ground as a floor. 'No light is admitted but at the entrance, and through a hole in the thatch, which gives vent to the smoke. This hole is not directly over the fire, lest the rain should extinguish it; and the smoke therefore naturally fills the place before it escapes.'

You no longer march up to people's houses and ask to be shown round, even if you are prepared to repay both the kindness and the welcoming dram as Johnson did, with a payment of snuff. The old crofts have, in any case, mostly gone from the land or are preserved, as at Colbost, as museums. They still trust a stranger here. No-one manned the little kiosk, no-one told me that I was too late – there was just a polite note asking me to leave my money at the desk and welcoming me to the croft. It is an extraordinarily successful little museum. If Dr Johnson's world can often seem a dim memory, then here at least the memory is preserved, though literally still dimly. As in the croft he described, the only light was from the doorway and the hole in the roof, and the strong, sooty smell of the peat fire still hung in the air. The reality of the old way of life may have gone, but this is as good a reconstruction as one could hope to find. It had been on balance a successful first day: nostalgia had been satisfied, nostalgia for my own youth and for the age of Johnson. It was now time to make for Carbost and the pub where I was staying for my days on the island.

The Old Inn was plain and friendly. In Johnson's time there were 'no houses where travellers are entertained for money', though he did, in fact, later find an inn in Portree where he managed to get a meal. I did not hunt out Johnson's inn, being perfectly happy at the pub, with a friendly gathering of walkers and climbers, among whom were a few locals who satisfied Dr Johnson's definition of a Highlander by speaking in Gaelic. Reading Johnson's accounts of the attitudes and way of life of the Highlanders, I often feel that he might as easily have been describing the habits and habitat of South Sea islanders. He was extremely irritated to find that, when he asked for information on a point of interest, the locals were eager to provide an answer but then were just as likely to provide a different answer in flat contradiction of the first, at the next asking. Their views on their own history proved equally unreliable.

The traditions of an ignorant and savage people have been for ages negligently heard, and unskilfully related. Distant events must have been mingled together, and the actions of one man given to another. These, however, are deficiencies in story, for which no man is now to be censured. It were enough, if what there is yet opportunity of examining were accurately inspected, and justly represented; but such is the laxity of Highland conversation, that the inquirer is kept in continual suspense, and by a kind of intellectual retrogradation, knows less as he hears more.

Such history as did appear tended, it seems, to dwell on the bloodier aspects of the past. On his first night on Skye at Armadale, in the home of Sir Alexander Macdonald, he was entertained at supper by the music of the pipes.

An elderly Gentleman informed us, that in some remote time, the *Macdonalds* of Glengary having been injured. or offended by the inhabitants of *Culloden*, and resolving to have justice or vengeance, came to *Culloden* on a Sunday, where finding their enemies at worship, they shut them up in the church, which they set on fire; and this, said he, is the tune that the piper played while they were burning.

Not, one would have thought, much of an encouragement to jolly, mealtime conversations.

The pipes were not heard in the pub at Carbost, though I remembered well on a previous visit to Skye hearing them played in what must be the ideal setting. High on the cliffs that stand above Coire Lagan in the Cuillins is a rock that stands out from the face, à Cioch. It was on this rock that the piper stood, a solitary romantic, sending his music ringing round that rocky amphitheatre. Even the non-musical – or, as a cynical Englishman might say, the musical – could hardly fail to be moved. There was no music in the pub, just friendly chat. The locals still seem a very independent people, able to turn to anything to make a livelihood. I spoke to a man who did a little crofting, a little fishing, and if anything else turned up, a bit of that as well. His companion, a man of seventy, had reached the age where he could sit and enjoy his dram in peace. I tackled him on the old controversy. How should you drink your whisky – neat or with water (no other mixture being, of course, admissible)? He was a firm

believer in the addition of water. By adding
water to his glass, he could, he claimed, finish
the whole bottle and feel no ill effects the next
day. I did not attempt the experiment, though I
was quite prepared to believe that had I done
so I too would have felt no ill effects. I do not
think I would have felt any effects at all. I felt
though that I had entered into the true Johnsonian spirit of enquiry even if, like him, I was
not entirely convinced by the accuracy of the
reply.

Dr Johnson had visited Talisker, not the
village where I was staying, but Talisker Bay,
some 5 miles away. It was time to take a
genuine Johnsonian excursion, and what a fine
place it turned out to be. 'Talisker,' declared
Johnson, 'is the place beyond all that I have
seen, from which the gay and the jovial seem
utterly excluded; and where the hermit might
expect to grow old in meditation, without
possibility of disturbance or interruption.' It
remains lonely and lovely; lonely I suspect
because it is only reached down a rough and
narrow road, and even that stops short a mile
from the sea. You need to walk and that alone is
sufficient to keep the spot blessedly free of
crowds. Entrance to the bay is guarded by the
shapely cone of Preshal More. To the north, a
waterfall draws a thin strand of silver down the
cliffs; to the south craggy hills rise up and
between was a beach of silver-grey sand on
which no Man Friday had left his footmarks. It
was a place that I found an absolute joy, relish-
ing its air of solitude. I tried to imagine Dr
Johnson coming here, but somehow that big,
shambling, essentially urban man seemed not
to have a place in such a landscape. Yet here he
had stood, viewing and describing precisely
that scene that lay before me two centuries
later. This was just the sort of scene, in fact, that
had drawn me to the island, and I had dressed
myself in all the correct approved gear for the
modern pleasure of walking to a wild, remote
stretch of country. Johnson must have cut a
very different figure, and what was the attraction that brought him to such a remote spot?
Talisker House and Mr Donald Maclean who
earned himself the Doctor's unstinted praise
for his efforts to bring the agricultural methods

The shattered cliffs of the Quairaing.

The Old Man of Storr, the pinnacle that stands guard over Skye's eastern coast.

of Hertfordshire and Hampshire to the Isle of Skye. It does not look much like the Home Counties, but Talisker House is still there, handsome behind its shelter of trees. It always brings one just a little closer to the original traveller when you come across a detail that remains unchanged, far more effective than any wider view. Boswell wrote that '... the court before the house is most injudiciously paved with the round bluish-grey pebbles which are found upon the sea-shore so that you walk as if upon cannon-balls driven into the ground.' There they are still, and just as uncomfortable. Suddenly I found I really could believe in my travellers after all.

One feeling that comes over more strongly than any other in Johnson's account is a sense of crossing and recrossing a trackless island. To recapture that feeling today means abandoning the obvious routes that join places together in favour of walking the wilder parts of the island. I contemplated going back to Glen Brittle where more of the Cuillins had emerged from the mists, though a cloud like an Andy Capp flat hat still perched on top and drooped down at the edges. I decided, however, to opt for something just as wild but even more fantastical. I headed off for the northern part of the island, stopping off for lunch in Portree. This is tourist-town Skye. There is a certain nobility in the harbour where fishing boats, bravely painted with decorated prows, stir gently on gunmetal water. Elsewhere it is pseudery craftery, microwave pie, and fizzy beer. I did not linger long but carried on up the east coast past the Storr and the sea stacks by the cliffs for the splendour of the Quairaing.

The road zig-zags up a hill, past reminders of the old life of the island, past a ruined shieling where a lonely herdsman would have spent the summer watching the cows on the sparse moorland pasture; past the dark streaks on the land where the peat has been cut for fuel. Then, at the top of the hill, you can leave the car and take to a one-man wide track that leads across the hillside, over gully and scree, for the cliff that seems to tumble away from the summit of Meall na Suiramach. The eighteenth century has left us with two contrasting views of the world. Johnson epitomizes one. Here man is the measure of all things; landscape is viewed for its usefulness not its scenic beauty; a good book or good conversation is infinitely preferable to a deserted moor. Then there is the other side, which was to grow and develop to become the Romanticism of the nineteenth century. The Quairaing belongs to the latter world: gothic pinnacles and spires rise above a tumult of shattered, weathered, crumbling cliff. Distant thunderclouds stood over the sea above pillars of rain and added their own sombre notes. Here, too, there was the slight frisson of danger, a walk in a wild place. A scramble over rocks, an uphill slog with a beat of blood in the ear, all part of the pleasures of the scene. There is a curious, perhaps puritanical streak in me, that says I have to earn the right to enjoy a view, and the greater the effort then the greater the enjoyment will be. I really cannot imagine the literary Doctor sharing such a view. Did he ever get a thrill from the dangers and hardships of the way, or was it always a necessary discomfort to be endured for the sake of the noble cause of acquiring knowledge? If he did ever get pleasure from the way, then he kept such feelings to himself and contented himself with noting details of agriculture and wildlife. We stand before the same scenes but see them quite differently. I see an ever-changing pattern of light on the rocks, and view the movement of sheep on the lower pasture as little more than a way of giving scale to the landscape. Dr Johnson notes drily:

> The goat is the general inhabitant of the earth, complying with every difference of climate, and of soil. The goats of the *Hebrides* are like others: nor did I hear any thing of their sheep, to be particularly remarked.

He notes that '. . . there are in *Sky* neither rats nor mice, but the weasel is so frequent, that he is heard in houses rattling behind chests or beds.' I can, alas, offer no more information on the Skye weasel, and did nothing at all to try to collect it. In fact, given the choice, I might well have spent all my time on the hills, but I still felt I needed to get closer, if I could, to the Skye of my distinguished predecessor.

A major excursion for Boswell and Johnson was a trip to the little island of Raasay. I went off there myself on a day of typical island weather. From the ferry there was a magnificent view that stretched from the Cuillins in the south to the Storr and the Quairaing in the north. Great wedges of cloud appeared on parade, each carrying its own parcel of weather with it. Grey rain sloped down to the hills but, between, the land gleamed in the sun: Raasay was floodlit, the Quairaing glowed. In the middle of it all was the ferry with its own personal cloud keeping pace with it, ensuring that we travelled in a perpetual downpour. The island presented just one area of greenery, surrounded by rock and heather and, in the middle of that, sat Raasay House commanding, as it later appeared, one of the finest views in the Western Isles. This was Dr Johnson's destination – 'a neat, modern fabrick' he called it, and here he spent most of his time, being right royally entertained. There were good food, good company, and Erse song to which he said he listened as he would to Italian opera 'delighted with the sound of words which I did not understand'. Seen from the boat, it was easy to believe that little had changed. The

A nineteenth-century version of Johnson and Boswell being taken by boat to Raasay.

house looked cosily elegant and I thought what a good day it would have been to travel in the old style under sail, for there was just enough breeze to flick white foam on to the tips of the waves. Instead, we had the conventional ferry which took a mere quarter of an hour to deposit its passengers at the quay and not, as the earlier boat had done, to a disgruntled Dr Johnson, on the rocks.

The first sight on landing came as something of a surprise, a muddle of old warehouses, ore shoots, and a disused railway that mark a nineteenth-century iron ore mining operation. You get another view of the enterprise at Inverarish where houses are built in two close terraces as if they were part of an industrial town in the north of England – packed together although there was a whole island to build on. I turned off into the Raasay forest, an area of woodland straight out of the Brothers Grimm. Trees were close set, impenetrable except where the path wound through to a little, plain church with equally plain furnishings. No frippery here, just whitewashed walls and uncomfortable-

looking benches. Johnson would have been pleased, but not perhaps overwhelmed at the sight. He had found an island where the churches lay in ruins due to the 'malignant influence of Calvinism'. He was much saddened by the sight of so many decaying churches through the island.

From these remains of ancient sanctity, which are every where to be found, it has been conjectured, that, for the last two centuries, the inhabitants of the Islands have decreased in number. This argument, which supposes that the churches have been suffered to fall, only because they were no longer necessary, would have some force, if the houses of worship still remaining were sufficient for the people. But since they have now no churches at all, these venerable fragments do not prove the people of former times to have been more numerous but to have been more devout.

Raasay House, looking out across the water to the Cuillins;
William Daniell.

He found worship in houses, not in churches. The church in the forest would, no doubt, have been thought an improvement, though it is doubtful if he would have approved its bare austerity. It would, at least, have been something to look at, for his verdict was: 'Raasay has little that can detain a traveller.' Boswell, however, found it rather more interesting, walked all over the island and danced a Highland fling on the top of Dun Caan. I was enchanted by the forest, and enchanted seems the only word to use for such a place. As I left the church, the forest grew ever denser, scarcely allowing more than a dim light to filter down on to a cushioned path of mouldering leaves and thick, uncannily green moss. In the trees, huge boulders and fallen trunks were all clothed and softened by the same moss. Green above, green below and that pale filtered light made the walk seem like an undersea exploration. There was certainly an unearthly feel to the place. And then, in the centre of all, a mound rose up, the path climbing it through gnarled roots and a tumble of stone. At the very top, a boundary wall could still be discerned. This was the broch, a primitive castle dating back to the Iron Age. In this setting it could as easily have belonged to a world of mythology as to any historical reality. The Raasay forest would be an ideal setting for a witches' sabbath, and the broch could scarcely be bettered as an ogre's castle. After that, it was almost a relief to walk on to Raasay House and civilization.

The house that looked so fine from a distance was somewhat less enticing on closer inspection. The grounds must once have been splendid, but no more. Iron fishes clambered up an iron fountain, but no water flowed, and cows munched in the bowers. The house, too, was changed. For Johnson it was a place of unalloyed pleasure:

> Such a seat of hospitality, amidst the winds and waters, fills the imagination with a delightful contrariety of images. Without is the rough ocean and the rocky land, the beating billows and the howling storm: within is plenty and elegance, beauty and gaiety, the song and the dance.

The music now was rock, the beauty has faded, and the lawn where the ladies and gentlemen had strolled was covered with kayak canoes.

This was once the formal garden of Raasay House where Johnson stayed.

The house is now an adventure centre, whose inhabitants actually prefer the rough ocean and the rocky land to the old elegance.

The area has one last curiosity on offer. Down by the old pier is a fortified round house dating back to the Napoleonic wars. It is guarded by two fierce mermaids, presumably set there to deter rather than to attract. They could never have been very beautiful maidens, and the loss by one of both arms has not turned her into a Venus de Milo, while the removal of one breast from her companion has done little to improve her. It was time to go back to Skye, so I rejoined the ferry which was off for its busiest trip, collecting the local children who had been at school in Portree. I returned as I came, with cloud escort.

I woke next day to a grey morning: grey clouds sat low on the hills and a thin, grey rain swept in bands down the loch. It was a world reduced to the tonal values of a badly printed black and white film. The two ducks by the back door preened themselves and ended up with feathers stuck all over their beaks. They abandoned the exercise and went off for a swim instead. A solitary hen sat under the garden table. If it is possible for a hen to look anything at all, then this one looked miserable. I sympathized. It was not a day to gladden the heart. It seemed, however, an ideal day for a second attempt at visiting Dunvegan Castle. How easy it now is to reach the place and, on a wet day, it is such an obvious attraction that, by the time I got there, the car park was nearly full and the first coach had already arrived. Global Tours was debouching its load of visitors whom I once heard referred to by the guide at one attraction visited by that company as 'the globules'. Visits made too easily can seem to lose something in the process. Dr Johnson's journey to Dunvegan was hard going but included along the way one remarkable encounter, or so it seems today.

Johnson left Raasay and carried on by sea and land to Kingsburgh where he was entertained by Mr Macdonald and rather more interestingly, as far as his readers are concerned, by Mrs Macdonald, the famous Flora who had helped Prince Charles to escape after his disastrous defeat at Culloden. Hers was, said Johnson, '. . . a name that will be mentioned in history, and if courage and fidelity be virtues, mentioned with honour'. The name is indeed remembered and honoured, but I was struck on reading those words that they were written by the quintessential Englishman, popularly supposed to be less than favourably disposed to Scottish nationalist fervour. The following day Johnson continued his journey, again partly by sea which made for easier travelling than did the crossing of a boggy squelchy moorland on horseback. It is not surprising that his enthusiasm for Dunvegan was somewhat greater than mine.

Dunvegan Castle is the greatest of the Skye castles, a place overflowing with historical incident, yet oddly disappointing to the visitor. The grounds are fine and cheerful, and they added a welcome note of colour to a gloomy day, but the castle itself seems little more than an overgrown country house, sadly lacking that romantic air which one feels should be an essential ingredient of any ancestral seat in Scotland. Inside, it is comfortably if not lavishly furnished, and, though there are glimpses of stone stairways and dungeons, and although the walls are liberally hung with the inevitable collection of swords, guns, and other lethal implements, it still seemed remarkably cosy. There are reminders of stirring times – the Fairy Banner, which it is said could change the course of battles, and mementoes of Flora Macdonald and Bonny Prince Charlie. Yet nothing quite disturbs the air of peaceful domesticity. The portraits on the walls of elegant ladies and gents add to this air of refinement, for only one out of all the paintings shows the prototypal chieftain in full Highland regalia. In fact, the fiercest-looking face on display is that of Dr Johnson, whose portrait scowls down from the walls. It is only to be expected that such comfort would have appealed to the eminent writer, who almost certainly looked a great deal happier during his visit than he does now in art. He was not in a hurry to leave:

> At Dunvegan I had tasted lotus, and was in danger of forgetting that I was ever to depart, till Mr. Boswell sagely reproached me with my sluggishness and softness. I had no very forcible defence to make; and we agreed to pursue our journey.

As a paying visitor rather than a house guest I was less reluctant to go, and decided to take a boat trip round the little islets that shelter Dunvegan from the sea. Now, at last, the castle assumed a suitably romantic aspect, even if much of the grandeur represented the embellishments of Victorian 'restorers' rather than genuine medieval defences. The old keep can plainly be seen set high on its rocky eminence, while the slightly later Fairy Tower stands out from its surroundings of fake battlements. Ah yes, you say to yourself, that is just what a castle should be like. But, of course, my whole view of the castle is that of the paying, sightseeing visitor, and much though I might hanker after medieval austerity, it is not a view to commend itself to the present generation of MacLeods who still live here. Such musings did not last long, for there were other things to look at on the boat trip besides an old castle. The major attractions of the islands are the seals. I suppose there are few more endearing creatures around than seals, part of the attraction being that they seem at least as interested in you as you in them. Sleek heads pop out above the waves, and black eyes peer at you. The young lounge around on the rocks, a blasé street corner gang with nothing much to do except scratch themselves. What is it that makes some animals attractive and others repellant? Not that everyone sees seals as lovable – fishermen regard them as predators, fish hunters in potential fur coats, but most of us regard them fondly. But why seals rather than, say, water rats? The latter are equally sleek water creatures, if somewhat shyer by nature, but you seldom hear anyone oohing and aahing over water rats. There is no doubt a deep philosophical thesis to be written on the subject – there may well be a deep philosophical thesis already written – but for the time being I was quite happy to make the seals' acquaintance and ooh and aah with the rest. They were the main attraction, the old, be-whiskered aldermen seals and the gauche youngsters: anthropomorphism is it seems inescapable when discussing the beasts. There were some other good turns on the bill, including nesting herons, and, after an appropriate time had been spent viewing the animal world, the boatman turned back towards the shore. Now the castle was really coming into its own, with ominous clouds blowing off the tops of the hills.

From Dunvegan I continued on the Johnson route to Ulinish. The house where he stayed is now a hotel where I was able to enjoy a local speciality, an excellent soup of haddock and potato. How rare it is these days to eat the food of the country, genuine local produce – and how very welcome. The hotel is as quiet and unassuming as the house must have been 200 years ago; plainly built, whitewashed, as are so many Skye buildings, its only note of grace a well-proportioned porch. Above one window, engraved letters mark a wedding.

17 AM ♥ MM 57

Little has changed around here. Nearby are the remains of a broch or dun, not dissimilar to that on Raasay. Dr Johnson inspected it with great care, being particularly intrigued by the en-

trance, which was then more or less intact, a narrow stone passage topped by massive slabs. How, he wondered, were they put in place? He thought that long levers had probably been used. 'Savages, in all countries, have patience proportionate to their unskilfulness and are content to attain their end by very tedious methods.' He also speculated on the building's age and purpose. Nowadays, we all have guidebooks full of information, but here was a structure which appeared to be that of a round building some 42 feet (almost 13 metres) in diameter, slightly tapering and having smaller compartments within it. It stood in a wild area, with nothing much around it to provide clues. Johnson was at least bold enough to put his own judgement down in black and white:

> If it was ever roofed, it might once have been a dwelling, but as there is no provision for water, it could not have been a fortress. In *Sky*, as in every other place, there is an ambition of exalting whatever has survived memory, to some important use, and referring it to very remote ages. I am inclined to suspect, that in lawless times, when the inhabitants of every mountain stole the cattle of their neighbour, these inclosures were used to secure the herds and flocks in the night. When they were driven within the wall, they might be easily watched, and defended as long as could be needful; for the robbers durst not wait till the injured clan should find them in the morning.

The reasoning is impeccable, but the conclusion, alas, wrong. We now know that there were some 200 of these brochs, tapering towers that were ideal strongholds, and we also know that they date from the Iron Age and are peculiar to Scotland. So, on this occasion, we can catch the Doctor out in a mistake, though if you walk to the broch you will have ample confirmation that he was an accurate observer. The moorland is, he declared, everywhere very boggy, and as you squelch around the area, you can only agree. Visiting the building, now far more ruinous than in Johnson's time, I thought how very differently I felt about it and its 'savage' builders. He saw a crude structure built by crude men: I saw a building of surprising sophistication. Given the lack of tools and equipment, the builders constructed a

tower that has survived extraordinarily well.
Enormous care must have gone into the drystone walling of the outer shell, and we can see
it now as being the ideal structure for this
exposed site. A totally solid, mortared wall
would have offered more resistance to the
winds from the sea or the moor, but the looser
construction used here allows it to 'give' with
the elements, allows the force of the wind to be
dissipated throughout the whole structure. The
mere fact of its survival is itself the strongest
argument in favour of the notion that the men
who built it had a very good idea of just what
they were doing. And if one turns to aesthetics,
then one has to remember that Dr Johnson had
not had the pleasure of seeing some of the
buildings the sophisticated technocrats of the
twentieth century have foisted on to the land.

I had now covered a good deal of the journey
made by Johnson and Boswell: Raasay to
Dunvegan, on to Ulinish and Talisker. Perversely perhaps, I had yet to cover the first part
of the journey. I marked that down for the next
day with a hope for better weather.

If the sea crossing from Mallaig to Armadale
is the best way to reach Skye from the mainland, in the sense that the longer sea crossing
gives you a chance to shake off thoughts of the
mainland and anticipate the pleasures to come
on the island, it does not follow that the road
away from Armadale will give you the best of
Skye. You are spared the suburban, gifte
shoppe atmosphere of Broadford but do not
immediately capture the feeling of a moun-
tainous Hebridean island. Indeed, as you leave
the pier for the main road – a term which does
not imply anything as exotic as a dual carriageway, nor even a road wide enough for two
vehicles to pass, you find yourself in what
could well be an English country lane. The
grass banks were speckled with flowers, with
beech trees to shade the way. Armadale Castle
has gone to be replaced by the Armadale Clan
Centre, an obvious conclusion to a process that
was well under way in Johnson's time, a process which he found as interesting as anything
he observed during his stay on the island.

Following the collapse of the Jacobite Rebellion, the power of the clan chiefs was abated

A somewhat exaggerated view of the Cuillins
by William Daniell.

and the clans disarmed. Johnson's long discourse on the topic shows him at his very best. One might well have expected him to have given the move every support but, in fact, he weighs the different factors with a nice appreciation of how matters affected different sections of the community.

> Their pride has been crushed by the heavy hand of a vindictive conqueror, whose severities have been followed by laws, which, though they cannot be called cruel, have produced much discontent, because they operate upon the surface of life, and make every eye bear witness to subjection.

The old days when the chief walked his domain with his armed followers had been ended. Johnson looked at both the good and the bad of the old system.

> Every man was a soldier, who partook of national confidence, and interested himself in national honour. To lose this spirit, is to lose what no small advantage will compensate.

Yet this was not a way of life to commend itself to Johnson. But why, he asks, need the country be made uniform? Why need all be the same? Equally, however, he was not blind to the iniquities of the old ways.

> It must however be confessed, that a man who places honour only in successful violence, is a very troublesome and pernicious animal in time of peace; and that the martial character cannot prevail in a whole people, but by the diminution of all other virtues. He that is accustomed to resolve all right into conquest, will have very little tenderness or equity. All the friendship in such a life can be only a confederacy of invasion, or alliance of defence. The strong must flourish by force, and the weak subsist by stratagem.

He saw the same balance in many aspects of life. The administration of law by the chiefs may not have been perfect, but it was law administered by local men who knew local ways. And far and away the most important aspect of the new life of the Highlands was the change of attitude towards the land.

> The chiefs, divested of their prerogatives, necessarily turned their thoughts to the improvement of their revenues, and expect more rent, as they have less

homage. The tenant, who is far from perceiving that his condition is made better in the same proportion, as that of his landlord is made worse, does not immediately see why his industry is to be taxed more heavily than before. He refuses to pay the demand, and is ejected; the ground is then let to a stranger, who perhaps brings a larger stock, but who, taking the land at its full price, treats with the Laird upon equal terms, and considers him not as a Chief, but as a trafficker in land. Thus the estate perhaps is improved, but the clan is broken.

Today, some of the sillier laws have been repealed – the tartan and the kilt are again permitted. They have, however, long since lost much of their old significance. They are no longer the uniforms of armed men, but remembrances of a period of Scotland's history that ended more than two centuries ago. So, instead of the reality of clan life, we are left with the Clan Museum. And many of the visitors of today are descendants of those who were leaving the islands in their thousands in Johnson's time, the men and women who made their way to Nova Scotia, the New Scotland. Johnson was saddened by the migration. He was ready enough to accept that those who wished to travel to live in other lands should be free to do so. That was not the case in Scotland as he saw it: it was less the appeal of the new and rather more the circumstances at home. 'But if they are driven from their native country by positive evils, and disgusted by ill-treatment, real or imaginary, it were fit to remove their grievances, and quiet their resentment.' Reading the whole section, which runs over several pages, I was struck again by Johnson's reasonableness, the care with which the arguments were mustered and weighed. It might seem somewhat lacking in passion, and today we fulminate, quite rightly, over policy in Scotland which led to the infamy of the Highland Clearances. It is worth remembering, however, that a mere twenty-seven years had passed since Culloden, and many, possibly the majority of, Englishmen regarded the Highlanders simply as the dangerous rabble which had invaded their country.

The road onwards followed a route much the same as that taken by Johnson and Boswell, hugging the coast before cutting across a narrow neck of land to Broadford. This is the sensible route for anyone wanting to drive from Armadale. I was tempted by a detour, a narrow twisting road that leaves the eastern shore of the peninsula and wriggles its way inland to reach the opposite coast. It follows that for about 5 miles, and then wriggles back again to the main road. It is a far longer route, far more difficult to travel and offers nothing along the way except a promise of wild scenery. It was as attractive to me as it would have been repugnant to my eighteenth-century predecessor. I abandoned Johnson's low road for my high road and it quite definitely answered expectations better than I could ever have imagined possible.

The twists and turns you can see on the map, even the ordnance survey map I was using, give only a hint of the extraordinary convolutions of the road itself, which combines acute bends with a switchback of changing levels. It is not a road for those in a hurry and there are constant temptations to leave the car and travel on foot. At Taskavaig I succumbed. Here you look across the rocks and sands of the bay, over a low headland to the dramatic outline of the Cuillin peaks. There is a scattering of houses but no more than a scattering; a lovely remote spot where I would gladly have stayed a week, but alas time on Skye was beginning to run out. So it was back to the serpentine way through woods and moors to the main route. 'It's not a very good road from Armadale', someone said to me. They should try the detour: after that, it would look like the M1. I still had one more section of the Johnson trail to follow, but first I still had to finish my personal tour. The view of the Cuillins with no more than tattered grey shreds hanging over their shoulders in place of the great cap of clouds that had been set so firmly on their tops, was simply too enticing. I went back to the place that was calling me – Glen Brittle.

The day had a wild note to sound. The little swing bridge across the river Brittle swayed and rattled in the wind. Clouds sped down the valley and tore themselves apart on the peaks and I set off to walk the track across the moors to Coire Lagan. Memories returned to good days climbing the amazingly rough gabbro of the crags, a rock so hard that they say it makes

ideal climbing for potential criminals, who can wear away their fingerprints in no time. There were sad memories, too, of my last visit when I joined a mountain rescue party only to find that there was nothing to bring down but the bodies of the dead. These hills have their dangers, but, for those who are prepared to take them seriously, they can offer great rewards. I have stood on the high ridge and seen an eagle swooping down into the corrie and it is a sight that remains perfectly clear in my mind after more than twenty years absence. This day I was to take no more than a short walk up to the foot of the crag, to the point where the little loch sits in its bowl of rock. It was a walk for recollections, and I was glad to have made it. This was always the Skye I came to, the wild Skye, the challenging Skye. It was not, in any sense, Dr Johnson's Skye, and I still had that last section of his route to follow. So I turned my back on the crag and made my way down-hill to the lower slopes which still bear the marks left by crofters who had once ploughed and sown this rough land. I returned to the route I had followed on the first day in the island, back towards Broadford.

Johnson stayed the night at Coriatachan, '. . . a house very pleasantly situated between two brooks, with one of the highest hills of the island behind it. It is the residence of Mr. Mackinnon by whom we were treated with very liberal hospitality, among a more numerous and elegant company than it could have been supposed easy to collect.' Coire-chat-achan is marked on the ordnance survey map, a building between two brooks beneath the shadow of Beinn na Gaillich, which stands in fact at a modest 2400 feet (730 metres) whereas many of the Cuillin peaks comfortably top the 3000-foot (900-metre) mark. When you reach the spot, however, the house shown on the map turns out to be modern to us not to Dr Johnson. All that remains of his house are ruined walls among farm buildings with no more than a chimney piece to tell you that it was ever a dwelling. It seemed a fitting place to say goodbye to the Doctor. The house where he was entertained has gone, just as the Skye he recorded, with its still vivid memories of clans, chieftains, and wars has gone. It was a spot, too, that encapsulated a special sense of dis-belief that had remained with me throughout

The ragged peaks of the Cuillins near Sligachan.

the journey in Johnson's footsteps. Did that committed Londoner, that devotee of urban life, really come here to this wild place in the hills? I tried to imagine the scene as the travellers arrived late at night, tired and hungry, to be greeted by that elegant company and offered the hospitality of a gracious house. The imagination refused to rise to the task. No picture of that scene would come to my mind. I found it difficult to think of Dr Johnson, of all people, here in Skye. But he did come here at a time when travel was infinitely more difficult than it is today, and he came when he was a man in his sixties.

The very difficulty which I felt in envisaging the scene is, in a way, a mark of respect. He often himself had doubts as to whether he would make the trip, and Boswell has recorded his own apprehension. But come he did and left us a record not just of observations of scenery and customs, but of ideas, carefully pondered. Rereading his journey it is the thoughts that impress with the insight that they give into the mind of a great man. My next traveller presents both similarities and contrasts. He, too, put his thoughts down – thoughts more forcefully expressed than Johnson's, but not always as carefully considered. And where Johnson seems a man out of place in the open country, it is difficult to imagine our next guide staying away from it for long.

WILLIAM COBBETT (1763-1835)

·

On Four Legs

Rural Rides 1830

Most people now meet William Cobbett for the first time as the author of *Rural Rides*. The Cobbett I first encountered, however, was Cobbett the radical, Cobbett the politician. I was looking at the early years of the British cotton industry when I came upon a speech he had made to the House of Commons in favour of a bill that was to limit the work of children to ten hours a day. No-one might have thought a particularly extreme measure, but the factory owners wrung their hands and prophesied doom. Cobbett was not impressed with their tale of woe. Here is a part of his speech which still seems to me to capture the wit and the fighting heart of the man: and it still sends waves of affection for the speaker rippling through my system:

> I have only one observation to make, and I will not detain the House two minutes in doing so. We have, Sir, this night made one of the greatest discoveries ever made by a House of Commons . . . Hitherto, we have been told that our navy was the glory of the country, and that our maritime commerce and extensive manufactures were the mainstays of the realm. We have also been told that the land had its share in our greatness, and should justly be considered as the pride and glory of England. The Bank, also, has put in its claim to share in this praise, and has stated that public credit is due to it; but now, a most surprising discovery has been made, namely, that all our greatness and prosperity, that our superiority over other nations, is owing to 300,000 little girls in Lancashire. We have made the notable discovery, that, if these little girls work two hours less in a

day than they now do, it would occasion the ruin of the country; that it would enable other countries to compete with us; and thus make an end to our boasted wealth, and bring us to beggary!

I still feel I ought to stand and cheer whenever I read those words which seem to encapsulate so much of the character of Cobbett. He was, it is clear, completely assured as to the rightness of his case and was prepared to argue it before all and sundry. I warmed to him at

William Cobbett; artist unknown.

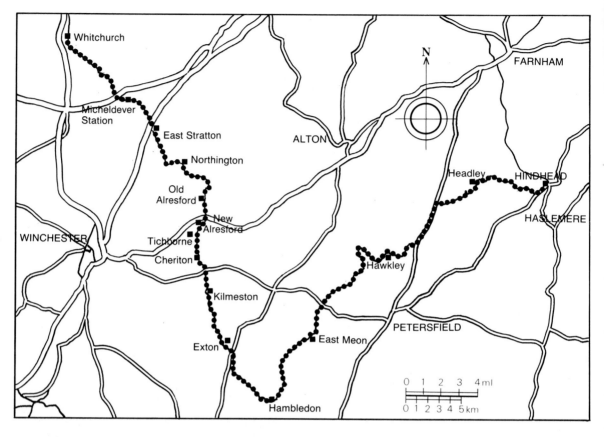

once – but was to discover as I turned to more of his writings that he could be as enthusiastic an exponent of causes of which I did not approve, could be indeed an exponent of causes of consummate daftness. That was, at first, a disappointment. But, as I read more Cobbett it became clear that this was a part of the man – opinionated, yes, but always ready to stick his neck out. He was a man who cared little or nothing for what the world at large felt about any subject that attracted his attention, and there seem to have been very few topics of the day which did not interest him. He was as ready to speak out for an unpopular cause as for any other. He was not, it is said, either a good or effective politician, which seems to mean that he was not prepared to appeal to special interests nor to trim his opinions to gain popularity. Would there were more of his ilk. And his opinions were not left behind on the office shelf when he went travelling. He clearly loved the purely physical pleasures of riding across country, but what he saw was invariably set within a social framework. 'Why do people have to bring politics into everything?' is a common cry of the twentieth century. Cobbett would not have understood it. For him, politics stood at the heart of everything, for it was only through political action that the good could be saved and the bad changed. In following Cobbett's trail, I have always been at least as conscious of the personality of the guide as I have been of the ground over which I travelled.

As always, a decision had to be made over which section of his travels to follow and which form of transport to use. The first choice was simple for, as soon as I thought of the book, I thought at once of the splendid account of the journey, unwillingly and unwittingly undergone, over Hindhead Common. How to travel? That was more problematical. Cobbett was a horseman. As far as he was concerned, the only proper way to travel was on horseback either across country or by narrow roads and lanes. He hated the turnpikes, the new, improved, well-surfaced roads that were beginning, in his day, to make a real impression on travel in Britain. If one were looking for a modern equivalent, one would turn to the motorist who ignored motorways and limited his journey entirely to B roads. But, with Cobbett, we have for the first time among our travellers, a man who regarded the process of travel as being at least as important as the places to be visited. He was also a man constantly on the lookout for things of interest along the way. That ruled out the motor car for me because even the slowest car moves too fast for a driver to take in much of the detail of the scenery along the way. My usual alternative, to travel by my own feet, suffered from the opposite disadvantage to that of the car – it was too slow. I simply would not have the time to take in a respectable fraction of Cobbett's travels. He himself had faced something of a similar problem. His very first journey was made in 1822 from Kensington to Uphusband, near Andover, and he explained just why he went cross-country on horseback.

> It is very true that I could have gone to Uphusband by travelling only about 66 miles, and in the space of about *eight hours*. But, my object was, not to see inns and turnpike-roads, but to see the *country*; to see the farmers at *home*, and to see the labourers *in the fields*; and to do this you must go either on foot or on horseback. With a *gig* you cannot get about amongst *bye-lanes* and *across fields*, through bridle-ways and hunting-gates; and to *tramp it* is too *slow*, leaving the *labour* out of the question, and that is not a trifle.

The arguments are sound, but I am no horse-man. There was no way I should be travelling on four legs. Or was there? The solution appeared in the ample shape of friend and neighbour John May and his sixty-year-old tandem. Four legs it was to be: two of mine, two of his. So we set off in early autumn for our own rural ride.

Our starting place was Whitchurch in Hampshire, a small and quite delightful small town, far pleasanter now than it was some years ago. Once the A34, the Oxford–Southampton road ran straight through the middle, but a bypass has restored the peace. It has been a double blessing: motorists have been spared long holdups, the locals can go about their affairs without a constant stream of

traffic. Further north, above Oxford, other towns still wait for similar blessings, but there the authorities have opted for a full-scale motorway, that will eat up vast areas of good land and overwhelm some beautiful country-side. The planners have been rather crafty. They have presented their case in terms of accept the motorway or keep the status quo, and have tried to pretend that all the alterna-tives are totally impractical. Why this is so they never explain. If the dual carriageway bypass is adequate for Whitchurch, why not for Wood-stock? A deathly hush descends for a moment before the all-too-powerful road lobby starts shouting again – motorway or nothing, motorway or nothing. None of this is, I sup-pose, especially relevant to Cobbett and his rural rides, but he does set a precedent. He was a great man for riding his hobbyhorse in public. At Whitchurch he was straight away into a tirade against what he saw as one of the great evils of the day – paper money. It had been produced in large quantities and one result was a serious inflation. At Whitchurch he saw the mill where the money was printed.

> I hope the time will come, when a monu-ment will be erected where that mill stands, and when on that monument will be inscribed *the curse of England*. This spot ought to be held accursed in all time hence-forth and for evermore. It has been the spot from which have sprung more and greater mischiefs than ever plagued man-kind before. However, the evils now appear to be fast recoiling on the merciless authors of them; and, therefore, one be-holds this scene of paper-making with a less degree of rage than formerly. My blood used to *boil* when I thought of the wretches who carried on and supported the system. It does not boil now, when I think of them. The curse, which they in-tended solely for others, is now falling on themselves; and I smile at their sufferings. Blasphemy! Atheism! Who can be an Atheist, that sees how *justly* these wretches are treated; with what exact measure they are receiving the evils which they inflicted on others for a time, and which they intended to inflict on them for ever!

It should be evident that Mr Cobbett was not

Whitchurch Silk Mill.

a man much given to delicate expression or too nice a concern for the feelings of others. He got so worked up about the iniquities perpetrated in the paper mill that he never got round to saying anything whatsoever about the rest of the town. I have known the place for some time not, however, because of its paper mill – to which, incidentally, no monument was ever erected – but because of its silk mill. This is a handsome little building, unmistakeably Georgian with its pedimented front, delicate cupola and most importantly, its proportions, so effortlessly right and proper. Its red-brick exterior is, however, just a skin covering a structure built up of blocks of chalk. It stands on the River Test, which is not exactly a raging torrent but which I find particularly attractive. Its shallow, clear waters, allow you to look down on to the softly streaming weed that waves gently in the current. I was reminded at once of a painting by Monet, simply called *The Boat,* which hangs in the Marmottan Museum

in Paris. The boat in the title sits up in one corner, and what really holds the eye are those waving weeds. Even though they are fixed in the perpetual stillness of paint and canvas, it is impossible not to see them as moving. How odd it is that Monet should have come to a river which must have been very like the Hampshire Test, painted it and now, 100 years later, I should still be seeing the river as if through his eyes. I suppose, that is just one way of stating the obvious fact that Monet was a great artist.

There was a mill recorded here on the Test in the Domesday Book. Many mills have been built to do many jobs, but, ever since the late eighteenth century when the present building was finished, this has been a textile mill, first for spinning and weaving wool and latterly a more exotic commodity, silk. The building itself has altered very little in the last 200 years and it was powered by a waterwheel right through to the 1950s. The machinery is still there, and water still flows down the leat. A fat trout lay all but motionless in the water under the shade of the wheel house, head facing upstream, open mouthed as the swift current fed him an endless supply of food. When I last visited Whitchurch, it had been a working mill loud with the clatter of looms, but now the commercial life has ended. 'Eighties' recession has done for Whitchurch just as it has for so many other textile mills in Britain. On this visit I found one lady weaver, running just two looms. The material, steadily growing, and winding on at the back of the loom was exquisite, but there was that air of forlorn loss that always belongs with an enterprise that is closing. Why does it have to close? It is certainly old fashioned. The looms are years out of date, cumbersome beasts compared with their modern equivalents. But the place was just too small to command the cash for modernization. It was added to the long list of sacrificial victims delivered up to the new economic gods. It is absolutely necessary, say the experts; our theories show that. We have to clear away the dead wood. But it is not wood, it is people. And what, if you can imagine such a thing, if your theories are wrong? Are they any more likely to be right than the last set of fashionable views? And if they are wrong, which is more than possible, who will sort out the wreckage of collapsed companies, lost jobs? You, the deciders, the rulers, can change your minds and move on to the next theory. Where does an unemployed weaver go?

Happily, the Whitchurch story is not all unrelieved gloom. Hampshire Building Preservation Trust is keeping the fabric of the building in repair and it will open again as – yes, inevitably, an industrial museum. I have this terrible vision that, if present policies continue, we shall end with the complete museumization of the country, where the only industry left will be the manufacture of tea towels and mugs, and the entire working population will be employed by the Manpower Services Commission. But I am still glad that Whitchurch Mill is to be saved, for all that.

Tour of the mill over, it was time at last to start travelling. I had laid out a route on the ordnance survey map which would take us to all the places Cobbett mentioned using, as far as possible, lanes and the most minor of minor roads. For the first 15 miles, the route went more or less south-east, after which it headed pretty well due south all the way to Hamble-

don. That was to be the turning point after which it was to be north-west to Thursley. That, at any rate, was the intention. So, off we set. Riding a tandem is a slightly curious experience. My role at the back was, you might say, stoker to John's driver. He controlled the steering, the gears, and the braking and all I was required to do was pedal – and once my feet were in the clips I had no choice about that either. A curtain amount of co-ordination between the two pedallers is required, but the one at the back has the best of it and, indeed, for my purposes it was ideal. Not having to steer I could sit up in the saddle, take the map out to check the way and view the world going by, and all without having to stop.

Cobbett was reasonably clear about his route: 'Quitting Whitchurch, I went off to the left out of the Winchester-road, got out upon the high-lands, took an "observation," as the sailors call it, and off I rode, in a straight line, over hedge and ditch, towards the rising ground between *Stratton Park* and *Micheldever-Wood*.' Tandems are not particularly good at going over hedge and ditch, so we took a series of minor roads which, if they were not exactly making a straight line, came quite close to it. The phrase '. . . got out upon the high-lands. . .' was probably all that Cobbett felt was necessary to describe his ride. It sounds very simple, but we were soon wheezing and puffing on our way up the hill. Once up, we came upon an amazingly empty landscape of fields, hedges, and woodland – empty, that is, of people. It was a landscape quite densely populated with other forms of life. Sheep and cattle grazed and the air was loud with bird song. And very notable among the bird population were the pheasants. They waddled from the woods to peck among the stubble of the adjoining fields. Occasionally, they showed alarm and either ran for cover, spindly legs going so fast you could scarcely see them, or took off with a noisy flurry of wings. What pleasure this landscape gives, this very English landscape: fields which alternate crops with grazing cattle, divided off by hedgerows. How long will it survive the drive towards greater efficiency? In Britain we grumble endlessly about the European farm subsidies which keep French peasants as peasants with holdings too small to warrant modernization. How much better to mechanize, to increase crop yields, which the government can then buy up and store away until it rots. If you want a symbol of modern Britain, come to Abingdon. They closed down the old MG car works because it did not pay – and the old works buildings are full of efficiently produced grain which cannot be sold. And this in a world where millions starve. We are prepared, and by we I mean those who have the power to take such decisions, to pay millions to keep the works of the great English landscape painters, such as Constable and Gainsborough, but not to preserve the beauties of the land they painted. At least this part of Hampshire has been spared the excesses of modern prairie farming, and long may that be true.

Pedalling down the lane, one inevitably fell to wondering whether this was indeed a route followed by Cobbett. Well, the lane was almost

BELOW *A reaper sharpening his scythe; by William Pyne, 1813.*

RIGHT *A rural ride through a formal avenue of trees on the hill above Micheldever.*

certainly there in his day, for its way was marked by very old hedgerows. In 1970, Dr Max Hooper came up with a sort of rule-of-thumb method for dating hedges. To do the job properly you have to make a systematic study of a number of 30-metre (100-foot) lengths of hedgerow, counting the different species of tree and shrub that you find. You then average the results, multiply the number of species by 100, and you get the age of the hedge in centuries. You cannot do that sort of thing from the back of a tandem, but I did keep noting the species in the laneside hedge, ticking off dog-rose, bramble, hawthorn, elder, beech and oak – and there could well have been more. I cannot date the hedge for you, but it was obviously old and would certainly have been there in Cobbett's day – and it was on his straight-line route. It was somehow pleasing to think that he probably did trot down this very lane.

This is a very chalky, flinty land, so it is no surprise to find flint widely used as a building material, even if you might not expect to find it in Micheldever railway station, a comfortable, homely little place, with a verandah. As so often happens at small country stations, the British Rail plastic logo stuck prominently on the front looks totally incongruous. One supposes it is necessary to identify the place as a railway station, though you would have to be pretty dim not to recognize it, but why does everything have to have 'the corporate image'? Why cannot we use a bit of imagination, and design something that actually suits the place? The building is now somewhat overshadowed by a large oil depot, which at least confirmed that we had reached a main line, in this case from London to Southampton. A good deal of turning this way and that now followed before we reached the village of West Stratton. Here we did precisely what he had done, when he had to make a detour because of some wet meadows:

> I, therefore, turned to my left, went down to the turnpike, went a little way along it, then turned to my left, went along by Stratton Park pales down East Stratton-street, and then on towards the *Grange Park.*

Now, however, the turnpike is an ordinary and rather quiet main road, beside which stands the lodge for Stratton Park. Its old function has

gone for now, between it and the park is a cutting through which run the six lanes of the M3. Cobbett was not overfond of turnpikes; Heaven knows what he would have made of motorways. Fortunately, our minor road now ran safely across the top of it and we could pedal on into East Stratton.

The village is almost embarrassingly picturesque, the sort of place which a Hollywood designer would produce for a schmaltzy musical set in olde Englande. Even the post office is quaint and thatched, while the cottages are masterpieces of rural charm, complete with sunflowers and roses at the door. But, and this is important, it was not designed by Hollywood, nor does it cater for tourists. It is real. People live here, go about their daily business just as they would anywhere else. The effect is not entirely without artifice, for this is very much the village of a great estate, intended to set off the Great House, so that even modern estate cottages are still dressed out in thatch. Look at old prints of the place and you will see that parkland and the house, Stratton Park,

aggrandized by a tall, stone pillared portico. The parkland is still there, the portico is still there – but the house has gone. In its place is a modern structure of steel and glass. The effect is surreal, and seemed even more so when a black horse wandered across in front of the scene.

East Stratton is a small and charming spot, which one feels deserves to be bathed in perpetual sunlight. I stopped and looked at the war memorial. Fifteen names were listed: what devastation for such a tiny place and this was just for the years 1914-18; the effect must have been overwhelming. At least nothing on that scale afflicted the place in Cobbett's day. Then poverty was relieved by charity doled out by the local lady-bountiful to local girls, who in return had to wear uniform and were taught to sing hymns and psalms. Cobbett was not impressed. He saw it as breeding hypocrisy in the children and was dubious of the motives of the providers.

Looking down on the motorway that now pierces Stratton Park.

ABOVE *Stratton Park as it was in Cobbett's day.*

BELOW *Stratton Park today.*

When persons are glutted with riches; when they have their fill of them; when they are surfeited of all earthly pursuits, they are very apt to begin to think about the next world; and, the moment they begin to think of that, they begin to look over the *account* that they shall have to present. Hence the far greater part of what are called *'charities'*. But, it is the business of *governments* to take care that there shall be very little of this *glutting* with riches, and very little need of 'charities'.

We went on our way, the route still over a country marked by hills and hillocks. There are two ways for the cyclist to view such a landscape. The optimist puffing up the hill will think cheerily that he is bound to come down again soon; the pessimist zooming down with gravity doing all the work can only contemplate the climb up ahead. The view opened out to a distant prospect of Northington church looking extremely grand, particularly as there

appeared to be no settlement of any size attached to it – a theme that recurs throughout Cobbett's writing and which we shall be meeting again later. The landscape now was becoming distinctly watery with streams and ponds, and very attractive they looked too, though the ponds are not there merely for ornament. The area around Alresford is one of the great centres for the growing of watercress. The wet land of the river valley was little use for conventional crops or for grazing, but ideal for this somewhat insignificant vegetable. The best thing to do with watercress is to turn it into soup, but most people seem to prefer to use it as a garnish. It is, however, rich in iron which is, I am reliably informed, a very good thing though I am not sure that I know why. The watercress has also given its name to the preserved steam railway that runs from New Alresford, the Watercress Line. Cobbett lived long enough to see the establishment of Britain's railway system and regarded it with about as much enthusiasm as he did the turnpike roads. Both got you to places faster than

The village post office at East Stratton.

had previously been possible, but, as you saw less along the way, he thought it at best, a dubious advantage. Now that steam has given way before diesel and electric, and the rail system has shrunk before the advances of the motor car, we view these old lines in the rosiest of nostalgic glows. I am as guilty as any and make no apology, but on this occasion there was a more pressing problem to be resolved – lunch.

We stopped at a pub beside Old Alresford Pond, an extraordinary sheet of water, notable for the vast numbers of wildfowl on its surface and on its banks. I must confess that the prospect of beer and grub were more enticing than natural history, and, suitably fortified, we were soon on our way again. Cobbett stopped the night at Alresford, where he was pleased to find a meeting for parliamentary reform, a subject very dear to his heart. We found a street fair. I like street fairs, especially when they are found in rather genteel settings such as this. You can measure gentility by counting, not shrubs and trees, but antique shops. New

Alresford rates pretty high, and the occasional dose of noisy vulgarity does no harm.

Our road now took us past Tichborne, a spot which achieved considerable notoriety late in the last century, when a claimant appeared to announce himself to be heir to the Tichborne estate. Was he genuine, was he a fraud? The whole country, it seemed, had a view on the matter. It was an extraordinary story. Sir Roger Tichborne, was on a ship bound for England from South America, which was lost with all hands. Sir Roger was declared dead, but his mother would never accept the fact. So that when a butcher from Wagga Wagga, Australia appeared to claim the title, Lady Tichborne rushed to embrace him. Others were less convinced, and certainly the 24-stone claimant bore little resemblance to the somewhat underdeveloped Sir Roger. In the end, the claim was denied and the claimant gaoled for fraud. We scarcely had time for more than a

The west front of old Titchborne House;
by James Cave, 1801.

glance at the great estate for it happened to coincide with a downhill section, and the temptation to get a free ride was simply too great to resist. Cheriton appeared next, a plain but sensible sort of place. Here Cobbett met 'a grand camp' of gypsies. Today, they are much reviled, but he was greatly taken with them, especially a tall, beautiful girl.

> I pulled up my horse, and said, 'Can you tell me my fortune, my dear?' She answered in the negative, giving me a look at the same time, that seemed to say, it was *too late*; and that if I had been thirty years younger she might have seen a little what she could do with me.

Nothing that exotic happened to us.

What you mostly see in this part of the world is farming country and, if the big, trim, well-tended farms are anything to judge by, rich farming country at that. It is also a country liberally spotted with clumps of woodland, which provide cover for game. It is, said Cobbett, 'a high, hard, dry, fox-hunting country'. It still is. Our most obvious, direct route would have kept us straight down

The ploughman's lunch – original version;
by William Pyne, 1813.

southwards to Kilmeston, but Cobbett had made a detour to Beauworth to enquire after the family of an old farmer friend, so we dutifully followed. It is one of those little places that seem to have changed little over the years, nothing more prominent to show than the old squire's house, the church and the school. But the new rural community is very different from the old. Just how different appeared at Kilmeston, which I was eager to see for Cobbett's description had intrigued me.

> A bridle road over some fields and through a coppice took me to *Kilmston,* formerly a large village, but now mouldered into two farms, and a few miserable tumble-down houses for the labourers. Here is a house, that was formerly the residence of the landlord of the place, but is now occupied by one of the farmers.

'Poor' Kilmeston has come up in the world. The Volvo estates were being emptied of their uniformed occupants straight out of school – we met the male adults later as the first BMWs appeared in the nearby lanes, marking the home-time traffic. There are few labourers here now. The farms that employed fifty can now make do with one or two men and the machines. The labourer's cottage is now a desirable country residence, no longer just a cottage but 'The Cottage' or, Heaven help us, 'The Cot' with shiny red burglar alarm on the wall. Anyone who has lived in a village will know just what the changes meant in terms of local communities. There is little point in either commending or deploring, for it is now a fact, a reflection of changing social patterns.

It is a curious circumstance that, as the day lengthens towards evening, the uphill sections become not only steeper but far more frequent. Our route took us past Beacon Hill, from which Cobbett assured us we would be able to see '. . . the Isle of Wight in detail, a fine sweep of the sea; also a way into Sussex, and over the New Forest into Dorsetshire. Just below you, to the East, you look down upon the village of Exton.' Thanks to the autumn mist which had lingered through the day, we could just about make out Exton, and that was all. It was, however, at least a downhill route and we shot through the village and pedalled on to Droxford. Here I had hoped to stay at the pub, but there was no room and they suggested the 'guest house' up the road, which turned out to be a motel. The motel is, of course, an American import. Over there it works really quite well. America is a country where everyone, it seems, travels by car and where the one thing which they have in ample supply is space. So each town you come to announces its presence by the neon motel signs strung out along the highway. If you do not like what you see on the way into town, pick another on the way out. You cannot always tell if you have been through the town at all. Everything seems to be moving to the outside – the out-of-town shopping mall, the out-of-town cinema, the drive-in church and the drive-in bank. That does not leave much to go into the middle, so that I have seen towns which have not only got very little left in the centre but, in some cases, no centre at all. But centre or not, everywhere has its motel, and you can rely on reasonable comfort and a private bathroom, colour telly, plenty of room – and a low bill at the end of it. They are impersonal, standardized, frankly dull, but good value. The British, however, do not have a lot of space. The British motel room was cramped and, by American standards, quite expensive. As so often happens, we have seen an idea work in America, where circumstances are very different from those of England, imported it, and simply got it wrong. I wish I could have stayed at the pub. We did, however, find a certain pleasure in parking the aged tandem between a Porsche and a Ford Granada.

The next morning dawned as grey and dull as the last, with something of an autumnal bite to it. But at least it was dry and we began with a downhill sweep instead of an uphill pant. 'Better start today,' said John as the wind whistled in our ears, which seemed to be tempting providence – and providence promptly accepted the temptation. There was an unhappy grinding noise and we stopped to find the lower part of the rear mudguard bent and twisted on to the wheel. It was not too difficult to disentangle and we cut off the mangled bit with a pair of pliers. Serve us right, we said, that will teach us not to be over-optimistic. The lesson, however, was not yet concluded. We went on down to Hambledon and paused, as Cobbett had done at this the most southerly part of the excursion. It was an occasion to look back and reflect on what had

This village pub at Hambledon carries a reminder of the birthplace of cricket.

been seen along the way. What Cobbett saw was a changing countryside; smallholdings were falling into decay while the big towns grew, villages shrank and the people moved from country to towns. The industrial revolution had taken hold of Britain and Cobbett loathed it. He stood for tradition and the rights of the labourer and the small farmer. He was a countryman to his bones. To get the flavour of Cobbett you have to read at least one of his tirades in full. In this quote, the 'tax-eaters' are the corrupt parliamentarians of London, who claimed the country as a whole was being improved.

At West End. Hambledon is a long straggling village, lying in a little valley formed by some very pretty but not lofty hills. The environs are much prettier than the village itself, which is not far from the North side of Portsdown Hill. This must have once been a considerable place; for here is a church pretty nearly as large as that at Farnham in Surrey, which is quite sufficient for a *large town*. The means of living has been drawn away from these villages, and people follow the means. Cheriton and Kilmston and Hambledon and the like have been beggared for the purpose of giving tax-eaters the means of making *'vast improvements Ma'am'* on the villanous spewy gravel of Windsor Forest! The thing, however, must *go back*. Revolution here or revolution there: bawl, bellow, alarm, as long as the tax-eaters like, *back* the thing must go. Back, indeed, *it is going* in some quarters. Those scenes of glorious loyalty, the sea-port places, are beginning to be deserted. How many villages has that scene of all that is wicked and odious, Portsmouth, Gosport, and Portsea; how many villages has that hellish assemblage beggared! It is now being *scattered itself*! Houses which there let for forty or fifty pounds a-year each, now let for three or four shillings a-week each; and *thousands*, perhaps, cannot be let at all to any body capable of paying rent. There is an absolute tumbling down taking place, where, so lately, there were such *'vast improvements Ma'am!'* Does Monsieur de Snip call

those improvements, then? Does he insist, that those houses form *'an addition to the national capital?'* Is it any wonder that a country should be miserable when such notions prevail? And when they can, even in Parliament, be received with cheering?

Today, Hambledon shows every sign of prosperity, but Cobbett was right to claim that the old ways were dying. The destruction of the smallholdings, the migration of workers into towns have been completed: the commuter village is the thing. Ironically, it is now those industrial areas of the north that wrought the change that are suffering. Cobbett bemoaned the fact that the wealth created in the country was sucked into the Great Wen as he called London – the same cry is still heard in the north, in Scotland, and in Wales. But the despair that clings to a ruined town such as

Hambledon in the nineteenth century;
by Birket Foster, 1825-99.

Consett in Durham has not yet touched the south-east. It is easy in Hambledon to believe with the Panglosses of parliament that all really is for the best in the best of all possible worlds. Cobbett was no great economist nor an original political thinker, but he knew when things were wrong and said so, not in a whisper but in a bellow. Who can say that things are not wrong in the Britain of the 1980s?

Cobbett's tirades were only a punctuation to his journeys, and he was soon seduced by the pleasures of his rural rides, just as we were seduced by the delights of Hambledon. As a Yorkshireman, which means almost by definition an enthusiast for cricket, Hambledon is a place of pilgrimage. It is said that it was here that the very first match was played in the 1760s between the local team and the rest of England. Hambledon won, and the site of the original cricket club is marked by a stone monument. It is also, as is only right and proper, recorded on local pub signs. The village itself is pleasingly unpretentious, but has a few surprises. The local grocer announces his presence by a conventional shop sign, but above that fading paint on the wall proclaims 'People's Market'. No-one I asked seemed to know why. A Hampshire commune, Hambledon revolutionaries? It seems unlikely – very intriguing. Facing the grocer's, a street climbs the hill towards the church. A very typical English country church, growing, developing, and changing on a time scale measured in centuries rather than years. You could do an architectural course on this one building: here is the Saxon part, here the Norman, and so on through the changing styles that denote different periods. The latest addition was the very pleasing organ loft. Outside in the graveyard, the grass was being kept down by sheep, munching away in a roped-off section of their own. But beyond the graveyard is what appears to be a second church. There is at any rate a second church tower even if, on closer inspection, there is no sign of a church, only a house alongside. It is, in fact, a folly built, it is said, around 1840 so that a farmer could sit in comfort at the top of his tower and still keep an eye on the labourers in the fields. An alternative story, which I rather prefer, is that a local man claimed that a certain landmark was visible from the top of the church tower. A wager was made but, as is always the way in

this kind of folly story, the landmark was invisible. The only thing to do to win the bet was to build a second church tower. I hope that is the true story, simply because it is so gloriously illogical. Anyway, the house is still called Folly House, and I think the tower is rather a sensible addition. I should very much enjoy having such a tower outside my home where I could work in peace or simply view the world below.

Cobbett's next objective was Thursley, which was easily reached by going across to Petersfield and then straight up the main road. But he did not like main roads, and it would in any case have taken him over the heathland of Hindhead, and that was even worse. If he disliked turnpike roads, he disliked heathland even more, places which were quite simply no use to farmers and therefore no use to anyone else. He would not, he vowed, go to Hindhead. He had a map of Hampshire, but none of Surrey, but reasoned that he should be able to skirt Hindhead hill, though not with ease. He was told he would have to go down the steep, wooded hill of Hawkley Hanger and through Woolmer Forest, and his friends told him that if he did not break his neck at the first he would certainly get stuck in a bog in the second. Cobbett was undeterred. That was to be his route, and that was to be the route we were now to follow through a somewhat complex maze of little roads. It seemed likely to be an interesting journey.

When I think of going out to enjoy the countryside, I usually think first of wild country, of cliffs, mountains, and moors. I find the restrictions of walking in agricultural country, where your way is limited to official footpaths, irksome. But cycling down these all-but-deserted country roads was a joy. The land rolled and swooped, and the furrows of the plough exaggerated the curves of the ground as on a contour map. This swell of land is broken and delineated, kept from monotony, by the trees: a tall stand of beech marches across the horizon, a cluster of oaks crouch in a valley bottom. The feeling of loneliness seemed absolute. We stopped to listen. At first, all you hear is the call of birds, a ragged chorus with tones ranging from the monotonous ground base of the woodpigeon to the soprano melodies of the warblers. But behind it there was a steady background of fast-moving traffic

Farming land near Droxford.

on a distant road, out of sight but still not out of hearing. The farms such as Big West End Farm – Little West End Farm is a mile away to the north – show every sign of prosperity. These are not the old style of jumbled-up buildings, with buildings scattered in an apparently random way around a yard ankle deep in muck. Big West End Farm is trim, organized, and planned. And the process noted by Cobbett has been extended over the years, for the farms are now widely scattered. Tegalease Farm is over a mile away by road and seems further, for there is a steady, unremitting uphill slog that ends, at long last, at a crossroads. This was probably the most attractive stretch of country we came across on the whole ride, and it was not just because of the promise of an easy passage after the sweaty climb. To the north, the valley dives down between hills defined by woodland, lovely, deciduous woodland already tinged with the gold of autumn. It was one of those magical places where all the elements unite in harmony, where the curved edge of woodland matches the more delicate swing and swoop of the land. Our way led across the head of the

valley to the edge of the hill above East Meon. There we met mother and daughter out for a ride, the horses' four legs coping a good deal better with the terrain than our weary pair of pairs. My daughter rides but I do not and I am always astonished by the way quite small women can control what seem to me to be enormous animals. Mother was equally intrigued by us and the tandem, and paused to watch us clamber aboard and pedal off with, I thought, a certain style. But then it is easy to show style at the top of a hill, for it was now downhill all the way to East Meon.

The little town is dominated by its church. Not that there is anything to be ashamed of in the rest of the town, snuggling up to the Downs where the River Meon has its source. Anyone would be happy to come across such a place, to stroll down its streets and poke around in its alleys. It is neither better nor worse than many another small town or village. But the church really is something special. There had been a church here in Saxon times, quite an important church at that, but that has gone and the present building had its origins in the years following the Norman Conquest. Inevitably it has seen changes, new generations adding ever more elaborate details to the original, solid, basic structure. Its finest moment came in the middle of the twelfth century when the font was delivered, carved in wonderful detail from a solid block of marble by the sculptors of Tournai in Flanders. It is more than a mere carving, it is the story of creation as seen by medieval man. I love the section representing the expulsion from Eden. Paradise is seen, not as a garden, but as a magnificent Romanesque palace guarded by a surprisingly bewhiskered angel. Adam and Eve retreat, clutching their fig leaves, and are then taught to work for a living. Adam is shown how to dig with a spade and Eve is given a demonstration of how to spin with the distaff. The carvings retain tremendous vigour and vitality. If I had seen nothing else along the way, the sight alone would have made the journey worthwhile.

Cobbett admired the church, but it inevitably led his thoughts off on to one of his favourite topics, the then popular theories of the Reverend T R Malthus. The hypothesis was that the population was expanding more rapidly than was the supply of food so that, inevitably, in time, there would be disastrous famine in the land. The only answer, declared Malthus, was control of the population by the prevention of marriage among the lower orders of society. Cobbett was outraged, but turned his arguments not against Malthus' conclusions but on to their fundamental basis. The new census returns showed that population was, indeed, increasing, but Cobbett would have none of it. He pointed to East Meon church.

> Where did the hands come from to make it? Look, however, at the downs, the many square miles of downs near this village, *all bearing the marks of the plough*, and yet all out of tillage for many many years; yet, not one single inch of them but what is vastly superior in quality to any of those great 'improvements' on the miserable heaths of Hounslow, Bagshot, and Windsor Forest.

East Meon was just another victim of paper

The downland of Hampshire.

money and London avarice: the claimed population increase was a fraud.

'Noonday Rest'; by J Linnell, 1792-1882.

> All *observation* and all *reason* is against the fact; and, as to the *parliamentary returns,* what need we more than this: that *they* assert, that the population of Great Britain has *increased* from *ten* to *fourteen* millions in the last *twenty years*! That is enough! A man that can suck that in will believe, literally believe, that the *moon is made of green cheese.*

We now know that the census was right and Cobbett was wrong – but I still cannot help enjoying his outbursts, which you feel were no sooner thought than committed to paper, so that now they jump from the page in all their original freshness.

It was only a little after midday when we left East Meon church, but a glance at the map suggested that it was going to be a long time before we found anywhere else to stop for refreshment, so we called in at the local pub. What a splendid decision that turned out to be. It still retained its public bar for locals, where you could have a game of darts, and there was a large bar where you could feast in fine style. John May was especially impressed. If John ever decides to lead a national campaign then it will be for English pubs to serve proper English food, and that means local produce. That was just what we had, lamb chops – chops, mark you in the plural – potatoes, sprouts and parsnips. It was the parsnips that did it for John, a splendid vegetable which seldom receives its due praise. It was after that and after the Gale's bitter, that two somewhat reluctant tandemers set out to face the hill out of East Meon, which seemed to have grown somewhat during our temporary absence.

Our route took us out past the ancient court house, the medieval manor of the Bishops of Winchester, whose presence goes a long way towards explaining the opulence of East Meon church. We paused partly to admire the manor and partly to put off the climb up Park Hill, but it had to be faced some time. A pattern for the afternoon was set: up a hill, pushing the tandem rather more frequently than pedalling

'Labour'; by J Linnell, 1792-1882.

it, then coasting down the other side. There seemed to be scarcely a flat piece of land anywhere along the way, but it was rich land and richly enjoyable. We were steadily approaching the section which had driven me to this particular one of Cobbett's rural rides. He had called in on a friend who advised him strongly against the proposed route, but Cobbett was adamant. ' "Well then," said his friend at last, "If you *will* go that way, by G –, you must go down *Hawkley Hanger*!" of which he then gave me *such* a description!' Cobbett went on regardless, and was directed up a green lane.

On we trotted up this pretty green lane: and indeed, we had been coming gently and generally *up hill* for a good while. The lane was between highish banks and pretty high stuff growing on the banks, so that we could see no distance from us, and could receive not the smallest hint of what was so near at hand. The lane had a little turn towards the end; so that, out we came, all in a moment, at the *very edge of the hanger*! And, never, in all my life, was I so surprised and so delighted! I pulled up my horse, and sat and looked; and it was like looking from the top of a castle down into the sea, except that the valley was land and not water. I looked at my servant to see what effect this unexpected sight had upon him. His surprise was as great as mine, though he had been bred amongst the North Hampshire hills. Those who had so strenuously dwelt on the dirt and dangers of this route, had said not a word about the beauties, the matchless beauties of the scenery.

We reached the same point where a lane turned off the road. The road was clearly going steeply down hill, and all we needed to do was get on the tandem, put our feet up, and let gravity do the rest. But Cobbett's descent of the hanger had been a real adventure, slipping and sliding on a wet soil which he described as 'grey soap'. His description alternates between ecstatic comments on the view and horrendous notes on the difficulty of the journey. There was no way that we could take the tame route: we would follow Cobbett, though how we should cope with the tandem we had no idea. The map showed a very definite track, something far better than a mere footpath and the first part was even surfaced, though the surface was not especially good. It soon began to deteriorate even further and, all the time on our right-hand side, we could see the tree-thick ground falling away so steeply that it seemed impossible that anything could grow on such a slope. And, all the time, too, we had the thought that we were at the top of this great escarpment and somehow, at some time, we were going to have to get to the bottom.

We had one thing in our favour on this part of the journey; the ground was dry and hard. Had it been muddy and wet we would never, I think, have got ourselves and tandem down the hanger for, once we started to plunge down, we plunged with a vengeance down a path cut deep by use through the surrounding trees. Our only companions were a pair of motor-cyclists practising rough riding. We did not try to emulate them – and even they gave up before the steepest sections were reached. The tandem is a heavy machine and it seemed in a hurry to reach the bottom, so that it was brakes full on and strain back to keep it from running away. Looking back on it afterwards, it seemed extraordinarily similar to Cobbett's descent. We, too, were torn between admiration of the autumn woodlands hanging on to the steep hill and close attention to the difficulties of the way. Cobbett mused over how many horses had come that way: I wondered how many tandems had been seen on that path!

Cobbett, who had not had the good fortune to lunch on lamb chops and good ale, got nothing to eat until he reached Headley at dusk, where he rested, had food, and contemplated calling it a day. But he had negotiated the terrors of the hanger, so why admit defeat? Why not press on to Thursley? All he needed was a guide to show him the way. He found a local who said he knew the route but, as they struggled on through the rain and the dusk, it soon became clear that the guide was totally and irretrievably lost. They had to turn and retrace their steps. At last they were put on the right way to reach the turnpike but, alas, not at all in the place that Cobbett had wished.

At the end of about a mile, we fortunately found the turnpike-road; not, indeed, at the *foot*, but on the *tip-top* of that very Hindhead, on which I had so repeatedly *vowed* I would not go! We came out on the turnpike some hundred yards on the Liphook side of the buildings called *the Hut*; so that we had the whole of *three miles of hill to come down at not much better than a foot pace,* with a good pelting rain at our backs.

It is odd enough how differently one is affected by the same sight, under different circumstances. At the *'Holly-Bush'* at Headley there was a room full of fellows in white smock–frocks, drinking and smoking and talking, and I, who was then dry and warm, *moralized* within myself on their *folly* in spending their time in such a way. But, when I got down from Hindhead to the public-house at Road-Lane, with my skin soaking and my teeth chattering, I thought just such another group, whom I saw through the window sitting round a good fire with pipes in their mouths, the *wisest assembly* I had ever set my eyes on. A real *Collective Wisdom*.

His journey was now all but over. He reached his friend's house and was none the worse for the day's trials.

My intention was to follow the wrong route as it were, over Hindhead, which would have presented few problems for it was daylight and we had good maps. The problems did begin, however, as soon as we came down off the hanger. It was not at all clear which point of the road we had reached. We turned right, expecting to reach a left turn up to Hawkley. We were still going downhill, and it quickly became clear that the previous descent with brakes full on to stop the machine running away had worn down the blocks, so roadside repairs were needed. We were greatly encouraged, however, to meet a sign pointing to Hawkley – somewhat less encouraged when it became apparent that it was taking us up a steep, winding hill road which certainly did not fit in with the road marked on the map. It is not unknown for signposts to be turned round by local humorists, and this we decided was what must have happened. It was a decision that, if nothing else, enabled us to turn and go down hill instead of pedalling up. So we went past our last turning and found ourselves approaching, not Hawkley as expected, but West Liss. The mystery was solved: it was our very first decision that had been wrong, and we had actually managed to turn back when we were less than a mile from Hawkley.

At the point we had now reached, was the main road that we had originally intended to join further to the north. Having reached it, however, we were disinclined to backtrack on a lengthy diversion, so we resigned ourselves to about 4 miles of main-road cycling. Cobbett was contemptuous of the new turnpikes of his day and, as a cyclist, I began to share his opinion. There is very little to be said in favour of travelling with speeding cars and heavy trucks for company. They can seem especially menacing if you have spent the last two days in virtually empty country lanes. But if we found the other road users unappealing, some at least of them were vastly amused by us. Children were being ferried home from school in parents' cars, and they were greatly diverted by the sight of two middle-aged gents puffing along on a tandem. The main road did, however, have one advantage, in that it was well surfaced and we were going along in fine order. All around was the Woolmer Forest against which Cobbett had been warned. Today's warnings are of a very different nature, for a good deal of it has been taken over by the army for rifle ranges. Danger signs sprouted everywhere, which made us disinclined to venture on any short cuts. And, we said, at this rate the main-road section will soon be over. How right we were. A sudden jarring shock hit the bike and we came to an instantaneous halt. Something had caught in the back wheel with a devastating effect. Seen head on, the wheel was now a figure-of-eight and stripped gear cogs had flown all over the road. The cycle trip was ended.

We padlocked our stricken steed to a fence, undid the panniers, and plodded up the road to Whitehill to 'phone the rescue squad – John's wife Penny. There is not a great deal to do on an October afternoon in Whitehill. The only café was shut, so we sat and waited for the pub to open. As six o'clock drew near, we watched for any sign of life. A light went out upstairs – we waited, for what seemed an age – and then a light went on downstairs. Two chilled cyclists headed for the warmth of the bar, and here we remained until our chauffeuse appeared and we were off to collect the tandem and head for home.

I never did get to Hindhead. I thought about going back another day but, when you set out on a journey, you have to take that journey as it comes. It had gone wrong at the end, but then so had Cobbett's. In a way it was almost pleasing to find that, even in this day and age, travel can have its surprises. Cobbett himself would not have been the least surprised. He believed in the old ways, not in machines, and would probably have regarded our tandem with as much distrust as he did the railways which, at the end of his life, were beginning to invade the countryside. By the middle of the century they had spread through most of the country, but one part at least remained aloof, cut off from the rest of Britain. It was not until 1859 that Brunel's bridge across the Tamar brought the rails down to Cornwall, and that was seven years after our next writer had made his aptly named *Rambles Beyond Railways*.

WILKIE COLLINS (1824-89)

•

Round the Coast and Under the Sea

Rambles Beyond Railways 1851

Until I came across *Rambles Beyond Railways*, I had only known Wilkie Collins the novelist, the man who, a decade later produced one of fiction's more splendid villains, Count Fosko of *The Woman in White*. It is not, however, a notably jolly piece. The main protagonists are either solemnly virtuous or darkly sinister in the best style of Victorian melodrama – Fosko being the one exception, a brilliant creation without whom the book would be unreadable. Nothing, therefore, prepared me for the breezy air and geniality of the young Wilkie Collins, striding off over the fields and round the cliffs of Cornwall. It is a book pervaded with good humour, the good humour of a young, fit man enjoying days in the open air in a part of the world he is discovering for the first time.

> Walk, and be merry; walk, and be healthy; walk, and be your own master! – walk, to enjoy, to observe, to improve, as no riders can! – walk, and you are the best peripatetic impersonation of holiday enjoyment that is to be met with on the surface of this work-a-day world!

He has a splendidly cavalier approach to his subject, writing about what interests him and leaving the rest alone. We join him after he has just popped across from Liskeard to Helston, a journey of which he has nothing to say other than to inform the reader that he is going to '... skip over five intermediate market-towns and two large villages, with a mere dash of the pen.' Over the next few chapters he goes on to describe the country round the Lizard, fishing villages, Lands End and finally, in what is for

me the climax of the whole book, he goes down Botallack Mine. If Wilkie Collins could pick and choose, missing out whole tracts of country and dwelling lingeringly over others, I see no reason why I should not be equally indulgent. His trips tended to be made as excursions out

Wilkie Collins; by J E Millais, 1850.

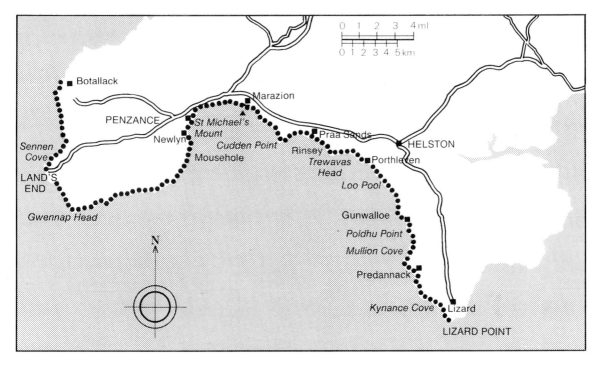

from fixed points, such as Helston. The places described, however, are almost all on the coast so I decided to please myself and visit those same spots by my own preferred route, along the coastal path. Here then is a personal account of a walk around the Cornish coast from the Lizard to Land's End and up the north coast to end near Cape Cornwall. We shall be meeting the jovial Mr Collins at numerous places along the way.

Wilkie Collins' first set of excursions were from his base at Helston, which was not a place which called forth any great enthusiasm.

> Its principal recommendation, in the opinion of the inhabitants, appeared to be that it was the residence of several very "genteel families", who have certainly not communicated much of their gentility to the lower orders of the population – a riotous and drunken set, the only bad specimens of Cornish people that I met in Cornwall. The streets of Helston are a trifle larger and a trifle duller than the streets of Liskeard; the church is comparatively modern in date, and superlatively ugly in design.

Not what one would call much of an incentive to visit but, as I was not planning to start the walk proper until the Monday, I decided to visit Helston on the Sunday to see how far the criticism was justified. I have to say, it is not a supremely interesting town, though few towns are seen at their best on Sundays. The most interesting-looking structure seemed at first to be a triumphal arch, looking one wondered over what magnificent spectacle. In the event, it turned out to lead to nothing more exciting than the municipal bowling green. So much for gentility; what about the drunken riotousness. Helston has two principal claims to fame. The first is 'The Furry Dance', when the citizens dance hand-in-hand through the streets. An extraordinary absurdity according to Collins, a view on which I offer no comment as the dance takes place in May and I was there in the middle of September. The second attraction is one of Britain's best-known pubs. The Blue Anchor is a thatched, medieval building in the centre of the town, which was once a monks' hospice. It is a very attractive place, with snug, panelled rooms leading off a central corridor, but its fame resides in the courtyard at the back of the building. Here you find the brewhouse where they produce some notably strong beers – cognoscenti might care to note that their ordinary bitter has an OG of 1050! Customers can wander out and peer into the murky brew – and then go to the bar to order what turned out, in my somewhat unhappy experience, to be an equally murky end product. Still the locals seemed to enjoy it. Proper locals they looked, too, with their fishermen's sweaters and old stained jeans. So you sidle up to glean the latest information on the state of lobster pots and the price of mackerel. What you get is a discourse on who got the new Cornflakes account and fluctuations on the stock market. They did not seem likely to prove a riotous set, nor very entertaining, so I left.

The following morning was a day for walking, but first there was a question of getting to the start by car. May is probably the best time of year to visit Cornwall, when the tall steep banks that border the narrow lanes shine out with colour in the sun, but September can be almost as good. School holidays are over; the crowds have thinned. Quite a few tourists do, however, still linger – and tour. This involves driving to beauty spots at an incredibly slow pace, looking at same beauty spots, preferably without leaving the car, and driving back equally lethargically. This produces agonies of frustration in other road users. Collins had warned me, told me it was pointless to expect anything but misery if I chose to travel by any means other than the locomotion of my own limbs. The hazards may have changed, but the message is the same.

> You, who in these days of vehement bustle, business, and competition, can still find time to travel for pleasure alone – you, who have yet to become emancipated from the thraldom of railways, carriages, and saddle-horses – patronize, I exhort you, that first and oldest-established of all conveyances, your own legs! Think on your tender partings nipped in the bud by the railway bell; think of crabbed cross-roads, and broken carriage-springs; think of luggage confided to extortionate porters, of horses casting shoes and catching colds, of cramped legs and numbed feet, of vain longings to get down for a moment here, and to delay for a pleasant half hour there – think of all these manifold hardships of riding at your ease; and the next time you leave home, strap your luggage on your shoulders, take your stick in your hand, set

> forth delivered from a perfect paraphernalia of incumbrances, to go where you will, how you will – the free citizen of the whole travelling world!

I had not heeded the advice, so there I had to sit and fume until I and my walking partners, Neil and Sheila, reached the Lizard. The most prominent feature is the lighthouse which, apart from being a working light, is also the centre of a small lighthouse museum. I visited there a couple of years before, and it turned out to be a quite extraordinary experience. The light itself is, of course, what matters in any lighthouse and it is concentrated and given direction through a complex of lenses and mirrors. There was no light on that day, so I was invited to stand in the centre of the lantern and, with no more than the push of a finger, the keeper set the glass turning. Each segment of glass held its own miniature world, so that reality became an endless shifting and fracturing of tiny images. I have never tried hallucinogenic drugs and, after the Lizard light, I have no need to, for no drug could produce anything as weirdly dislocating as that. This, however, was not a day for lighthouse visits, but for walking out into the grey morning to the cliffs and the sea whose pounding beat we could hear but which we could not yet see.

Wilkie Collins had set off to walk here from Helston on a day of mist and rain; we had the mist but, as yet, nothing worse. He had called in first at the inn – too early for us – but even if we had followed his example it is unlikely that we would have been faced with a scene such as that which confronted Collins.

> We beheld a small room literally full of babies, and babies' mothers. Interesting infants of the tenderest possible age, draped in long clothes and short clothes, and shawls and blankets, met the eye wherever it turned. We saw babies propped up uncomfortably on the dresser, babies rocking snugly in wicker cradles, babies stretched out flat on their backs on women's knees, babies prone on the floor toasting before a slow fire. Every one of these Cornish cherubs was crying in every variety of vocal key. Every one of their affectionate parents was talking at the top of her voice. Every one of their little elder brothers was screaming, squabbling, and

One of the original illustrations by Henry Brandling who accompanied Colins on his travels. This shows a somewhat wild and windswept Kynance Cove.

tumbling down in the passage with prodigious energy and spirit.

The explanation for this alarming scene was an impending visit by the local doctor who was about to vaccinate the entire infant population of the peninsula against the smallpox. The travellers, wisely, retreated and turned from the cries of the children to the calls of the gulls. Collins was off to discover the wild cliff scenery and he loved it. I was off to do the same with equal enthusiasm.

Those who have never been on long coastal walks often think they must be somewhat monotonous and a quick glance at the map seems to confirm the view. The red dotted line hugs the coast all the way, but look a little closer and you will see it cut by contour lines, where the waters draining off the land have carved deep valleys to the sea. The coastal path is a switchback, and the rises and the falls give totally different perspective to the scene, quite apart from the exercise they ensure for the walker. One moment you are striding in comfort over the turf and heather of a high cliff top, then you are scrambling down into a deep combe. One minute you are level with the gulls

that ride the winds off the cliff top, close enough to see the gaps in the wing feathers that indicate the autumn moult. Then you are heading down to sea level, where you see the sea rise into ridges that seem almost to stand still, waiting in line until their turn comes to gather momentum and drive in a final explosion of foam on to the rocks. Spray flies in fine showers spurting from the crashing waves. After that, there is the climb back up the cliff and a steep climb it generally proves to be. The one thing the coastal path does not offer is an easy stroll.

The great spectacular of the morning was to be Kynance Cove. In summer it is just about as popular a spot as you can find, but on a grey morning in mid-September we had the place to ourselves. We were not, however, the first visitors of the day. A single line of footprints led off to the centre of the sands, to a huge, inscribed letter A then led back to the rocks. Was it a signal for passing helicopters or an egotistical gesture by visiting Arthur or

Amanda? It was not a puzzle to linger over, for Kynance is a spot that demands attention. Even on such a dull day it is a surprisingly colourful place. The sea, at a distance, was a uniform grey that blended all but imperceptibly into the grey of the sky, leaving the horizon as a faint smear which scarcely registered in the monochrome picture. Inshore, however, it suddenly appeared in quite startling emerald and turquoise, from which the dark-tipped rocks emerged in sharp outline. Down by the tide-washed shoreline, the waves have smoothed and worn the rocks which appeared as purplish brown lumps, like piles of kidneys on a butcher's tray. But it is not to these that the eye is first drawn but to the high rocks that ring the cove and stride out across the sand. Collins approached them with all the fervour of the New Romantic glorying in their wildness. Here, for the first time, we have a totally modern outlook of a man who has come simply to admire the scenery and to enjoy the landscape without any reference to its usefulness to man. Collins' description of Kynance could, making allowance for the Victorianisms of the language, have been written today. It could certainly have been written on our visit, when conditions were almost exactly as he described them.

> What a scene was now presented to us! It was a perfect palace of rocks! Some rose perpendicularly and separate from each other, in the shapes of pyramids and steeples – some were overhanging at the top and pierced with dark caverns at the bottom – some were stretched horizontally on the sand, here studded with pools of water, there broken into natural archways. No one of these rocks resembled another in shape, size, or position – and all, at the moment when we looked on them, were wrapped in the solemn obscurity of a deep mist; a mist which shadowed without concealing them, which exaggerated their size, and, hiding all the cliffs beyond, presented them sublimely as separate and solitary objects in the sea-view.

Collins even went climbing on the rocks for no better reason than that it looked as if it would be fun to do so, an attitude that would have been totally incomprehensible to Defoe or Johnson, but which we now accept.

From Kynance we continued to walk on round the cliffs. I had measured the distance round to Mullion Cove from Lizard Point and made it around 5½ miles, which looked like a pleasant meander that would get us safely there by lunchtime. I had not allowed for the ups, the downs and the convoluted path forced on us by the many small inlets which looked so insignificant on the map but which add so much to the journey. We walked past Predannack air-

Tiny Mullion harbour on a dull, autumn day.

field which seemed to stay with us forever, and still could see no sign of the island that marks the entrance to the cove. It appeared at last as we descended the steep path down to the little harbour, an enclave of calm as the waves spent their force on the breakwater. We asked the way to the pub. 'Just over a mile up the road, in the village,' we were told. 'Nothing nearer?' we asked. We were pointed to the hotel, high on the cliffs to the north. No-one was very im-

pressed by that either. So we settled for the little café, and very good it was too. They actually had proper Cornish pasties with meat in chunks not a ground, indefinable mass, potato but not too much, and the essential ingredient, turnip to keep it moist. And there were excellent, fat crab sandwiches. That with a cup of tea, suitably fortified from the hip flask, made everyone feel very much better, which was just as well for the weather was getting very much worse.

The day was getting wetter and wetter. A west wind whistled off the sea, spotting the surface with white flakes of foam so that it looked like a pointillist painting. There is something about such a day that gives one a special sense not so much of exhilaration as of satisfaction. It is that old Protestant ethic at work again telling you that the longer the walk and the worse the weather, the more worthy is the effort. So I begin to feel that there is a special virtue in stomping over the cliffs on a day when a force 9 gale is driving the rain into your face. No-one had asked me to do it, no one benefitted from my doing it, but it remained a virtue.

From Mullion, the route continues its up-and-down progress. The footpath is often very narrow, so that you can only process in Indian file. You have to walk by placing one foot straight down in front of the other, which means that, for someone like myself who tends to walk slightly splay footed, the way was marked by frequent stubbing of toes on the path's edge. There are landmarks to watch for along the way. The Marconi memorial above Poldhu Cove marks the first transatlantic radio transmission of 1901 and tells you so in somewhat repetitive detail. Gunwalloe appears, almost it seems too tiny to boast the name of village, with its own church by the beach dating back to the thirteenth century. It manages to be both an actual church and a perfect image for a church, being both literally and metaphorically a refuge from the storm. This is a lovely little place, sheltering as well as it can from the rigours of this stormy coast, crouching down into its hollow. The separate tower is actually built out over a cave, but the rigours of the weather have left their marks. This is a church of the sea as well as of the land, and sea disasters are remembered even in the fabric of the building. The rood screen was carved from the wreckage of a Portuguese vessel that sank off this coast in 1527. And the sea is eating at the land that surrounds the church, threatening to take its wreckage back again. But on this day at least it provided a welcome, if temporary, haven for a group of very wet walkers.

Beyond the church of Church Cove, the coastline changes. Instead of the serrated margin of cliff and cove you have the 2-mile straight of Porthleven Sands. An odd enclosed little path runs on a ridge above a green slope that drops down to the creaming waves and the beach. Just when you think it might be getting monotonous, Porthleven Sands spring their surprise. You reach the Loe or Loo Pool as it was known in Collins' day. It is as if one had come across a Scottish loch or a piece of Lakeland accidentally dropped down by the Cornish sea. It has nothing of Cornwall about it: it is totally foreign, alien, quite out of place. As the misty rain thickened in the late afternoon, it took on the appearance of a Japanese watercolour. The hills that stood by this freshwater lake were reduced to two dimensions, represented only by their outlines and variations in grey. The bordering trees, conifers mainly, stood out against these pale silhouettes in contrasting, spiky outline. Between lake and sea is a great sand bar, a barrier that separates two contrasting worlds. Collins approached this spot from the opposite direction, from the land not the sea, but was equally struck by the contrast.

> On one side, close at hand, water is dancing beneath the breeze in glassy, tiny ripples; on the other, equally close, water rolls in mighty waves, precipitated on the ground in dashing, hissing, writhing floods of the whitest foam – here, children are floating mimic boats on a mimic sea; there, the stateliest ships of England are sailing over the great deep – both scenes visible in one view. Rocky cliffs and arid sands appear in close combination with rounded fertile hills, and long grassy slopes; salt spray leaping over the first, spring-water lying calm beneath the last! No fairy vision of Nature that ever was imagined is more fantastic, or more lovely than this glorious reality, which brings all the most widely contrasted characteristics of a sea view and an inland view into the closest contact, and presents them in one harmonious picture to the eye.

We lingered over the fairy vision, but soon had to face a less pleasing reality. Having left the narrow walk, we were faced by a walk across the beach, over piles of shifting pebbles which tried their best to pull you back as you attempted to march forwards. It was horribly hard work, and not very enjoyable either. It was with great relief that we reached Porthleven itself, the end of the beach and the end of the day's walk. It was good place to finish, and if you ever wanted to know just why harbours were built, then Porthleven gave an object lesson that day. Wooden boards were set in place at the entrance to the inner harbour, and the waves which thrust through between the stone crab-claws of the outer harbour hurled themselves against the timbers. The outer harbour boiled and thrashed; the inner rippled and the fishing boats sat motionless at their moorings.

On the next day, we continued where we had left off, but now the storm had died, the winds had dropped and waves no longer clattered the boards in the harbour entrance. A theatrical light played its spotlight across the scenery of land and sea. In the darker areas there was still a lack of resolution that had been so much a feature of the previous day, where grey land, grey sea, and grey sky merged and melted, one into the other. There was another, more mundane, memory of the previous day in the narrowness of the path cut through the turf above the cliff. I was not getting noticeably better at coping with it, still stumbling and tripping over my feet. Not that I minded very much, for I had a definite objective in view which I was eager to reach, the mining area of Rinsey Head.

Not everyone is drawn to this aspect of Cornish history, though few, now, are unaware of it. The engine house is as much a symbol of the county as the popular scenes of cliffs, sands and sea. I have been fascinated and intrigued by Cornish mining history for many years, for there is something almost heroic – no, there is no need for the qualification – there is something heroic about the scale and enterprise of the old tin and copper mines. Cornwall can justly claim to be the region where the true Age of Steam was born. The mines of the area go deep, and deep mines can only be worked if they can be pumped dry of water. The invention of the steam engine made this possible: build an engine, light the fire in the boiler and away you go. But Cornwall has no natural coal supplies. Fuel was expensive, and the only way

the pumping engines could be made to pay was through greater efficiency. Local engineers went to work with a will, building ever bigger and better engines. They built the finest engines in the world, and sold them to the world. I have seen Cornish engines as far apart as Spain and Holland, and they remain unmistakeable. These were huge engines, not the size of a house but the size of a small block of flats. They were beam engines: a massive iron beam pivoted at its centre, perpetually nodding over the shaft. At one end was the piston of the engine, driving up and down; at the other, the pump rods descending into the shaft to pump the water. And the stone engine house was something more than just a cover to keep off the rain; it was the frame that supported the ponderous engine. Look at the ruined engine houses that are such a feature of the Cornish landscape, and you will see that one wall is shorter than the rest but much thicker. This is the 'bob wall' that supported the great beam or bob. Look closely and you will still see the grease from the bearings that stained the granite blocks of the wall. Without the steam engine, the mining industry would have collapsed – and, without the genius of Cornish engineers such as Richard Trevithick, we may never have seen that great spurt of development that culminated in the steam locomotive. Most of the engines have, alas, gone – but the engine houses remain. Built to survive the pounding of their engines, they also survive the pounding of the natural elements of air and water. I have visited literally scores of Cornish engine houses, but I still get a feeling of excitement whenever the familiar silhouette appears on the horizon. And there is a special thrill on seeing the engine houses of Rinsey and Trewavas Heads.

A lot of people look at engine houses without being quite clear what they are, without being able to envisage the engine inside. This is not surprising, for we find it difficult to appreciate the monumental nature of these early machines. You have to think of the engine as almost filling the house, top to bottom, side to side, a mass of intricately moving machinery. We think of engine cylinders like car cylinders, as being a few inches across at most – the cylinder of the big pumping engine at Trewavas was nearly 6 feet (1.8 metres) in diameter, a

monster indeed. That alone would make the site remarkable, but what makes it truly spectacular is the situation of these high, remote headlands. Think of the effort of hauling the stones for the houses and the great iron components for the engine to such a spot, and then putting them together while an Atlantic gale does its best to rip you from the cliffs. Just try to conceive of the problems of building the tall stack for the boiler house. No wonder we talk of work on a heroic scale. And if that does not impress, consider the effort that went into sinking the shaft you can still see by the houses and then burrowing out beneath cliff and sea. I must emphasize, however, that I certainly do not recommend crawling to the edge of the shaft to peer down into it. I could have spent a day here, but objectives had been set, destinations were still to be reached – and there was the thought of lunch. The gloom of the previous day had been replaced by a day of racing clouds, which at least meant that each patch of darkness was sure to be followed by a gleam of light: and the natural world responded to the change. Incredibly for the time of year, butterflies appeared along our path: blues, delicately powdered with colour, richly toned purple emperors. The gulls no longer held a monopoly of the airways. Stonechats obligingly chattered, kestrels hovered, and a peregrine soared above them all in majestic disdain. Ravens appeared, shouting hoarsely at each other like a boozy, raucous football crowd. If there is any truth in the theory of the transmigration of souls, then these were probably long-departed Chelsea fans. Underfoot, too, the land was transformed as colour flickered in the shifting sun on gorse, heather, and the more timid plants that peered out from behind the shelter of the rocks. The cliff scenery was similar to that of the first day, but the effect was totally different.

Then the cliff gave way to the long expanse of Praa Sands, just the sort of place to avoid in high summer but splendid now. A great sheet of wet sand gleamed ahead of us, populated only by the sea anglers and one resolute couple who sat quite alone on their folding chairs in the very centre of the beach. We joined the less-than-crowded shore, while at the other

LEFT *Looking out from the engine house on Rinsey Head.*

RIGHT *The stoicism of the English: Praa Sands.*

Sea anglers on Praa Sands.

end a second visitor appeared, a rider on horseback who galloped across the empty spaces, splashed down to the water's edge and vanished again. We plodded on, through the soft sand to the Summer Mecca of caff and boozer, now looking a little dejected with the out-of-season blues. Here was a car park with a few, occupied vehicles. A couple had driven down, parked and fallen asleep to the treacly strains of Radio 2 that oozed out through the car window. At least we knew why we had come – and went to find a pint.

Praa Sands proved to be no more than an intermission to the now familiar pattern of cliff and cave and, even when you think that there is a certain similarity between this zig-zag path up a cliff and the one you seem only just to have recovered from climbing, something turns up to surprise you. Coming up to Prussia Cove, the sound of a string trio playing Haydn with a deal of expertise was wafted towards us from one of the outbuildings of a rather fine house. It was, according to a young man clutching an armful of scores, a convention of young musicians. He spoke slowly and carefully with a heavy Germanic accent. 'Each year,' he said, 'it is good.' So it sounded, very good indeed, and it was tempting to sit, put up one's feet and simply enjoy the music. But there was still some way to go before the end of the day's walk.

The cliffs up ahead provided a fantasy of rock shapes, some simply weird contortions, others showing remarkable similarity to animals or birds. The granite blocks had cracked, splintered, and worn with the weather, so that now they stack like unusually shaped children's building blocks. Several, in silhouette, reminded me of the animal shapes you see in Egyptian hieroglyphics: a monkey looked out over the sea; a dog sat up, perpetually begging. Up ahead lay Marazion and famous St Michael's Mount – Mont Saint Michel's English cousin. I shall say no more on that subject, taking my lead from Wilkie Collins, who also came this way.

From Helston we proceeded to Marazion – stopping there to visit St. Michael's Mount, so well known to readers of all classes by innumerable pictures and drawings, and by descriptions scarcely less plentiful, that they will surely be relieved rather than disappointed, if these pages exhibit the distinguished negative merit of passing the Mount without notice.

Beyond Cudden Point we turned inland on a path that looked initially to be somewhat dreary, and proved, in the event, to be even drearier. What do they do in this part of Cornwall to earn a living? The answer seems to be: grow cabbages. They do not grow peas, carrots, cauliflowers, beans, nor any other vegetable or fruit – just cabbages, field after field of them. I was reminded of little children being told to eat up their greens because they were good for them. The local populace, when not engaged in cabbage growing, seem mostly to be out taking their dogs for walks, including one owner with a three-legged dog, a remarkably agile tripedal canine. The local council have put up signs, such as one sees beside roads, showing a small pooch depositing a circular turd, the whole

crossed out with a red diagonal. The signs have not been effective. I was not greatly taken by Marazion, even though I was interested to discover that the name was a corruption of Mart of Zion, the market of the Jews who brought tin ore for smelting. From here we shall leap ahead to the centre where I stayed for my Cornish tour, Penzance.

Collins was presumably not impressed by Penzance, for he has nothing whatsoever to say about it, which is rather a pity but it is possible to see why. It is not a place to offer an immediate appeal. You have to hunt out the good things, but they are there all right. It is odd that, approached from a distance, quite the most obvious feature is the dome that crowns the magnificence of Lloyds Bank. It was not as one might guess built as a bank but as part of a market project, when Jew's Market Street was designed as a rival to Marazion. An architectural competition was held and won by a London architect but, as is often the way with such contests, the winning design was first lauded for its style and grandeur but then, when the costs were looked at a little closer,

Penzance from the sea by a local artist W Willis, c1850.

rapidly discarded. The irate Londoner was bought off with a £300 sweetener and William Harris came down from Bristol to do a scheme on the cheap. He did quite a good job of it, and there is still a market in the hall behind the bank.

Penzance was once a fishing village little different from many others along the coast, and might have remained so had not the gentry of the eighteenth century become convinced of the medicinal benefits of sea water. They bathed in it, preferably in tubs rather than in the sea itself, and even drank it, arguing no doubt that anything that tasted so nasty must be doing them good. Then came the great day that was to change Penzance's fortunes: the Great Western Railway arrived and the seaside town was born and thrived, in spite of what one might have thought of as the disadvantage of possessing virtually no beach. But it does have all the *proper* things: a municipal park

Fisherwoman with her traditional basket or cowal.

with bandstand and ordered lawns; Sea View Villas from some of which one can even see the sea; and a wonderful, old-style, open-air pool that looks as if it is waiting to stage a Busby Berkeley musical extravaganza. But best of all, Penzance still has a harbour, a genuine working place. Fishing boats come and go, and fish is sold on the quay; repair yards are still at work so that you find quite large vessels stranded like arks beside the main road. Here is the Customs House, small and neat, the Pilotage and the Scillies Steamship Company. And here, too, is the Trinity House workshop, a colourful place of huge buoys and the rainbow prisms of lighthouse lamps.

From the harbour the town clambers up the steep hill, and granite rules: granite refined and polished or left in great, raw chunks. Just look at the chapel which gives Chapel Street its name. That is the real, brooding stone, a dark stone to put the congregation in mind of the wrath to come. But just opposite, peering up cheekily at it, is the old Turk's Head, and the reason I did not call in had nothing to do with any sense of foreboding occasioned by the chapel, it was quite simply too full. Just up the street from here is Penzance's oddest building, the Egyptian House, a polychrome fantasy like a temple to Osiris slap bang in the middle of all the shops and pubs. That was my base for the walks. There I stayed, feeling amazingly grand and eventually getting used to being stared at as tourists stood open-mouthed in front of this splendid, slightly ridiculous building.

Our route went on through Newlyn to Mousehole, which is everyone's idea of what a Cornish fishing village should be. It is still a working port but times have changed since the last century when the fishermen set out to hunt not for herring and mackerel, crab and lobster, but for pilchards. I never think of pilchards as being caught here – in fact I find it difficult to think of them in the sea at all, never having seen them in anything but a can. But they were once plentiful and are now said to be returning, though it is doubtful if pilchard fishing will be quite as entertaining as it was in Collins' day. It was so interesting that he devoted a whole chapter to the subject. This is how it begins:

> If it so happened that a stranger in Cornwall went out to take his first walk along the cliffs towards the south of the county,

in the month of August, that stranger could not advance far in any direction without witnessing what would strike him as a very singular and alarming phenomenon.

He would see a man standing on the extreme edge of a precipice, just over the sea, gesticulating in a very remarkable manner, with a bush in his hand; waving it to the right and the left, brandishing it over his head, sweeping it past his feet – in short, apparently acting the part of a maniac of the most dangerous character. It would add considerably to the startling effect of this sight on the stranger, if he were told, while beholding it, that the insane individual before him was paid for flourishing the bush at the rate of a guinea a week. And if he, thereupon, advanced a little to obtain a nearer view of the madman, and then observed on the sea below (as he certainly might) a well-manned boat, turning carefully to right and left exactly as the bush turned right and left, his mystification would probably be complete, and the right time would arrive to come to his rescue with a few charitable explanatory words. He would then learn that the man with the bush was an important agent in the Pilchard Fishery of Cornwall; that he had just discovered a shoal of pilchards swimming towards the land; and that the men in the boat were guided by his gesticulations alone, in securing the fish on which they and all their countrymen on the coast depend for a livelihood.

The man on the cliffs was the 'huer', and, if he did his job well, the shoal was trapped between the shore and the open sea, then netted and brought to the salting house for curing. A hundred years ago it was a major industry, sending nearly sixty-five million fishes to foreign markets in 1850 alone. Then, for no obvious reason, the pilchards left and the trade was ended. There are still reminders of those days in Mousehole, notably Ye Olde Pilchard Press. There is a good deal of Ye Olde goes on in Mousehole, which can be justified in the sense that a lot of it is old. Every alley has, it seems, its picturesque view and attractive cottage, but these buildings often have such genuine character that all this phoney archaism subtracts from rather than adds to the feeling of antiquity. This was a working place before it was a tourist spot, and people built sensibly and sturdily against the winter gales. So you find houses with porches built of monumental granite slabs, guarding tiny domestic doorways. The principal attraction, however, is the harbour itself and its immediate surroundings. It has been photographed a million times, but it is still worth pausing to look at the details of its dark walls, at the pattern of stone blocks, grey to the waterline, yellow with lichen above. It seems a random arrangement of stone, not chosen to fit any pre-ordained design but simply based on what was available. It is beautifully satisfying and it is not difficult to see why abstractionists, such as Ben Nicholson and Barbara Hepworth, came to settle and work in Cornwall. Everywhere you look there are patterns to satisfy the eye: the curve of mooring lines that swing down from bollards and rings and then at low tide streak the gleaming mud; there is satisfaction in the shape of the boats themselves and so it goes on. What you are seeing is a practical world made by practical men and no nonsense about aesthetics, but aesthetic pleasure is what you get anyway. And if you get tired of standing and staring, you can always retire to the Ship Inn, a good, honest sort of place which may depend on the tourist trade but has not compromised itself to go out and look for it. The best of Mousehole is like that.

Our route now continued on around the coastal path. As a walk it provided the same mixture as before, which was a constant delight to the walkers but could prove tedious to the readers. So I must ask you to accept that round the cliffs we walked with great enjoyment, but to be content with descriptions of just a few, particular places met with along the way. Most were places where I shared in the enthusiasms of Wilkie Collins – but one was a personal exercise in nostalgia. On the rest of the journey down the south coast, Collins' chief pleasure came from a visit to the Logan Rock, a huge stone which stands above a promontory and is so precariously balanced that one man can set it rocking with a hard push. He was absolutely delighted by it. 'You have treated eighty-five tons of granite like a child's cradle; and like a

child's cradle, those eighty-five tons have rocked at your will!' I, however, hurried on to see a man-made – or rather woman-made – wonder.

The Minack Theatre represents the realization of a dream. The dreamer was Rowena Cade, and the dream was of a theatre in the Greek style, an amphitheatre backed by the sea, not the Aegean but the Atlantic. There were very few who shared her vision, so she got on with the job herself helped only by her gardener. Terraces were dug in the cliff, a platform made for the performers and, over the years, more and more amenities were added. It is unique in Britain: a theatre in a splendid setting, the stage backed by the sea and accoustically superb. It is not a place for cosy, domestic comedies, but is ideal for plays of real breadth and stature. I first came here many years ago as part of a London-based company, performing Shakespeare. We chose *The Tempest*, a play made for this setting. At night, a large spot shone out across the players to pick up the foam of waves on the rocks below the stage. The island was always with us. As a seaweed-draped Caliban, I almost froze to death, but it was worth it. Seldom can a play and its setting have achieved such perfect harmony: except, that is, for the matinee. At night, with distress rockets zooming up from our make-believe shipwreck, it was totally credible; but, on a balmy sunny day, poor Miranda had to turn to Prospero and say:

> If by your art, my dearest father, you have
> Put the wild waters in this roar, allay them.
> The sky, it seems, would pour down
> stinking pitch,
> But that the sea, mounting to th' welkin's
> cheek,
> Dashes the fire out.

And the sea was glassy calm, and not a cloud spotted the endless blue of the sky. The following year, however, as if by way of compensation, the elements decided to play their full part in the production of *Macbeth*, though they were to prove somewhat overenthusiastic. It was a night of storms; separate, distinct storms which could be seen quite distinctly thundering and sparking all down the coast. Each entry of the witches brought out the heavenly tim-

PREVIOUS PAGE *The Minack Theatre on the cliffs at Porthcurno.*

pani and the electric flashes, but the best effects of all were reserved for the finale as Birnham Wood was advancing on Dunsinane. By now, the separate storms had joined to deluge over the Minack. The stalwart audience stayed on beneath protecting brollies while we, the unprotected actors, struggled on, wishing they would all go home. Lady Macbeth was in hysterics in the dressing room, and the somewhat depleted army of extras was gingerly making its way, fir trees clutched to bosoms, up the slippery cliff paths behind the stage. Then the lights went out: not just our lights, but every single light in the whole area. Howls of terror joined the crash of thunder as the unhappy, tree-carrying army found itself suddenly stranded in pitch darkness above a precipitous cliff. The audience, bless them, rose to the occasion. Torches were produced and the unhappy army was led to safety. The performance was abandoned, but no-one asked for their money back. It may not have been the best-acted Shakespearian performance of the age, but it must rank among the most spectacular.

I have only the happiest of memories of the Minack since, in retrospect, the disasters have become no more than after-dinner anecdotes. I thought of trying out the stage again, a quick soliloquy from my extensive repertoire but thought better of it and turned back to the coastal path. Gwennap Head offered perhaps the finest scenery of the whole walk. The cliffs were still the now-familiar ramparts of hard granite, hard edged, ruler divided into blocks. But away from the cliff was, if not a softer land, one of softer colours. The moorland above the cliffs is like an impressionists' palate, where the yellows of gorse and the purples of heather splash against the dull ochre of the lichened rocks. But it remains essentially hard, especially for those who come to work the land. Tiny fields stretch down almost to the sea's edge, each delineated not by stone but by boulder walls, great rocks heaved together by who knows how much sweat and effort. And, at best, the fields can produce a thin grass on a thin soil on which a few cows can graze.

The cows were confined, but not the multitude of birds wheeling and singing above, among which must have been – though unrecognized by me – some rare visitor, for the area was being invaded by 'Twitchers'. This is, in itself, a strange breed recognized by its colouring, green anoraks, green boots, and usually green trousers; and its characteristic display of binoculars, telescopes and tripods. These are birdwatchers with a highly specialized function. They do not watch just any bird, only the rarest. If a bird that can be found in profusion in, say, Siberia, turns up unexpectedly looking dazed and bewildered after taking a wrong turn, then the twitchers will be there to see it and add it to their lists. A really important rarity – a 'megatwitch' – will bring them from all over the country to stand in rows inspecting some hapless denizen of Outer Mongolia. It is an activity which I find about as comprehensible as stamp collecting.

We were now headed for Land's End, a prospect which was far more enticing to Wilkie Collins than it was for me.

> Something like what Jerusalem was to the pilgrim in the Holy Land, the Land's End is – comparing great things with small – to the tourist in Cornwall. It is the Ultima Thule where his progress stops – the shrine towards which his face has been set, from the first day when he started on

his travels – the main vent, through which all the pent-up enthusiasm accumulated along the line of route is to burst its way out, in one long flow of admiration and delight.

Lucky man, to be able to visit the tip of Cornwall before it was quite overtaken by the tourist industry. At least those of us who arrive by foot are spared having to pay for the privilege of arriving at this famous spot, unlike those who come by car and coach. It is a place where no-one is left in any doubt as to what is expected of them, and that, at least, was true a century ago. 'Here are certain "sights" which a stranger is required to examine assiduously, as a duty if not as a pleasure, by guide-book law, rigidly administered by guides.' Today you are invited to pose for a photograph beside the signpost, on which the signs will be obligingly changed to accommodate the visitor. 'American are you sir?' In goes the sign, pointing west and inscribed with the mileage to New York. Home-grown tourists can call up boards from Macclesfield, Manchester or Maidenhead. You need no map to tell you when you have reached

Logan Rock, another of Brandling's sketches.

taste than I expect them to convince me to follow theirs. We go our own ways. They point to the tap – I to the pump handle. So why put an imitation handle over a keg beer? It can only deceive and confuse, which may be good news for the landlord who sold me the beer I would otherwise have rejected. I left and went to the village of Sennen and an honest pub with a good honest pint.

The north coast of Cornwall has a very different character from the south. Shingley coves give way to soft sandy beaches, though both are bounded by the same dramatic landscape of high cliffs. This is the coast I know and love and have been back to time and time again. This is where we came when our children were young, and if there is one thing I regret about their growing up it is that I have lost the excuse to play beach cricket. I often think that I was the only one who enjoyed it anyway. But on this trip I was not looking forward to the nostalgic rerun of the seaside past. Ahead lay for me what was to be the climax of the whole journey, just as it had been for Wilkie Collins before me – a trip down a Cornish mine. Collins gave this explanation to his readers who had been waiting for such an account:

> Readers who have questioned thus, may be assured that their impatience to go down a mine, in this book, was fully equalled by our impatience to go down a mine, in the county of which this book treats. Our anxiety, however, when we mentioned it to Cornish friends, was invariably met by the same answer. 'Wait' – they all said – 'until you have turned your backs on the Land's End; and then go to Botallack. The mine there is the most extraordinary mine in Cornwall; go down that, and you will not want to go down another – wait for Botallack.'

Botallack is indeed amazing, even now when it has long been disused. Those who might have thought that the engine houses at Rinsey occupied an impossibly dizzy site on the cliffs will realize that the situation is easy compared with that of Botallack. A path winds down the cliffs and there, on a tiny ledge, stands the engine house, the waves beating round the rocks at its feet. Even in its ruin it is a superb sight and, in its working days, it must have been overwhelming. Wilkie Collins' descrip-

Land's End. The litter starts to appear and steadily accumulates the nearer you get to the magic spot, then diminishes again as you move away. But it reaches no more than a few hundred yards, the maximum distance most visitors are prepared to walk from their vehicles. Yet the place clings to a last vestige of magic and its wildness has never been truly abated, as was tragically shown in 1985 when a party of children was swept from the rocks. We have not yet tamed Land's End.

I preferred not to linger too long here but to walk on away from the crowds to Sennen Cove. There we entered the local pub where they practise what I can only describe as a cruel deception. There was the all-too-familiar array of taps attached to assorted kegs of beer and lager and, in among them, just one pump handle, labelled bitter. I asked for a pint from the pump, at which the gentleman behind the bar pulled the lever, and held it down – no pumping action, just held it. The handle was a snare and a delusion, simply opening the way for horrid gassy beer. Now I have no objection to people drinking keg beers or anything else they fancy. I no more expect them to follow my

tion of his descent down this mine and his walk out under the seabed is the finest thing in the whole book, full of information, full of atmosphere and, above all, full of humour.

Collins and his friend, having persuaded the miners that they were prepared for danger and discomfort, were fitted out in miners' clothes. His companion was suitably clothed; then came Collins' turn:

> The same mysterious dispensation of fate, which always awards tall wives to short men, decreed that a suit of the big miner's should be reserved for me. He stood six feet two inches – I stand five feet six inches. I put on his flannel shirt – it fell down to my toes, like a bedgown; his drawers – and they flowed in Turkish luxuriance over my feet. At his trousers I helplessly stopped short, lost in the voluminous recesses of each leg. The big miner, like a good Samaritan as he was, came to my assistance. He put the pocket button through the waist buttonhole, to keep the trousers up in the first instance; then, he pulled steadily at the braces until my waistband was under my armpits; and then he pronounced that I and my trousers fitted each other in great perfection. The cuffs of the jacket were next turned up to my elbows – the white nightcap was dragged over my

Botallack Mine in its working days.

ears – the round hat was jammed down over my eyes. When I add to all this, that I am so near-sighted as to be obliged to wear spectacles, and that I finished my toilet by putting my spectacles on (knowing that I should see little or nothing without them), nobody, I think, will be astonished to hear that my companion seized his sketch-book, and caricatured me on the spot; and that the grave miner, polite as he was, shook with internal laughter, when I took up my tallow candles and reported myself ready for a descent into the mine.

In this unlikely garb, he went into the pit, clambering through a trap door and down vertical ladders, the only light being supplied by a candle stuck to the front of his hat by a blob of clay. After descending over 400 feet (120 metres), the guide announced that they had reached a gallery, but exploring that proved no easier than the climb down. Narrow planks crossed pits whose bottoms were lost in the darkness. Then came one place crossed by widely spaced beams which Collins, in his oversized outfit, was quite unable to manage.

Our friend the miner saw my difficulty, and extricated me from it at once, with a promptitude and skill which deserve record. Descending halfway by the beams, he clutched with one hand that hinder part of my too voluminous nether garments, which presented the broadest superficies of canvas to his grasp (I hope the delicate reader appreciates my ingenious indirect-ness of expression, when I touch on the unmentionable subject of trousers!) Grappling me thus, and supporting him-self by his free hand, he lifted me up as easily as if I had been a small parcel; then carried me horizontally along the loose boards, like a refractory little boy borne off by the usher to the master's birch; or – considering the candle burning on my hat, and the necessity of elevating my position by as lofty a comparison as I can make – like a flying Mercury with a star on his head: and finally deposited me safely upon my legs again, on the firm rock pathway beyond. 'You are but a light and a little man, my son,' says this excellent fellow, snuffing my candle for me before we go on; 'only let me lift you about as I like, and you

shan't come to any harm while I am with you!'

It is only then the visitors were told the secret of this mine: that they were walking under the sea bed.

After listening for a few moments, a distant, unearthly noise becomes faintly audible – a long, low, mysterious moan-ing, which never changes, which is *felt* on the ear as well as heard by it – a sound that might proceed from some incalculable distance, from some far invisible height – a sound so unlike anything that is heard on the upper ground, in the free air of heaven; so sublimely mournful and still; so ghostly and impressive when listened to in the subterranean recesses of the earth, that we continue instinctively to hold our peace, as if enchanted by it, and think not of com-municating to each other the awe and astonishment which it has inspired in us from the very first.

His account is full of the practicalities of mining for tin and copper, but what you re-member is the sense of excitement, and the sense of awe experienced by a grown-up schoolboy enjoying a special treat. I could not follow Collins down Botallack, for the mine has long been closed, but I did go further along the cliffs to Geevor, the old Levant mine, which was then still at work.

My introduction to the mine was not unlike Collins', for I too was presented with an in-congruous uniform: rubber boots, blue dun-garees that only had a fastening on one side and a brown dustcoat that was of little use in keeping off the dust, since it had no fastenings at all. I was, however, spared the candle and the lump of clay, being provided with a conven-tional hard hat and cap lamp. Our guide was every bit as cheery and friendly as Collins', a working miner with the practical engineer's distrust of the theorist. He told me of the famous three-handed geologist – on the one hand, on the other hand, then again on the other hand . . . We chatted comfortably as we waited for the cage that was to take us down the shaft. It was a shock to see men smoking, for I

Miners preparing to go down Dolcoath Mine, photographed by J C Burrow in the 1890s, and looking much as Collins described them.

was used to coal mines where such a thing is unheard of, but these Cornish mines are free from the risk of gaseous explosions. The descent, however, was the same falling away into darkness, with flashes of light as we passed the different levels of workings, until we slowed down to rest as gently as a feather 1500 feet (460 metres) below the surface. The first time you go down a mine, it all comes as something of a shock. No black holes here, but strip lights like a department store, space to move and, just in case you thought you had done something amazingly daring in coming down here, there is a plaque announcing that the Queen had been down in 1980 for the official opening of the new levels. The second surprise is the temperature. People think of mines as being like caves but, in fact, the further you go down the more the temperature rises.

The sense of adventure begins to increase as you start to move away from the shaft, splashing through the water that slops around at the bottom of every passageway. Water is still the Cornish miner's greatest enemy, but now the work of pumping is not done by steam engines at the surface but by electric pumps below ground – two of them, one for salt water, one for fresh. It is a sobering thought that the sea water creeps into these workings at such a rate that they have to pump out 160 000 gallons (700 000 litres) of it every day. Fresh water comes in at an even greater rate, 360 000 gallons (1 600 000 litres), of which some is recirculated for processing the ore.

There are four groups of workers down here: rock breakers, no explanation needed; trammers and diggers; timber men; and day pay. Everything has its own name, and the first activity I saw was tramming at a grizzly, or, in plain language, men pushing a tram or small truck along lines and then tipping the contents into a hole covered by widely spaced metal bars which hold back the bigger chunks which are later broken by a hammer. Timber men are responsible for the woodwork that supports the roof and the staging on which the miners stand to attack the ore. But, as yet, we were nowhere near the metal itself. We splashed off, ankle deep in orange, greasy water, down a maze of tunnels. The lighting came to an end and the cap lamps provided the only illumination. The beams picked up the shine of metal ore in the roof, the line or lode which the miners followed. Somewhere in the distance was a noise, a low grumble that got louder and louder, until we turned a corner and there at the end of a passage was the rock wall and two spectral figures enveloped in dust and a halo of light. They were drilling preparatory to blasting, extending the passageway on, moving it forward 8 or 9 feet (2.7 metres) every day and blasting out around 25 tons of granite in the process. These were the day-pay men, paid by results. Throughout this three-dimensional labyrinth, others were similarly at work following a lode or attacking a pocket of ore, eating away a cavern as the pneumatic drill gnawed at the roof.

If you have never been down a mine, then you can perhaps never grasp the special nature of the work: the ear-shattering noise, the darkness, the heat, the damp, and the total lack of facilities. No popping out to the loo here – no loo. There is no canteen either, just sandwiches from a tin as you sit on a bench with your feet in the ever-present water. I found the mine fascinating, but there is no way I would want to work there. It was lunchtime and I was able to go back to the surface for a pint and a pie in comfort. We returned via one of the old shafts, not vertical but full of slight bends – going up the banana they call it. It is only when you get back up and have to walk back to the place where you started that you realize how far you have travelled underground. Like Collins before me, I greeted the fresh air with pleasure.

> Habit teaches us to think little of the light and air that we live and breathe in, or, at most, to view them only as the ordinary conditions of our being. To find out that they are more than this, that they are a luxury as well as a necessity of life, go down into a mine, and compare what you *can* exist in there, with what you *do* exist in, on upper earth!

I could also look out over the sea and think the scarcely credible thought – not very long ago I was walking *under* that. It provided a superb climax to the coastal walk, and I had enjoyed the ghostly presence of Wilkie Collins, chuckling at my side at the incongruity of his own mine adventures. He is a man whose company I think I should have enjoyed. I cannot say the same for all my predecessors.

GEORGE BORROW (1803-81)

Hills, Mines, and Bards

Wild Wales 1862

George Borrow is a supreme literary egotist; whatever scene is described, you may be sure that he is at the centre of it and generally seen to good effect. The book would be insufferable but for one fact: George Borrow actually was a most interesting man. He was born in Norfolk in 1803 to a Cornish father and a French mother and something Celtic passed into his bloodstream to pervade his whole life. He was, from an early age, a brilliant linguist, but had to start life with a dull existence as a solicitor's clerk. It was during that period that he befriended a local groom with whom he learned to speak Welsh, though he had already begun studying the language in books. When his father died, there was nothing to keep Borrow in Norfolk and he began wandering the country, often in the company of gypsies. From his travels came his other well-known books *Lavengro* and *The Romany Rye*. Later he married, settled down – more or less – and travelled when opportunity arose, as it did in 1854 when the family set out for Wales. This is the briefest sketch of the man: a linguist who, in 1835, wrote *Targum or Metrical Translations from Thirty Languages and Dialects*, who could note quite casually that he was leaving Llangollen for a few days to walk over to Anglesey; and a man who, above all else, liked to talk to the ordinary men and women he met along the way. His book is called *Wild Wales* but, if you open it expecting long accounts of scenic splendours, you will be disappointed. They are there, but they take second place to his accounts of chance meetings. What you also get is the extraordinary, obsessive passion of the man for all things Welsh, but most especially for Bardic Wales, the old Wales of poetry and song. I do not think

I would have cared to travel very far in Mr Borrow's company, for he was never a man to hide his prejudices, never slow to trot out an opinion with total and absolute certainty. He stopped at Pengwern Hall near Llangollen, once a convent but reduced to a barn. His companion asked if he was admiring it.

'I was not admiring it,' said I; 'I was thinking of the difference between its present and former state. Formerly it was a place devoted to gorgeous idolatry and obscene lust; now it is a quiet old barn in which hay

George Borrow; by H W Phillips, 1843.

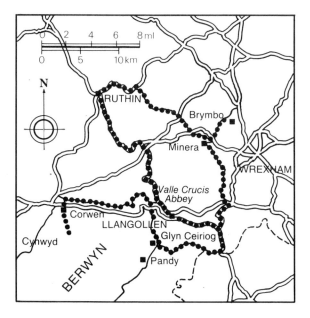

and straw are placed, and broken tumbrils stowed away: surely the hand of God is visible here?'

The companion, a good Welsh Methodist, heartily agreed and then told Borrow of a near-by holy well, where Catholics were said to worship.

'And so they do,' said I, 'true to the old Indian superstition, of which their religion is nothing but a modification. The Indians and sepoys worship stocks and stones, and the river Ganges, and our Papists worship stocks and stones, holy wells and fountains.'

He put some questions to me about the origin of nuns and friars. I told him they originated in India, and made him laugh heartily by showing him the original identity of nuns and nautch-girls, begging priests and begging Brahmins.

This extraordinary information was retailed without further comment.

One could continue listing Borrow's faults, for he tends to shout them at you, but he had another side to his nature, a generosity of spirit and a total lack of many of the conventional prejudices of the day. Englishmen were still taunting the Welsh with the old rhyme:

Taffy was a Welshman, Taffy was a thief:
Taffy came to my house and stole a piece of
beef.

And few Englishmen showed any interest in Welsh culture and language. It was rare, too, for men of his position in society to have anything to say to the 'lower orders', let alone seek out their company. These are the reasons for reading Borrow, but why follow his footsteps? That is a more difficult question to answer, and one I pondered over for some time. I eventually realized that what appealed to me was the enthusiasm with which he greeted each new event along the way and his ability to see behind the very obvious appeal of beautiful scenery to the life of the people, both now and in the past. In a way, we are back full circle to Celia Fiennes, or Daniel Defoe, but there is a subtle difference. The early travellers were all but oblivious to the delights of wild scenery but, in Borrow's time, the literary world had been all but surfeited with works in praise of the picturesque and the romantic. Borrow unites the two themes and presents us with both in versions highly coloured by his own personal views. It is in this that I feel closest to Borrow, for I too have spent a deal of time in walking around Britain, partly to admire and enjoy the countryside, partly in pursuit of a personal passion for one aspect of the past. Where we differ is in our choice of passions: for Borrow it was bards and ancient songs, for me the physical reminders of the industrial revolution. The Borrow family made Llangollen their headquarters, from where Borrow himself walked out in all directions in a series of excursions. Happily, this is a centre as well suited to my industrial meanderings as to his poetic travels. I made my own headquarters near, but not in, Llangollen, and I too made excursions. In part, I followed the paths trodden by George Borrow – but I also felt free to take my own ways, paralleling his journeys by a personal quest to match them.

I started out with an advantage over Borrow – I had no need to engage in any complicated persuasion. His wife, 'a perfect paragon', he informs us, who, '...can make puddings and sweets and treacle posset...', was all for a fashionable spa, Harrogate or Leamington. Her daughter supported her. Borrow promptly showed his true, self-sacrificing nature. 'I told them that there was nothing I so much hated as fashionable life, but that, as I was anything but a selfish person, I would endeavour to stifle my abhorrence of it for a time.' The ladies were unable to resist such subtle pleadings, so to Wales they all went. My wife, Pip, who does not make treacle posset, was very happy to go to Wales and found us a marvellous place to stay, a converted barn in a lovely valley. Borrow would, I think, have approved for this is very much wild Wales surrounded by hills but with a pub not far away in which he would have delighted, for he could have indulged his taste for good ale and impressed the locals by his knowledge of their native tongue.

Borrow was a great enthusiast for beer, even if the locals were not always overenthusiastic about the conversation. On one of his journeys he stopped off at Tafarn Tywarch, the Turf Tavern where he asked an elderly woman for his breakfast, in Welsh of course.

'Sar?' said she.

'Bring us some bread, cheese and ale,' I repeated in Welsh.

'I do not understand you, sar,' said she in English.

'Are you Welsh?' said I in English.

'Yes, I am Welsh?'

'And can you speak Welsh?'

'O, yes, and the best.'

'Then why did you not bring what I asked for?'

'Because I did not understand you.'

'Tell her,' said I to John Jones, 'to bring us some bread, cheese and ale.'

'Come, aunt,' said John, 'bring us bread and cheese and a quart of the best ale.'

The woman looked as if she was going to reply in the tongue in which he addressed her, then faltered, and at last said in English that she did not understand.

'Now,' said I, 'you are fairly caught: this man is a Welshman, and moreover understands no language but Welsh.'

'Then how can he understand you?' said she.

Llangollen – from the 'Garden of the Inn'
by Costello, 1845.

'Because I speak Welsh,' said I.

'Then you are a Welshman?' said she.

'No I am not,' said I, 'I am English.'

'So I thought,' said she, 'and on that account I could not understand you.'

'You mean that you would not,' said I. 'Now do you choose to bring what you are bidden?'

'Come, aunt,' said John, 'don't be silly and cenfigenus, but bring the breakfast.'

The woman stood still for a moment or two, and then biting her lips went away. Borrow then proceeded to give the Welsh lady a Welsh lesson, which put him in such a good mood that he ordered a second jug of beer, which he declared to be first class. He was a great connoisseur of beer was Mr Borrow, as ready to condemn as to praise. His appreciation was generally shown in practical form by ordering more but, when given a 'poorish' ale at a pub, he could only exclaim, 'O, for an Act of Parliament to force people to brew good ale!' Yes, indeed, but I had no complaints over the ale served at the Blue Lion in Cynwyd for it was brewed by Marstons of Burton-on-Trent and there are few finer beers on offer anywhere. The company was excellent, friendly and, among themselves, Welsh speaking. I certainly could not emulate my predecessor and speak in Welsh but, as they were all bilingual, they had no problem in communicating with the ignorant 'Saxon'. As an outsider, it is a pleasure to hear Welsh spoken and sung, though the spread of a sort of universal culture can produce strange combinations. I recently stayed in a pub on Anglesey, where Welsh is widely spoken. That night, a notice informed me, was to be music night. It was a sign that gave rise to forebodings. The singer arrived, went to the bar and conversed fluently in Welsh. Perhaps the old culture was alive after all. Borrow was much addicted to the works of the bards: were we to have Welsh song for the evening? Conversation over, the singer plugged in his guitar and began to tell us of his old home in Kentucky, the words delivered in the nasal whine that seems inseparable from the country music of America. I thought it very strange. Those who want to retain local culture have a long struggle ahead of them.

We made our visit to Wales in mid-May, a splendid month for travelling and walking. The chances of finding fine weather are good, but it is rarely so hot as to make you thoroughly uncomfortable. We found conditions to be perfect, and the sight of the hills above the farm was irresistible. To say spring was in the air was no more than a plain statement of fact, for the sounds of spring everywhere surrounded us. The young lambs had just been separated from the ewes, and the pained bleating of the one was answered by the mournful baahs of the other. The birds, however, seemed happy enough, and what a variety there was. You could lean on the stable-type door and see and hear them without all the paraphernalia of hides and binoculars that are usually necessary. Redstart, wheatear, and chiffchaff all came visiting while, more distantly, came the voices of lapwing, willow warbler, curlew, whitethroat, and the sweet song of the lark. A swallow passed by with its promise of summer. There was no staying indoors so we set off to investigate our surroundings.

The scenery of Britain is at its best when everything comes together in harmony, when the buildings seem to belong absolutely to that particular landscape. I saw it in walking the Pennine hills, and in cycling through the downland of Hampshire, and I met it again here. The small farms are scarcely seen before you are right on top of them. They hide themselves away in folds and hollows: stone walls, slate roofs, and not much time for frills and frippery, buildings that reflect the serious business of hill farming. Away from the farms, the stone walls lead on high up the hillside to the rough moorland. The stone wall has been such an integral part of the landscape of my youth, that I would expect scarcely to notice it any more, yet it still seems to me to be a marvel of patient craftsmanship. Infinite care goes into constructing a good wall from stones and boulders, but here a special skill is needed for the walls are made up of slender slate blocks arranged with precision and reinforced at corners and gateways by great slabs. Here they were really well maintained, and the temptation to go for the easier option of wire fencing has been resisted.

However attractive the farms of the valley might be, the walls led the eye upwards towards the hill, Moel yr Henfaes. Not a very high hill – it stops just short of the 2000-foot

(600-metre) mark – but high enough to send out a challenge. There is something about being at the foot of a hill that always makes me want to be at the top. It is not simply the prospect of enjoying a good view, but that challenge to test my limbs against its steepness. Here I am, the hill says, climb me and put a bit of effort into your life; pant a bit, sweat a bit, and remind yourself that the natural world demands an effort from you if you are going to enjoy it to the full. I was glad to accept the invitation. As I climbed I reached a point where the rock began to break through the covering of soil, turf, and bracken, and here the Welsh ponies munched away, eyeing us somewhat cautiously. As I climbed, so the view opened until it seemed a whole panorama of Wales was there in front of me. It was not just the view of the landscape that widened: the sky seemed to widen with it. Logically, I know that there is the same amount of sky over my head no matter where I stand, but there are certain places where the heavens seem to expand: East Anglia is the supreme example, for it seems a phenomenon of the plain rather than the hill. It happened here, though; a huge sky it seemed, patched with clouds. As they parted, the pallid, distant landscape burst into colour under the shifting beams of the sun. When Borrow came to these hills, he hoped for views of distant Snowdon: I got them, in a perspective with colour. Close at hand, the browns of the hill contrasted with the lush greens of the river valley but, beyond that, were the fainter, delicately tinted shapes that were the high peaks of distant Snowdonia. I could hardly have asked for a better introduction to wild Wales.

All Wales is not, however, wild, or at least not in the more romantic sense. Even here where moorland takes over at the road's end, there were parts as cosy as a corner of Kent. The following day I wandered down a lane between high banks, brightly spotted with springtime flowers, with violets and primroses, beyond which was an area of dark woodland that could have seemed gloomy, except that the space between the trees was filled with marsh-marigolds and bluebells about to come into their own. I walked on down the road, and found a sign pointing to Llwybr Cynoeddis, a name which did not appear on my map. I walked on towards Cynwyd and there was another sign,

same name, pointing across the fields and soon another, each pointing in a totally different direction. Where was this mysterious, shifting place? George Borrow would have known, for he would have been quite capable of understanding the Welsh for 'public footpath'. He would also have been smugly amused by my stupidity.

Down in the valley of the Dee, the farms seem less guarded, less huddled against the elements. The flat, watered lands grow good crops, and there was even a meadow, not a field of coarse rye grass but a genuine meadow, with meadow flowers scenting the air. Here was clearly a farm with a difference, for shire horses cropped the grass in a field and diminutive Shetland ponies kept them company in the next; giant horse and tiny horse both being treated to that curiously supercilious air that is unique to sheep. These were Jacob sheep and had, I suppose, a right to feel superior. This is altogether a softer landscape from that of the hills and the difference seemed acute as I reached the fringes of Cynwyd where suburbia meets the country and you might as easily be in Wembley as in Wales. The heart of the village remains purely Welsh, with stone houses topped by slate in every shade of blue and grey.

Beyond the village, the road crosses a disused railway on a dull bridge and the Avon on a fine bridge, one of those narrow constructions where niches stand above the piers to give pedestrians protection. Below, the river mumbled peaceably to itself, and chaffinches swooped across the shaded water. Up the lane, still banked and shaded by trees, stands an old house where I had stayed on a previous visit, Plas Uchaf. There seems little enough to it from the outside but it does impress by the massive quality of the masonry, a house built from boulders. Its true virtues remain hidden. This is a medieval hall house, where the main room, the hall, extends all the way up from stone-flagged floor to raftered roof, an enormous area which only shrinks at night when the light fails to reach the more distant, shadowed spaces. But enjoyable as the valley exploration was, the hills still kept demanding attention. It was time for a somewhat more ambitious walk, up the Berwyn.

'The Berwyn' is a somewhat ambiguous term, covering the whole range of hills to the south-west of Llangollen. Borrow made several trips over them, but I planned to walk to one of the more remote areas, to the rocky ridge that joins Cadair Bronwen to Cadair Berwyn, the highest point in the range. Here all the feelings about this particular landscape that developed on the first walk were reinforced, in much the same proportions as the effect of walking the steep hillside was increased. In these remote areas, a community needed to be self-sufficient. A farm showed signs of once containing a mill building, the water courses still clear; plough marks were still visible where crops were once grown on a seemingly inhospitable land. After the arable, came the pasture, spring lambs looking a little absurd with huge red capitals TE marked on their rumps as badges of ownership. There were occasional intrusions: a new metal barn gleamed like an electronics' factory in the sun and, inevitably it seems, a large chunk of land had disappeared beneath conifers. When a hill farmer gives up the struggle, who is there to take his place? Not another farmer in all probability, but the foresters are always there. So we get these dense plantations, tight packed and dark where nothing grows but evil-looking fungi. Why is it that when subsidies are being handed out all around the farming community, more cannot be done for the hill farmer, whose work actually enhances the land, while his counterpart in the lowlands is too often busy creating featureless prairies? They might even encourage the farmers to let the lambs grow to a decent size, so that mutton might again feature on our menus, a succulent meat full of flavour. Borrow was lucky enough to get the real thing, and his description seems now, to us mutton-bereft citizens, almost unbearably enticing.

> As for the leg of mutton, it was truly wonderful; nothing so good had I ever tasted in the shape of a leg of mutton. The leg of mutton of Wales beats the leg of mutton of any other country, and I had never tasted a Welsh leg of mutton before. Certainly I shall never forget the first Welsh leg of mutton which I tasted, rich but delicate, replete with juices derived from the aromatic herbs of the noble Berwyn, cooked to a turn, and weighing just four pounds.
> "O its savoury smell was great,

Sheep and spring lambs on the Berwyn.

> Such as might well tempt, I trow,
> One that's dead to lift his brow."

Need I add that this was washed down with good Llangollen ale.

There was no mutton to eat, but I had the pleasure of coming out from beneath the dark shade of the conifers to be faced by a grassy hill topped by a circle of stones. There are structures you meet on the land that seem to bring

you closer to people of the past, the remains of homely, domestic buildings where you can still in imagination feel the warmth of the fire in the grate and hear the sound of children playing. Stone circles seem instead to make the past recede into an impenetrable mystery. I can get no sense of the meaning of the rings, no notion of possible rituals, no idea of why men laboured so hard to create them in such remote spots. I have read accounts of mystic experiences – but never encountered any. So I turned back to the countryside, still loud with bird song. A pair of wheatears sat on top of the wall watching our approach. They flew off, landed, waited and flew off again before deciding that we were safely out of their territory and could be left to go on about our business. They are endearing birds and I enjoyed their company.

A haze dulled the moorland edge and a hard wind blew in from the west, promising little good. But for the moment the weather stayed fine as I reached the open moor blissfully empty for now though the track was churned up in places to a treacly morass where motor-cyclists had come this way. No engine now disturbed this empty land; the twentieth century was nowhere in sight. Here I could feel that this was still the Wales which Borrow walked, striding the land with a deal less effort than I seemed to be needing. This was the Wales I had sensed in his book, still untouched by the modern development of housing, industry, or what I often think is the most pernicious of all, tourism. No-one had made it easy for me to get here, and the reward seemed all the greater. It was, I thought, time to follow more directly in Borrow's steps.

Llangollen, Borrow's headquarters for all his early trips, did not itself excite me greatly. He stayed in a cottage situated between the canal and the river, and the only matter of note was the arrival of the church cat. It appears that the vicar of Llangollen had owned a cat which his successor's collection of cats and dogs drove away. It might have found a new home had it not been for its ecclesiastical upbringing, for the good dissenters of Llangollen had no room for anything that smacked of Anglicanism. The cat was damned by association until the Borrows took it in and turned the miserable, spurned stray into a model of sleek domesticity. There are cats in Llangollen today but whether church or chapel is no longer plain. Borrow's house seems, however, to have gone and the town itself is much changed. It is on the Tourist Map. This means a rash of teashops, coffee shops, and what would once have been gift shops but are now craft centres – different name, same products. The tourists come, zoom around at high speed in the brief intervals allowed by tour organizers or simply collapse into the nearest pub and abandon the whole thing. I met just such a crowd of OAPs in the Bridge Hotel, looking dazed and shellshocked, whisked from place to place with no time to potter so that the whole of Wales was reduced to the view from a coach window and scampi-and-chips in a basket.

Probably the one thing about Llangollen that has remained unchanged is its setting, surrounded by hills and divided by the river which tumbles through the town over rocky cascades. There are things still to catch the eye: the Royal Hotel standing grandly by the bridge, a pub with ornate plasterwork flowers brightly painted and a sign announcing that

stabling is available, and the old mill building down by the river. I walked up to the latter and heard a very familiar noise, the clatter of shuttles in looms. There was a flannel mill in Llangollen in Borrow's day, but this mill originally had nothing to do with textiles. It was a corn mill, and you can see the old grindstone in the actual fabric of the building. The woollen industry was once quite important in Wales but, like so much of Britain's textile industry, it went into seemingly irreversible decline. Now we seem to be coming back to where we started. The factories took over from the cottages and the small workshop: now the cottage and small workshop are coming back into their own. Craft to industry to craft in no time at all it seems.

Llangollen is one of those towns where you have to poke about a great deal to find much of real interest, but it does boast one unique building – a building which itself is even more fantastic than the story of its most famous inhabitants. This is Plas Newydd, home of the Ladies of Llangollen. They were not merely famous themselves, but received equally famous visitors, ranging from the Duke of Wellington, whose visit is commemorated by an inscription over a fireplace, to William Wordsworth who commemorated the visit himself with a notably inferior poem. The ladies in question were Sarah Ponsonby and Lady Eleanor Butler who had eloped from Ireland to the dismay of their families to set up home together. They dressed in dark riding habits, wore tall hats, and cropped their hair, looking, according to which contemporary account you prefer, either like 'respectable superannuated clergymen' or 'hazy or crazy old sailors'. Such was their notoriety that, when Borrow came to Llangollen over twenty years after their death, people still talked of them and regaled visitors with anecdotes of their eccentricity. The house was, as it still is, a favourite tourist attraction and it is not difficult to see why. Borrow recounts some of the general gossip about the ladies, but says nothing about this extraordinary building which seems all the more remarkable for its setting surrounded by modern houses.

How can you describe such a place? It began its existence as a plain Welsh cottage, but the ladies soon set about improving it inside and out until it was thoroughly and completely gothicized. Oriel windows were added with stained glass but, above all, it was filled and covered with carved oak. Gods of the Greeks and the Hindus cavort above windows; grotesque heads peer from the walls; cherubs look somewhat warily at the lions that guard the porch. Inside, not a surface is left untouched; elaboration lies upon elaboration and, even when a bit of wall appears between the pieces of carved oak, you find it is covered by embossed leather. It is rich to the point of surfeit. Had it only been the home of a Welsh bard instead of two Irish eccentrics, what a time Borrow would have had here. Instead, he walked on past and left it to his wife and daughter to explore.

Borrow did, however, spend a good deal of time looking at the transport route that first brought me to Llangollen, the canal or the camlas as Borrow called it in Welsh. I combined several Borrow excursions into one for a grand exploration of the Dee Valley. The canal itself is cut into the hillside above the town, and the passage along the valley of the Dee is as beautiful as you will find on any canal in Britain but ironically this section, now so popular with pleasure boaters, was not built primarily for boats at all. Its true purpose only becomes clear when you walk to the end of the line. Along the way, however, there is much to enjoy. You can see how the artificial channel has been blasted out of the rock, but artificiality need not mean ugliness. Time has healed the crude scars on the land, so that now the transparent waters of the canal can seem as attractive as the turbulent waters of the river that runs alongside. Where the river has the edge is in its sense of drama, for it is punctuated by a whole succession of small waterfalls. To balance that, the canal can offer illustrated lectures in natural history: fish chase their shadows through this watery lane while ducks shepherd their families along the way, leading the ducklings under the overhangs of the bank whenever human menacing forms loom over the water. The air was heavy with the scent of wild garlic so that you might, if blindfold, have believed you were on a tour of the kitchens of Montparnasse. The canal is a haven, but only because its real working life has ended. When Borrow came this way it was still part of an important trading network. He

was not particularly interested in this aspect of Wales, but he duly noted it all and the information still reads like jottings in a notebook.

> Presently I came to a barge lying by the bank; the boatman was in it. I entered into conversation with him. He told me that the canal and its branches extended over a great part of England. That the boats carried slates – that he had frequently gone as far as Paddington by the canal – that he was generally three weeks on the journey – that the boatmen and their families lived in the little cabins aft – that the boatmen were all Welsh – that they could read English, but little or no Welsh – that English was a much more easy language to read than Welsh – that they passed by many towns, among others Northampton, and that he liked no place so much as Llangollen.

For me, even this baldest of descriptions has a wealth of information to convey and how I would have loved to question his boatman on a whole range of topics – what was the journey like to London, when did he start living on the boat, who owned it, what sort of a livelihood did he make? Alas, Borrow never asked the questions and I cannot. I have to accept that Borrow was a romantic, whose imagination was fired by dramatic tales not by dry accounts of a transport system at work. Perhaps, however, I would have been somewhat mortified as Borrow was when he came upon his next canal boat being loaded with slabs of slate.

> In the boat was an old bareheaded, bare-armed fellow, who presently joined in the conversation in very broken English. He told me that his name was Joseph Hughes, and that he was a real Welshman and was proud of being so; he expressed a great dislike for the English, who he said were in the habit of making fun of him and ridiculing his language; he said that all the fools that he had known were Englishmen. I told him that all Englishmen were not fools. 'But the greater part are,' said he. 'Look how they work,' said I. 'Yes,' said he, 'some of them are good at breaking stones for the road, but not more than one in a hundred.'

The sort of thing that Borrow preferred was the story of the Robber's Leap. The river goes its turbulent way below the level of the canal, and a point is reached where it boils over a ledge and it is here that the thief is said to have made his great jump into freedom, for his pursuers were far happier letting a felon escape than in risking their lives in the Dee.

River and canal continue their companionable way until they merge at Horseshoe Falls. This is not a natural beauty spot but a weir across the river, constructed so that water can be fed down into the canal. This is the whole point of the Llangollen Canal in the Dee Valley: it was built not for transport but for water supply. Not that anyone cares any more, for the pleasure boaters are happy to enjoy its beauty without worrying too much about its history. Yet that history is there to be read at the Horseshoe. A view of lime kilns reminds us that this was a waterway with a job of work to do, while notices by the towpath chart the varying fortunes of the canal. We walk there, we are told, 'on sufferance' thanks to the generosity of the Shropshire Union Railway and Canal Company, and already we have moved one generation away from the old Ellesmere Canal Company who first built the line. A second notice gives details of water control by the L.M.S. the London, Midland and Scottish Railway Company, still later owners of the concern and today we have British Waterways in control.

A short detour on the way back takes you to Valle Crucis, the Vale of the Cross and two antiquities, the Pillar of Eliseg and the ruined abbey. Naturally enough Borrow wanted to see the pillar and received a brief note on its history from his Welsh companion.

> 'Sir,' said my guide, 'a dead king lies buried beneath this stone. He was a mighty man of valour and founded the abbey. He was called Eliseg.' 'Perhaps Ellis,' said I, 'and if his name was Ellis his stone was very properly called Colofn Eliseg, in Saxon, the Ellisian column.'

In fact, it was erected to the memory of Elise a contemporary of Offa's who, rather than peacefully inaugurating abbeys, was noted, according to the long-vanished inscription on the column, for taking Powys back from the English 'with fire and sword'. It is not, truth to

Valle Crucis Abbey from Thomas Pennant A Tour of Wales, *1809.*

tell, an especially exciting object of contemplation and the view from it is worse, for you look out over a monstrous caravan park that separates you from the abbey.

The abbey itself is beautiful, though Borrow, who was inevitably impressed by the pillar, was equally inevitably somewhat hard on a Catholic foundation, 'a place of great pseudo-sanctity'. In our largely secular age, we care

little about the abbey's religious life and tend to regard it simply as a piece of architecture divorced from its function, a Romantic Ruin. It was in the eighteenth century that the cult of the picturesque reached its peak, when all scenery was viewed in terms of how it would look in a picture. Ladies and gentlemen came with sketchbooks and watercolours, delighting in such spots and the more ruinous they were, the more they liked them. We do the same, but with less patience and less care – click goes the instamatic and the ruin is recorded. Where our forebears would have discussed perspective and shades, I talked lenses and apertures with a fellow visitor. But though the methods of recording may have changed, our tastes remain those of the earlier age. The tall arches of the nave reflected in the still waters of the fish pond

thrill us now as they have thrilled visitors for 200 years.

I turned away to climb the shapely hill that dominates the town of Llangollen, and to explore the castle that crowns it. What a striking silhouette this is when seen from the valley, what a promise of romantic ruins. Then you arrive to find the walls held up by steel scaffolding and somehow the romance begins to diminish. It becomes no more than a castle on a hill, decayed and still decaying. To Borrow, Castell Dinas Bran was a place where fact and legend were woven into one seamless Welsh tapestry. He quoted this translation of verses written on Dinas Bran, the Castle of the Crow.

> 'Gone, gone are thy gates, Dinas Bran on the height!
> Thy warders are blood-crows and raven, I trow;
> Now no one will wend from the field of the fight
> To the fortress on high, save the raven and crow.'

The way up is steep but, because of the steepness, you leave the town behind so much the quicker. The hill is a place of escape, for the schoolgirls who had come to lie in the grass and giggle among themselves at the comments of the boys, who kept their distance as they smoked their bravado cigarettes. My reward for the effort of climbing was a fine view of Llangollen, the silver ribbon of canal tying the parts of the town together, of the Eglwyseg valley with the outline of its rounded hills broken by a hard line of pallid crags. I took the path down beneath the fractured outline of Trevor Rocks, shattered by quarrying, and continued on a solitary path that led me back to the canal and across Cysylltau bridge to Froncysyllte.

This is where you meet one of the great wonders of the industrial revolution. You catch glimpses of it at various points along the way: you see much of it rearing up from the river bed as you stand on the ancient bridge across the Dee, but is is only when you see it all that you appreciate its true character. I think of that sentimental Landseer painting *Dignity and Impudence*, for those are the characteristics

Valle Crucis today.

embodied in the aqueduct, Pontcysyllte. There is an air of impudence about the whole notion of setting a canal high up in the air, sending boats, of all things, soaring high above their natural element of water, the River Dee; providing those boats with an artificial channel over 1000 feet (300 metres) long and more than 100 feet (30 metres) above the valley floor. And there is dignity in the steady procession of stone arches that carry the iron trough full of water. It is part of the mundane world of industry, trade, of earning a living and yet, at the same time, it is a grand gesture, perhaps the grandest gesture of the whole industrial revolution. Often we see some structure of the past and we are told that it was revolutionary in its day, and we accept the information as fact – but it fails to touch us, it remains an academic point. Pontcysyllte stirs you, overwhelms you still. Borrow went there on one of his very first excursions and, although he reserved his more ecstatic outpourings for older and more truly Welsh matters, he was nevertheless impressed.

> 'This is the Pont y Cysswllt, sir,' said my guide; 'it's the finest bridge in the world, and no wonder, if what the common people say be true, namely that every stone cost a golden sovereign.' We went along it; the height was awful. My guide, though he had been a mountain shepherd, confessed that he was somewhat afraid. 'It gives me the pendro, sir,' said he, 'to look down.' I too felt somewhat dizzy, as I looked over the parapet into the glen.

I find it even more dramatic than that description suggests but then I was considerably less moved by a natural pool in the river far below.

> It was shaded by lofty trees, and to all appearance was exceedingly deep. I stopped to look at it, for I was struck with its gloomy horror. 'That pool, sir,' said John Jones, 'is called Llyn y Meddwyn, the drunkard's pool. It is called so, sir, because a drunken man once fell into it, and was drowned. There is no deeper pool in the Dee, sir, save one, a little below Llangollen, which is called the pool of Catherine Lingo. A girl of that name fell into it, whilst gathering sticks on the high bank above it. She was drowned, and the pool was named after her. I never look at either without shuddering, thinking how

*A suitably picturesque view of Castell Dinas Bran from
Pennant's Tour of Wales, 1809.*

certainly I should be drowned if I fell in, for
I cannot swim, sir.'
Borrow cannot resist the temptation to point
out to the guide, and to his readers, that he
himself would be in no such danger and he
would be quite capable of diving for stones at
the bottom of the pool.

Once you cross the aqueduct you begin to get
salutary reminders that the whole enterprise
did not originally depend on tourism. Pontcysyllte was built for the world of work. From
its height, Borrow looked out over the forges of
Cefn Bach. There are traces of those days in the

to view the valley, where distance often lends the proverbial enchantment which closer inspection might dispel. There is quality here alright in severely classical Trevor Hall, in traditional farms and an old mill with mill pond and waterwheel still very much in evidence. But there is the real tat as well: the caravan park, the straggling villas, that belong to Acacia Avenue not a Welsh valley, and the main road with its noisy intruders. The height can produce transformation: the golf course looks really rather splendid, bunkers spread out over the land like giant yellow footsteps, and greens of scarcely credible lushness. But the parts I like best are those where the view is quite closed off by the trees and the canal clings to the hillside winding itself tightly round the rocks. Losing a wide view helps you concentrate on the details, a quiet stirring of water as it moves between light and shade.

Back in Llangollen, the sun had acted like a trigger to set events in motion. Local lads fresh out of school leaped alarmingly from the centre of the Dee bridge. The water looked tempting but I resisted temptation and went back to the car, back to the barn, and felt content that the day had shown not just that the world Borrow had known was still there to be enjoyed, but that the canal scene I had first experienced twenty years before was essentially unchanged. Encouraged by success I decided on another day's Borrowing, a trip to Ruthin. I did not, however, do as he did and walk, but lazily took to the car: 16 miles there and 16 miles back seemed a little much for one day. I had, in any case, been reading Borrow again and I was struck by the way in which his excursions seemed tied as much to his enthusiasms for matters Welsh, poetry and legend, as to Welsh scenery. If he could follow his own whims then I should follow mine. I would go to Ruthin and leave the rest of the excursion to fancy.

It is a town I prefer to Llangollen, for tourism has not yet got it firmly clenched in its jaws. There was an early note of alarm when I spotted a notice outside the Castle Hotel advertising medieval banquets. These appalling institutions owe more to Hollywood than to any medieval reality, and may Heaven preserve me from ever again having to drink that sickly concoction, mead. Elsewhere, however, the town seemed a good, honest, and unpreten-

piles of slag, all but overgrown at the canal side. There are traces, too, and no more than traces, of the route that was expected to replace the canal, the route of the railway. But the rails have gone, while the canal survives, though trading now in holidaymakers rather than slate, iron, and coal. Thank goodness that it does, for it provides a perfect route from which

tious place. It is a market town which still has a market, where cloth-capped hill farmers exchange the gloomy prognostications that form the main conversation of all farmers. It usually begins with the weather, which if not too wet will certainly be too dry, and continues on through the high price of fodder and the low price paid for produce to the inevitable conclusion of imminent ruin. At which point they repair to the pub.

Change is not marked very clearly in Ruthin. It still boasts fine timber-framed buildings. The inn where Borrow dined is still there, but now called the Wynnstay Arms instead of the Crossed Foxes. The Wynnstays owned the castle in Borrow's day, though in the book they are only referred to rather coyly as the 'W-s', and such an important family clearly deserved to have a pub named after them. So deserving were they that they got a second Wynnstay Arms in Holywell. The shops of Ruthin are appealing, especially the food shops: greengrocers where fruit and veg are displayed in

arrangements that are works of art; butchers with local meat which has not been over-trimmed and pampered, so that you still get suet with the kidney to encourage the cook to prepare a pudding. Other buildings of Borrow's day are still there, even if their function had changed. The old market hall is now a bank, while the gaol now houses the County Records Office, where at least one can feel assured the records are secure. Borrow, however, made great play of the excellence of his meal and the virtues of the locally brewed ale, so I decided to move on in search of the latter. I found it at the City Arms, Minera near Wrexham.

The landscape round this pub is as uncity-like as one could imagine, a wasteland of spoil heaps above which stands the unmistakeable outline of an engine house, so that for a moment one might have been transported back to Cornwall. Here, however, they mined for lead not for tin or copper. This was City Mine, so at least the pub's name makes sense, even if the mine name is still a mystery, and the engine house and mine are portrayed in splendid bas-relief on the wooden sign. Next door is a stone building emblazoned with a Welsh dragon and

LEFT *Castell Dinas Bran seen from the Llangollen Canal.*

BELOW *A narrow boat on the Llangollen Canal with Pontcysyllte in the background.*

here they brew Minera ale, and a good beer always seems to taste at its very best when drunk on home territory. Suitably fortified, I went on my way but, if one thirst had been satisfied, another had been aroused. Just as Borrow felt excited on hearing news of a bardic grave close at hand, so too I was excited by the knowledge that I was close to one of the key areas of the industrial revolution.

On the road to Brymbo, I screeched to a stop beside a low building with a tall chimney. Surely this was once a foundry? It was, and turned out to be my first introduction to the works of the Wilkinson family who had pioneered a boring process – hole-making not tedium-inducing – which was first used for cannon and then for making cylinders for the early steam engines. The tradition lives on at the massive Brymbo Steelworks, but a lot of the world of the old ironmasters also survives though not always where you might expect it. Bersham offers fine parkland with a busy stream falling across a wide weir, which might lead you to expect water gardens or ornamental pools. Then a farm appears dominated by a huge octagonal building, and the name, 'Mill Farm', at once provides an explanation for the weir. Here we have water power and a building far too large for a simple grain mill. These are the remains, it seems, of an old forge. You keep stumbling across such remains. Nearby is Davies Brothers of Croesfoel where they made the iron gates for Chirk Castle. How well things come together: Borrow goes off pursuing the Celtic past, I chase the industrial past, and we meet up at a place that delights us both, Chirk Castle.

Those castle gates certainly are magnificent as, indeed, is the castle itself even if, on closer inspection, this ancient seat of the Myddleton family seems now to owe as much to the notions of what eighteenth- and nineteenth-century architects thought a castle should be as to its original builders. The fortification has been thoroughly domesticated so that, once inside, as at Dunvegan, you find yourself on a stately home tour of admirable furnishings and tasteful pictures. Borrow brought his wife and daughter and mused on the heroic past.

As my two loved ones sat I walked up and down, recalling to my mind all I had heard and read in connection with this castle. I thought of its gallant defence against the men of Oliver; I thought of its roaring hospitality in the time of the fourth Sir Thomas; and I thought of the many beauties who had been born in its chambers, had danced in its halls, had tripped across its court, and had subsequently given heirs to illustrious families.

I was more interested in the other life of the castle, the life of those who kept the place going. The servants hall was, in fact, the old dining hall of 1529 and was only handed over to the servants when far grander premises were provided for the gentry. Here you get the feel of the old castle and an intriguing view of life below stairs. An inscription reads:

No Noise, No Strife, Nor Swear At All
But all be decent in the Hall.

Failure to obey these rules was punished with great severity: the beer ration was stopped! The castle had its own brewhouse and was famed for its good malt liquor and the small beer brewed for harvest time. That this was an important part of castle life can be gauged by the fact that only the head gardener drew higher wages than the brewer and under-brewer. Brewing, alas, is as much a thing of the past as sieges and battles so I made my way back to my temporary home and the pleasures of Marston's Pedigree.

Although Borrow's Welshifying can become a little irritating, there are times when his absolute sincerity shines through and you forgive him everything. Nowhere is this more apparent than in his search for mementoes of Huw Morris, known as the Ceiriog nightingale. So to the valley of the Ceiriog he went, and I came after though not with quite the same objective in view. The start, however, was very similar, across the Berwyn on a less-than-perfect morning. Borrow described his weather as 'lowering' and the word fitted mine just as well. It was not pouring with rain, but low cloud sat on the hills and a mist hung in the trees like thin grey sheets put out to dry. A sparse drizzle scarcely seemed to fall, but hung in the air and attached itself to you in beady drops.

Down in Glyn Ceiriog itself I was quite unable to resist the temptation to deviate from the Huw Morris trail to follow my own devices

The majestic aqueduct, Pontcysyllte.

Ruthin town hall; by W Willis after H Gastineau, 1830.

with a visit to Chwarel Wynne. This is a slate mine of considerable antiquity, even if no-one is quite certain of its age. Slates were being sent out of this valley 1000 years ago, but records for this particular mine date back no further than the seventeenth century, and it saw its busiest period early in the present century. These days, artificial roofing tiles are far cheaper, if not far better than genuine slates and Chwarel Wynne is a museum where the aimiable owner, Brian James, acts as engineer, curator, and guide.

At first approach you might think it has been unduly prettified for tourists: trees cover the hillside which echoes to the harsh calls of rowdy peacocks. Things are not, however, quite what they seem: the verdant hill is an overgrown spoil heap and the peacocks are no recent additions, for the colony was first established here a century ago. But here it is not the surface that demands attention, but the underground workings. The mine is a series of vast, echoing chambers, each one representing a huge amount of human labour. The men came here, much as their counterparts did in the Cornish mines, to hack and blast away the rocks, their way lit by the feeble glow of candles all but lost in the dust-filled air. When Brian James first put lighting in the mine, the old men came back and stared in awe at the immensity of the caverns they had made. They had never seen them before. Day in and day out they had worked here, but had never viewed more than a fraction of the whole. The rest had been lost in the dust, that same dust that ended the lives of so many slate workers. Go to the Methodist churchyard and you will see the gleaming headstones sparkling with light – but that sparkle comes from the silica which clogs and scars lungs and was responsible for the many young men buried here. It was never an easy life in the mine, and prodigious efforts were needed to make it pay. For some 30 tons of rock had to be removed for every ton of slate.

The slate miner suffered from the killer that hung suspended in the air, the lethal dust, rather than from accidents. Only one death was recorded as a result of accident, a man who drowned while checking water levels. Inevitably, the story got around that he was still haunting the mine. Brian James was recounting this tale to a Women's Institute group somewhere in the darker recesses of the workings. One of the women screamed and everyone turned to stare as a bearded man caked in clay emerged from a hole and ran, naked as it seemed, along the gallery. He was not, however, quite nude. And as ghosts are not usually to be found wearing Y-fronts, it was generally agreed that this was not a psychic phenomenon. In fact, a group of potholers had been exploring the lower workings and this man had found himself in a narrow passage through which he could only pass by removing his clothes. That is the nearest Brian James has come to a ghostly sighting.

At the surface, the Ceiriog Valley seems remote and peaceful, yet underneath is this system of man-made caves, the piles of spoil from which once threatened to overwhelm the town. There were woollen mills here, too, but they were already closed by Borrow's time. He walked down to the fulling mill of Pandy, which he claimed to be the first in Wales. It still stands, as does the pub where Borrow called in and met a spectacularly drunken local, who turned out to be a great admirer of Eos Ceiriog, Huw Morris.

'I am a poor stone-cutter – this is a rainy day and I have come here to pass it in the best way I can. I am somewhat drunk, but though I am a poor stone-mason, a private in the militia, and not so sober as I should be, I can repeat more of the songs of the Eos than any man alive, however great a gentleman, however sober.'

The pub has long closed and no-one, it seems, now recites Welsh poetry at Pandy. I walked on as Borrow had done to Pont y Meibion, Huw Morris's birthplace. Here he set out with an old lady and a girl to guide him to hunt for the chair of the bard, a carved stone set in a wall. They struggled through brambles and thickets, falling over roots and striving to keep close to the overgrown wall. At last the old lady shouted out: 'There's the chair, Diolch i Duw!' Borrow rushed forward and his companion, John Jones, invited him to sit down. The old

The Wynnstay Arms Hotel, Ruthin where Borrow dined.

lady offered to wipe the chair clean, but Borrow would have none of it.

I then sat down in the chair, and commenced repeating verses of Huw Morris. All which I did in the presence of the stout old lady, the short, buxom, and bare-armed damsel, and of John Jones, the Calvinistic weaver of Llangollen, all of whom listened patiently and approvingly though the rain was pouring down upon them, and the branches of the trees and the tops of the tall nettles, agitated by the gusts from the mountain hollows, were beating in their faces, for enthusiasm is never scoffed at by the noble, simple-minded, genuine Welsh, whatever treatment it may receive from the coarse-hearted, sensual, selfish Saxon.

The chair has been moved to Erwgerrig Farm where, by the roadside, you will see an obelisk raised to the memory of Huw Morris. I walked back to what Borrow called the 'gloomy valley' above Pandy which I found to be a place of delight, of bird song and mountain stream,

The inn by the fulling mill at Pandy where Borrow listened to the verses of Huw Morris.

where bluebells hazed the woodland floor. I took in a little more industrial history with a stroll along the long-disused railway, but my thoughts kept coming back to that image of George Borrow, sat bare-headed in the rain, reciting his verses to an audience of three. How fortunate he was to travel to a spot where such deep, heartfelt emotion could quite possess him. How few of us, who can travel the world more easily than he could travel in Wales, will ever achieve such feelings? I find it impossible to imagine expending so much emotion on an obscure Welsh poet. Well, that is my loss. I travelled on other paths walked by Borrow, but I prefer to leave him there on his bardic seat – and move on, before I get too maudlin and pompous. All journeys must end, and the best of them end with a rewarding comfort. That is precisely what happened with my final expedition.

ALFRED BARNARD

•

A Dram At the End of the Day

The Whisky Distilleries of the United Kingdom 1887

'Having long been possessed with an ardent desire to see the Distilleries of Scotland and Ireland, I took the first opportunity that presented itself, and knowing the task before me would occupy at least two years, made arrangements to transfer my duties to others.' Thus begins London publisher, Alfred Barnard's account of his excursions in pursuit of whisky in Scotland and whiskey in Ireland, and was there ever a more enticing opening to any travel book? Alas, I did not have two years to spare, nor indeed did I have a spare liver, so instead of visiting one hundred and sixty-one – yes, 161 – distilleries as Barnard did, I took just the week to look at a few of the establishments of the Spey Valley. I rapidly discovered that even such a modest ambition produced envious sighs from friends and colleagues, and numerous offers of assistance. In this at least nothing has changed, for Barnard discovered the same when he set out on 'the iron road' to Scotland.

Nothing of note occurred on the journey, except that we got a little amusement out of our fellow travellers – one of them a gentleman in clerical attire, catching some fragments of our conversation on spirits, evidently mistook us for important officers in the Salvation Army. Seeing this we puzzled him, and in answer to his enquiries, informed him that we had just started on a long and tedious pilgrimage to the spirit land, and that ours was a mission of investigation into the creation, development and perfection of crude spirits into 'spirits made perfect'. One of our party here produced his flask and explained to our reverend friend what kind of mission-

aries we were, when, to our surprise, after taking a 'wee drappie', and like Oliver Twist, asking for more, the pious-looking brother offered to join us in our excursions, that he might do the tasting, and we the writing. This generous offer we declined.

I travelled, somewhat reluctantly, by road, mainly because of the difficulty of visiting the distilleries of the area without a car. The scenery of the region is Highland, the grandeur of the Cairngorms, yet there are few places in Britain where the works of man and the works of nature seem to be more at odds. The new superior main road eased the traffic and brought thousands to the area and then the area had to think where to put them. So caravan

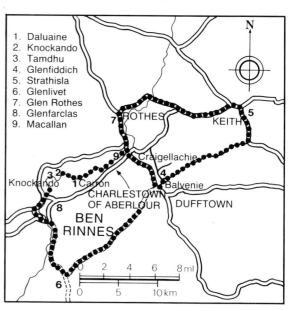

1. Daluaine
2. Knockando
3. Tamdhu
4. Glenfiddich
5. Strathisla
6. Glenlivet
7. Glen Rothes
8. Glenfarclas
9. Macallan

parks spread, gleaming white like fungal spores in the green valley. Then you reach Aviemore with high-rise blocks of a crushing, dull anonymity – the sort of thing inner-city authorities are just starting to demolish. I was not going to let that be my introduction to the Spey Valley proper. The main London to Aberdeen railway still runs through Aviemore, but, more importantly, part of the old route down the valley has been saved by enthusiasts and, best news of all, on this line the steam engine rules supreme.

If you want to get in the right mood for following a Victorian through Britain, you cannot do better than travel by steam. True, there were the Wilkie Collins of the world to advocate the superiority of human legs, but it was the steam train that opened up the country for tourists. The old steam trains were frequently cold, often dirty, unlit, uncomfortable, and un-hygienic though, by the 1880s when Barnard travelled, things were on the mend. But we forget all that and wallow in nostalgia. There is something comforting about an occasional retreat into the past, and the preserved Spey Valley line satisfies that need quite admirably. Carriages have old and faded pictures of sea-side resorts in the days when resorts meant donkeys on the sand at Morecambe rather than tower blocks by the pool at Marbella. Old coaches can seem just that, still carrying echoes of the road coaches from which they de-veloped. And there at the front is the steam locomotive. What is there about the steam engine that gives rise to such genuine affection among so many people? It is a troublesome object. You have to start work on it hours before you want to go anywhere, and, when it does get going, it is not very efficient. In part, that very troublesomeness adds to the appeal: the steam engine has to be coaxed and wheedled into giving of its best. Machine it may be, but there is something almost animal-like about it. It is temperamental; no two engines, even when built at the same works for the same design, are ever quite the same. The steam engine has a character. It is also com-prehensible. Sit in your car, press a starter and off you go, but all the work is going on out of sight. The steam locomotive is all there, open to inspection. Coal is shovelled into the firebox, which blasts out its hot air whenever the doors are opened. Smoke leaves the chimney and steam appears through several orifices as a reminder of the force that provides the power. Then, as it begins to move, with a steady beat of the exhaust and great exhalations of steam, you can see the pistons move in the cylinders, the rods move with the pistons and the wheels turn with the rods. The motion is satisfying, and it comes complete with an equally satisfying sound and a heady aroma of smoke and hot oil. From all of which the reader might perhaps by now have gathered that I can be counted among the ranks of the enthusiasts, and that my trip on the Spey Valley Railway was as much an indulgence as an attempt to follow Barnard.

The trip, however, did help to put me in the right mood. It provided a sense of occasion, as we chuffed away up the valley, rabbits scamp-ering furiously towards the woods at our ap-proach. At Boat of Garten, a delightful little Victorian station, there were also the first real feelings of entering the land of distilleries. There was snow on the distant hills while, closer at hand, were several augurs of things to come: a Glenfiddich coach, a distillery locomo-tive. Once we could have travelled all the way by train but, now alas, it was back to the car. Drinking and driving do not mix, but Barnard had no such problems on his journey by rail. At the end of the introduction to his subject, he gives this recipe for a hot toddy designed to see the traveller safely on his way.

> Four be the elements:
> Here we assemble 'em
> Each of man's world
> Or existence an emblem.
>
> Press from the lemon
> The slow flowing juices –
> Bitter is Life
> In its lessons and uses!
>
> Bruise the fair sugar lumps –
> Nature intended
> Her sweet and severe
> To be everywhere blended.
>
> Pour the still water –
> Unwarning by sound,
> Eternity's ocean
> Is dark'ning around!

Mingle the Spirit
The life of the bowl –
Man is cold mortar
Unwarmed by a soul.

Drink of the stream
Ere its potency goes –
No bath is refreshing
Except while it glows.

That recipe, if hardly suitable for the modern motorist, is, however, excellent as a remedy for the common cold, though I would commend the addition of a pinch of nutmeg. An eminent scientist who worked on cold research, once recommended to me the following way to combat the ailment. He called it 'the two-hat trick'. Take a large jug of hot toddy and a hat to your bedroom. Place the hat at the end of the bed, get

LEFT *Boat of Garten station at the entrance to the Spey Valley.*

BELOW *A sign of things to come: a distillery locomotive on the Strathspey Railway.*

into bed and start drinking the toddy. Continue drinking until you can see two hats, then go to sleep. It does nothing to cure the cold, but makes you feel a whole lot better.

One thing about approaching the Spey Valley from the west is that you never lose that sense of grandeur in the scenery. In this we fared better than Barnard who came to Rothes, his first stop in the valley, by rail from Elgin.

The route traversed was not so interesting at first, but became more so as we pursued our way; indeed, on emerging from the hills and entering the valley it became suddenly beautiful, and we found ourselves in sight of the village, nestling in its cosy nook of the lovely valley of the Spey. This he soon discovered was no more than an introduction to the delights of the area, for he was soon making an excursion from Spey-side Junction to Carron by coach.

How the road winds! what hills we ascend and descend, what peeps amid the trees of the tortuous course of the beautiful stream,

with its banks strewn with boulders, or in other places lawns sloping to the water's edge. Gazing from this Eden-like valley to the horizon, we see, on all sides, picturesque outsteppings of mountains and hills; most conspicuous of them all being Benrinnes, along whose broad base we drive all the way to Dail-Uaine. As we leave Aberlour the road begins to ascend, and presently we gain the level of the first height, which overlooks one of the most beautiful reaches of the Spey. Continuing our progress up the acclivity, we come to one spot where we would fain have lingered for hours. Here the whole glory of the scenery below suddenly burst upon us, and new points of beauty presented themselves. Words can convey but a feeble idea of the enchanting loveliness of Strathspey as it is now opened before us enclosed in its frame of hanging woods.

Somewhat purplish prose perhaps, but it decided us that this would be a good spot to make our headquarters – aided perhaps by a description of a little visit made from the local distillery by Barnard at the end of his stay.

> Before taking our departure, at the suggestion of the Manager, we ascended an eminence, from which can be seen, almost in a circle, no less than seven other Distilleries: The Glenlivet, Glenfarclas, Cragganmore, Cardow, Benrinnes, Aberlour and Macallan, forming most of the celebrated Speyside Distilleries, Glen Rothes, Glen Spey, Glen Grant and Mortlach being hidden from our view by hills and woods.

The cottage my wife and I took lay across the river from the Daluaine distillery, but seemed to belong to a quite different part of the world of the Spey. Once it had been home to a gamekeeper, and it stood next to the grand house, but suitably screened away behind trees and shrubs. It was indeed an idyllic spot, with a burn rushing down from the hillside to the Spey, where the occcasional flash of silver and plop of water were all that was evident of the other attraction of the area, the salmon. Fishing is one of those activities which totally baffle and bewilder the non-initiates. The fishermen lived in the big house and paid several hundred pounds each for the privilege of spending

the day waist deep in cold water not, as far as I could tell, catching anything. I almost saw a fish landed. It is a lengthy business catching a salmon and I was in no hurry and leaned on the bridge watching the rod that had been whipped into a parabola, jerk and twitch with the strain. Slowly the salmon was reeled in, the ghillie was ready with the net. You could see

The Daluaine Distillery, one of the original illustrations from Barnard.

the fish thrashing the water as it was edged ever closer to the bank until, when only inches from the net – it was free. The fisherman did not seem pleased!

Happily, I had nothing to do with the river other than enjoy its beauty, and it seemed a good idea to begin with a walk by the river, but out along a track followed by Barnard. He went by train from Carron, south down the valley to Cromdale, where he admired the scenery with few irritating interruptions from other travellers: nor, indeed, it seems would he have had any interruptions on any other day either for

The sparkling waters of the Spey.

'. . . although the Carron Station has been open for more than twenty years, we were the only persons who had ever booked to Cromdale first class, the numbers of our tickets which were faded with age, commencing at ought.' There are no interruptions and no trains either these days, for the line had barely reached its centenary when it was closed in 1965. Now it remains as a walkway and very delightful it proved to be. Keeping the main objective in view, I began with a walk across to the Daluaine Distillery which had excited a great deal of admiration from Barnard. It was in a way a good place to begin, for it has the romantic air that one expects of the Highlands. The office inside the gates is a miniature version of the Scottish baronial grandeur of Laggan House down by the river. There were once, or so they say, other distillers at work here.

A short distance up the glen, by the side of one of the burns, there dwelt in olden times a nest of bold smugglers, and the ruins of one of their so-called bothies was pointed out to us on the Distillery premises. A popular legend has it that the midnight wanderer may yet see evidences of their craft, and that the darker the night and the wilder the weather the more likely is he to stumble across the haunted bothy, which is situated in a rocky cavern in a ravine through which rushes one of the Dail-Uaine Burns. There the Still-fires are seen weirdly sparkling like eyes of diamonds, and the ghosts of the departed smugglers busy at their ancient avocations.

But it was daylight not midnight, and I wandered up the hill in front of the distillery to the workers' cottages. There was a sad air about the place, many cottages empty and the little sportsfield scarcely recognizable apart from the goal posts collapsing into the nettles. Things have not been easy in the whisky business in recent years, and the workers are reluctant to move into tied cottages, preferring council houses in the nearby town. It is an understandable, but miserable, state of affairs for the little settlement has a quite superb situation: on one side, the hills and in front, the river, now sparkling down below in early summer sunshine. I stopped to talk to Mr Anderson from the distillery, a man who had no intention of leaving that spot unless he was forced to. For him it was a place for all weathers and all seasons, and he loved it. It was easy to see why. We parted after arranging to meet later in the week.

The railway ran beside the road and crossed the river on a bridge that carried both road and rail, but which is now limited to road traffic. Then it swung off towards the next distillery, the Imperial, as impressive as its name at first glance, but appearances are deceptive. No whisky is made here any more. It is simply a warehouse forming part of the whisky loch, Scotland's equivalent of the wine lake of Europe. This is the fate that all who work in the industry fear – this is what keeps the Daluaine cottages empty. It was, however, far too nice a day to remain gloomy for long, and the Spey itself had a cheerful appearance whatever might be happening on its banks. The side of the river where I walked was covered with mixed woodland, silver birch and oak being especially prominent, and what a wonderful contrast they made: the one upright, pallid; the other darkly spreading out its boughs, opposite, the all-too-familiar conifers blanketing the hills. But between lay the Spey, shallow but fast, an intermittent sort of river. It reminded me of the old Boy Scout rule for covering long distances – walk ten steps, run ten steps, walk ten, run ten, and so on to the end. The Spey is like that. It goes along quietly for a while, then takes a sudden rush at the rocks, splashing and bubbling around them before settling down for another quiet session to gather itself for the next dash.

It was a June day, but scarcely seasonable. The great bulk of Ben Rinnes, not high but spread over a large area, dominates the whole of this region and its top was dusted with snow. Early risers reported finding ice on their windscreens. Now, however, it was at least a clean, clear sort of day with sunshine to compensate for the cold north wind. As I walked, I could see why there was so much forestry plantation, for this is by no means rich agricultural land. Tiny farms were surrounded by tiny fields, strips scarcely more than a dozen furrows wide cramped between the river and the stony hillside. Outside the houses you are apt to find an astonishing array of junk. One never knows when things will come in useful, but who will ever want a piece of that ancient, rusting A30? There was something here of that forlorn air that hung over the distillery cottages. Fortunately, one can turn to cheerier themes. There is no shortage of wildlife, especially rabbits. Some present you with a brief glimpse of a vanishing white scut, others seem almost blasé. One big chap was sat back on his haunches, head up, chest to the sun like a holidaymaker on the beach. He sat motionless presumably on the 'if I don't move they'll never notice me' theory. I studiously ignored him. Then came a rare treat, at least for a visiting Englishman – a red squirrel, not the common grey but the indigenous, attractive little creature that was once so common in British woodlands.

The Knockando distillery is a fine-looking place but just a touch too modern to have been visited by Barnard. The railway may have gone, but the sidings are still there looking very smart with the little crane ready to lift a barrel of Scotch on to a waiting waggon, should any waggon ever again appear. The adjoining Tamdhu distillery, another comparative youngster only begun in 1897, has made even better use of its railway connections. The old station has been refurbished and turned into a Visitors' Centre. This is one of many distilleries which now welcome tourists and provide them with an introduction to one of Scotland's great arts, the art of converting three simple ingredients – barley, yeast and water – into one of the world's finest drinks, malt whisky. That it is an art rather than a science is a fact beyond all reasonable argument. Just as you may ferment the grape to produce an infinity of different tastes and aromas in wine, so, too, the simple ingredients of the distiller give rise to the subtle differences that distinguish the great malts from the merely palatable. Here at Tamdhu you can see all the processes at work, which is quite unusual these days, for the first stage has in recent years become detached, the malting of the barley. So we could stop here and see it all, but an endless repetition of

descriptions of the same processes would lead to tedium – though Barnard seemed as interested by distillery number 161 as he had been by the first. I, however, want to invite the reader on a tour of just a few distilleries of the Spey Valley picking up the story as we go along.

The first essential must be to arouse one's interest in the subject under discussion. Who cares about the making of the whisky who has not first discovered its delights? Now, in these travels, we are going to be looking exclusively at a very special type of drink: the single malt.

There are very many popular brands of whisky which are made of blends of malt, and the inferior grain whisky. They have their adherents but, for me, no blend can boast the complexity of aroma and flavour of a first-rate malt. So I made my way on past the distillery, along the railway, to cross back over the Spey for a preliminary dram. What a very strange company I met there. On the one hand were the residents come for the fly fishing. Two bemused-looking Americans, tartaned up from socks to tam, cowered in their chairs while an upperclass English lady of more than ample proportions

Dalbeallie Station, now the Visitor's Centre for the Tamdhu Distillery.

shouted at them at point-blank range. The locals ignored them. I was greeted by one local who approached me with the monumental solemnity of the very drunk, an effect somewhat ruined by the flag of shirt waving through his flies. Fortunately, talking proved somewhat tiring to the brain, so he settled down to snore in a corner and I was free to savour my malt. Conviviality settled over the place. I was challenged to darts and did the right thing by winning one game to show that I was not wholly incompetent but losing two to satisfy local honour. After that I was very much at home and

happily mellowed when the time came to return to the cottage.

Look at the bottles behind any bar in any pub in England or Wales and, if there is only one malt whisky – an inconceivable notion in Scotland – then that will be a Glenfiddich. Somehow, its very popularity leads you to believe the name is an invention disguising a multinational corporation lurking in the background. The names Glen or Mac or Highland on a label are certainly no guarantee of authenticity. In Bombay, I was offered a dram from a bottle whose label had enough kilts, heather, and thistle to make an ex-patriate Scot weep. It bore some such name as Macpherson's Fine Old Highland Whisky. There may once have been a Macpherson involved in its manufacture but I doubt it – and it was not fine, nor was it old; it was assuredly not Highland and it was an abuse of the name whisky to apply it to such a beverage. It was a vile, raw spirit which had never been nearer to Scotland than the port of Bombay. Glenfiddich is happily different.

I drove down from Carron to Craigellachie, a delightful spot where the Spey is crossed by a fine bridge built by Thomas Telford between 1812 and 1815. It very much shows the thinking of the age. In its structure it was daring and modern, a single span of cast iron bridging the river in a graceful 150-foot (45-metre) arch. But to fit it to its romantic setting, Telford romanticized the bridge with little castellated turrets at either end. A plaque on one turret took me back momentarily to the last excursion, to another cast-iron span and another river, for it proclaimed that the ironwork was cast at Plas Kynaston, Ruabon. It was here that the ironwork for the Pontcysyllte aqueduct was cast and, in all probability, the parts for the Scottish bridge were carried over that same aqueduct by canal boat on their way to a port for the sea passage north. But my purpose was not really to stand around admiring bridges nor even to admire the Spey, though it is especially fine here. I was concerned with a tributary, the Fiddich which joins the Spey here. So the Glenfiddich whisky has every right to its name for it is made in the glen of the Fiddich. It has, indeed, an interesting story.

The tale begins with William Grant who worked at the Mortlach distillery. He worked there for twenty years, dreaming of the day when he could start his own business. Then, in 1886, just at the time when Barnard was visiting the area, his chance came. This is, in fact, recorded by Barnard though he had no way of knowing that an offhand remark of his was related to the foundation of the now world-famous distillery. He was visiting the Cardow distillery at Knockando 'a handsome pile' of new buildings which he described in detail. Remarking that '... as the old distillery will

shortly be demolished, we need not describe it'. The old was indeed knocked down and the equipment went to William Grant at a bargain price. Grant left his job at Mortlach in 1886 and, during the next year, he and his sons laboured to build the new distillery. That was the beginning, but only a beginning. A second distillery was added to the first and named Balvenie after the Balvenie Castle which stood nearby. It was during the early years of the present century that they began to be more ambitious. They opened an office at Blackburn in Lancashire and, encouraged by modest success, set out to conquer the world. Canada had a large proportion of Scottish emigrants who might be expected to look favourably on the drink of the old country. They did. Then, in 1909, one of the directors set off for the Far East, taking a year to travel from India to Australia. Glenfiddich found favour there as well so that, by 1914, they had sixty agencies in thirty countries. The last outpost to fall was England. There was general scepticism over the wisdom of attempting to sell genuine malt whisky to the ignorant hordes south of the border but, as we all know now, it worked. Grants have prospered mightily and those hordes now make the pilgrimage up to the north to see how it is all done.

The Visitors' Centre reflects the continuing international success of the Grant family with an audiovisual display in six languages, which pushes the Highland image with pictures that have rather more to do with Scottish romance than Scotch whisky. I amused myself by switching channels on the head set to receive a babel of voices among which the single word whisky was the only common denominator. There is something very odd about listening to Japanese being spoken to a bagpipe accompaniment! But a lot of effort has gone into creating the right image here, even the truck garage has a pagoda roof like a malting. Visitors are taken on a tour, but we diverged to go to the Balvenie distillery to see the very last of the old-style maltings in the Spey district.

The first ingredient to appear in the processes that lead up to the dram in the glass is the conversion of barley to malt. Each grain of

Traditional maltsters' shovels ready for use at the Balvenie maltings.

The Milton Distillery, now the Strathisla, as seen by Barnard.

barley is a little chemical laboratory of its own. The growing seed needs food, so there is a supply of insoluble starch wrapped up inside the grain. When growth begins, an enzyme is produced which attacks the starch, eventually turning it into sugar. It is this sugar that will go to make the whisky and the art of the maltster lies in delivering the grain at just the perfect point in its development. First the barley is soaked in water and spread out, being turned regularly to stop the little rootlets tangling and matting as they grow. Then the growth must be stopped at just that point when the starch has been converted to sugar but the young plant has not yet started to draw on the food supply. To judge this moment there is no substitute for the maltster's thumb. He needs a long strong nail to break the seed and a sense of touch that

will tell him by rubbing at the kernel just when germination should be stopped. At the right time, the rubbery, white kernel of starch will smear on to the finger. Then the malt is taken to the kiln. This is the building with the unmistakeable pagoda roof which symbolizes all whisky distilleries, for the roof acts in a way as a kind of giant chimney. The barley is spread on the kiln floor and a fire lit beneath, and not just any old fire for this is one of the points where flavour is fed in. At Balvenie, the furnace is fired with peat and the aromatic fumes penetrate the barley. The grain is turned over and over at regular intervals for around sixty hours after which the process is complete. Barley has become malt.

The malting is a lovely spot. The shape of the building is deeply satisfying, but nowhere near as pleasing as the sight of what goes on inside. In the furnace, the dark peat stands out against the rich red glow and the air is filled

with the pungent aroma of its smoke. Up above, the golden grain is spread and the malt-sters' shovels stand ready for use, huge wooden spades are always used here, for wood does not damage the grain. And does all this concern for tradition make any difference? Just taste the Balvenie with its lingering flavour of peaty smoke, and, if after that you think it has made no difference, then I suggest you return to Scotch and ginger ale. Tamdhu also had its own maltings, but of a more modern design. Nowadays, however, most distilleries buy in their malt, so I thought I should take a look at a thoroughly modern production centre.

Buckie Maltings was only built in 1979 on its site close to the port, close to the fields of barley and close to fifty-two distilleries. The other great advantage of the site is the purity of the air along the Scottish coast: when they set up pollution meters set at the most sensitive levels, the only thing they could record were

the occasional quivers from the exhaust fumes of a passing car. No pagodas here, just massive industrial buildings that give little hint of the process inside. Here you find grain stored in warehouses the size of airship hangars, and single vessel malting – everything going on in the same huge container, all controlled by microprocessors and computers. No need for men to tread delicately over the grain in rope-soled shoes – not much need for men at all. The machines do the lot, though the maltster's thumb still comes in useful. And, if a distiller still wants that special aroma of peat, then they are only too happy to blow peat smoke through for him. Forty-thousand tonnes of barley are taken in every year. Barnard would, I am sure, have approved. Only sentimentalists would suggest a return to the old methods, but I, for one, am glad the old floor maltings at Balvenie are still with us.

We are now ready for the crucial phase –

distillation, and it seemed only sensible to start at the oldest distillery in the region, Strathisla, though it is not a name that Barnard would have recognized. He knew it as the Milton dis-

tillery, Keith. His journey was, once again, by train, following the valley of the Isla down from the present Glenfiddich distillery past Loch Park. It was, and is, a pleasant journey with a

notably pleasant finale that comes with the arrival at the distillery itself.

It is bounded by the river Isla, which rises at Loch Park, Drummuir, seven miles distant, and falls over a small cascade just before it reaches the works. On our journey from Rothes, the railway traversed this loch. It is a mile long, and situated at the foot of a steep but beautifully wooded hill. The surface is dotted with pretty little islands and covered with rare water-fowl. The position of the Distillery is most romantic; a wood-crowned hill overtops it on one side, whilst the opposite side of the valley is ornamented with pretty villas, whose grounds stretch down to the water's edge, and the old kirk on another hill looks serenely into the busy establishment below.

The river is crossed by a rustic footbridge, and all the Distillery buildings have an old-world look, suggestively characteristic of the long established character of the works, which are approached from the main road to Keith by a carriage drive, and, with the exception of the new Warehouses, are all enclosed. The Distillery was established in the year 1786; originally a small work, it has from time to time been considerably enlarged, and under the superintendence of the present managing partner most of the newest appliances have been added, and the premises remodelled, so that the Distillery is quite comparable with the recently built Distilleries on Speyside, in modern improvements, whilst possessing the charm of age few others have.

Most of those comments still stand: there is still a railway down the Isla valley, now limited to freight, though there are still passenger connections to Keith. The scenery is still majestic and the town retains much of its air of antiquity. The distillery not only 'possesses the charm of age', but can, in fact, claim to be one of the oldest, if not the oldest, in Scotland. The doubt about the claimed precedence in terms of antiquity arises because one has to decide how to measure the age of a distillery: do you choose

The distinctive 'pagoda' roof of the Strathisla maltings.

the date at which it was licensed for distilling, or do you select the date on which distillation actually began? The two rarely coincide, for Keith was a great area for the bothy, the illicit still. Barnard quotes many stories of those days which, for his contemporaries, represented a well-remembered past. Here is one of his tales of a persevering excise man on the hunt for a still.

A determined gentleman of this department resolved to find it out at all hazards, and, on one moonlight night, unaccompanied by any person, he followed a horse led by a peasant, having a sack across the back of the animal, which, he suspected contained materials for this mysterious manufactory. When the horse had arrived at a certain place, the sack was removed from his back, and suddenly disappeared. The officer made his observations, returned to his residence, and having procured military assistance, repaired to the place where the horse had been unloaded, all was silent, the moon shone bright, the ground was unmarked by any peculiar appearance, and he was almost inclined (as well as those who accompanied him) to think that he laboured under a delusion. Perceiving, however, some brambles loosely scattered about the place, he proceeded to examine more minutely, and on their removal, discovered some loose sods, under which was found a trap door leading to a small cavern, at the bottom of which was a complete distillery at full work, supplied by a subterraneous stream, and the smoke conveyed from it through the windings of a tube that was made to communicate with the funnel of the chimney of the distillers' dwelling-house, situated at a considerable distance.

We left the manufacturing process with the malt duly prepared and ready for the beginning of its transformation into 'Uisga Beatha' the Water of Life. This is not quite the most picturesque of processes for it involves no more than crushing the malt to make grist which is then washed in hot water to remove the sugar in solution. The liquid is then run out into great wooden vessels, each able to hold 12 000 gallons (54 500 litres), yeast is added, and fermentation begins. The liquor froths and bubbles and carbon dioxide is given off. There are some who say that the best way to clear a stuffed nose is to take a good whiff of a wash-back, as the fermentation vessel is known and, if you try it, the gas seems to remove the top of your head. Conventional medical opinion does not commend the practice. There is, however, an undoubted fascination in seeing this mass of foaming liquid gradually turning itself into alcohol – and it is the strength of that alcohol that will itself eventually stop the yeast from working. After that, we come to the true heart of the whole process, the stills. Here, all the essential ingredients will combine and will contribute their share to the quality, the flavour, the aroma of the final product. Malt we have seen, yeast has been added, but the most mysterious of all is the most commonplace – the water. Why is Scotch whisky only made in Scotland? Because nowhere else has Scottish water, and no amount of analysis and computerized testing can reproduce it. And even if it could, would science add that touch of romance that adds its own nuance to the whisky?

> The water used in distilling comes from the Broomhill Spring, rising in the hill above the works. We visited the reservoir, wherein it is collected, said to be haunted nightly by the fays and fairies. The water is so bright and clear that a pebble we dropped into it seemed magnified into a

BELOW *An early engraving of an illicit still, with the customs men approaching in the distance: reproduced in Barnard.*

RIGHT *The gleaming copper and sinuous forms of the still room.*

huge crystal boulder. After the water leaves this receptacle, it is mixed with a small quantity of that from the Isla. The original proprietors had great faith in the efficacy of this marriage of the elements, and the old custom is continued to this day. This operation gives the name of 'Strathisla Whisky' to the make of this Distillery, which we need scarcely say is pure Highland Malt.

That same spring was used by monks for distillation as far back as the twelfth century. The knowledge of such a long history inevitably adds to one's enjoyment.

The still room is one of the most beautiful places you could ever wish to see, and that is a judgement which has very little to do with the process that goes on there. You can hate the taste of whisky, be an absolute teetotaller, and still delight in the purely visual splendours of the place. Being a devotee of the malt is simply a bonus. The still vessels are of burnished copper. The lower part is onion shaped and, from this, rises the long neck, narrowing as it ascends before bending over in a graceful curve. It is a perfect marriage of material and form, for you get double value here, as each shining copper still carries the reflection of its neighbour bent still further into yet more sinuous curves. And the reflection will always be there for no still room has less than two stills. All of this you will find in virtually any such room in Scotland, but Strathisla is the finest I have ever seen. The timber roof would be a credit to a medieval hall; the stills or pots are coalfired in the old way so that the air has a pleasing pungency. The brass and copper work is unusually ornate and, in the somewhat dark room, it glows out with a rich light. If you visit here and get no pleasure from the place, then abandon distillery visits for ever for you will not find its better.

The liquor in the still is heated and the vapour passes up the neck to be condensed in the 'worm', a suitably convoluted pipe that passes through cold water. The spirit is still impure, a rather nasty oily concoction which has to be reheated in the second still. The Strathisla distillery had an advantage in Barnards's day when refrigeration was in its infancy.

Here the imperfect spirit undergoes the same process as before, and emerges from

the worm a perfected spirit, passing through Condenser No. 2, in the Still House, to which water is raised from a spring, which, in the hottest day in summer, is icy cold, thus allowing distillation to be carried on at a time when most other works are obliged to stop.

The distillate passes through a sealed brass box with a glass front, the spirit safe – and this is no fanciful name – for it is as secure as HM Customs and Excise can make it. The liquor can be tested without opening the safe, but no-one can tamper with the precious fluid. When all the impurities are gone then the spirit is ready. All the distiller has to do now is sit around and wait for a few years for it to mature – and we shall be looking at that part of the story later.

The processes just described are essentially the same in all distilleries so you might wonder why anyone should bother to visit a whole string of them. The processes may be the same, but there are subtle differences between one distillery and the next. Each has its own character – and, often enough, its own characters. You might just as well ask a devotee of the grape why he bothers to visit different vineyards: don't they all just pick grapes, roll up their trousers and jump up and down on them? The differences are all important, for it is in the differences that the subtle characteristics that distinguish one malt from another are born. And extra savour is often provided by the histories of the individual concerns.

Those who wish to see a Highland distillery in a Highland setting, and one with a story that might have been penned by Robert Louis Stevenson could scarcely do better than visit Glenlivet. Barnard was quite overwhelmed by the whole experience.

> We shall never forget our ride of twenty miles to Glenlivet on a bright spring day. We proceeded by the Spey side, one of the most rapid and beautiful rivers in Scotland, through the plantations and copses of Ballindalloch, up mountain roads, across highland moors and past old Benrinnes, standing out like a mighty giant against the clear sky, the scene changing at every turn of the road like a bit of fairyland, until at last we came in sight of Glenlivet. The Distillery planted on its slopes has a background of distant mountains,

grim and bare to their very summits, and we wished for the pencil of an artist to enable us to transfer to canvas this scene of majestic grandeur.

My own approach was through Tomintoul, a town which grew up as a planned settlement, a garrison site on the eighteenth-century military road. You can still see something of that

old road at the southern end of the town, and you can see the military mind everywhere. The right-angle rules Tomintoul: roads meet at right-angles, a square sits in the dead centre, and houses line up with parade-ground precision. It is a town strangely at odds with its surroundings, uniform and rather dull, amid the wild hills. The romantically inclined might prefer to stop off at the old bridge of Livet, a satisfyingly picturesque structure in its decayed old age. It was probably built some time around the sixteenth century, and now all that is left are the arches with no roadway on top. It

The old bridge of Livet.

puts you in the right sort of mood for listening to a story of the old days when the distillery was founded.

This neighbourhood has always been famous for its Whisky. Formerly smuggling houses were scattered on every rill, all over the mountain glens, and at that time the smugglers used to lash the kegs of spirit on their backs, and take them all the way to Aberdeen and Perth for disposal. Now all is changed, and in the year 1824 a legal Distillery was built by the father of the present proprietor, who was a man of great moral courage and physical strength. So great was the opposition of the smugglers to his settlement in the district that for a long time until they were dispersed he had to carry firearms for his protection; hence he commenced work under great difficulties, but his indomitable perseverance overcame all obstacles in the end, and his efforts were crowned with such success that 'Smith's Glenlivet' has become a household word . . .

What Barnard does not mention is that George Smith was poacher turned gamekeeper, a former smuggler who, when the excise laws were changed in 1824, actually took out a genuine, legal licence, a thing unheard of in these parts. The dangers were certainly real enough and Smith's pistols are on display at the museum attached to the distillery. The place itself has greatly changed and is now a very modern complex, part of the big Seagram group. The setting, however, is as splendid as it ever was. It is a place to linger, so linger I did and found the nearby Minmore House Hotel offered traditional Scottish fare. I had mince, tatties and skirlie, the latter consisting of a mixture of oatmeal and onion fried in butter – and very delicious it was too. I would, however, have had to linger a very long time indeed to do justice to the stock of whiskies, for there were nearly 100 on offer, among the oldest being a Strathisla distilled in 1937. It works out a little expensive at £3.00 a tot! Others, if not quite so ancient, were more modestly priced.

Glenlivet was the most southerly distillery I visited. Glen Rothes the most northerly, but they both began life on significant dates, though the latter had nothing to do with distillation. It commenced production on the day

The Glenlivet Distillery from Barnard.

of the great Tay Bridge disaster, an event immortalized in verse by Mr William McGonagall, poet and tragedian.

> Beautiful Railway Bridge of the Silv'ry Tay
> Alas, I am very sorry to say
> That ninety lives have been taken away
> On the last Sabbath day of 1879.
> Which will be remember'd for a very long time.

We would never have remembered at all, but for you Mr McGonagall.

Glen Rothes is a remarkable place, a modern and very handsome group of buildings, every bit as attractive as any of its older counterparts. But, in operation, it is very different: automation rules, with only seventeen men at work. It can be very impressive. The warehouses are vast with rack upon rack of barrels and tall, forklift trucks running on railed tracks. A century ago they were producing 80 000 gallons (360 000 litres) a year: now it is over a million gallons (4 500 000 litres), most of which finds its way into Famous Grouse. Even more remarkable than the distillery is the graveyard next door, where the tombs are arranged in long terraces up the hillside, like a mill town for the dead. One may safely assume, however, that, given their situation, they contain happy spirits.

One of the delights of moving from distillery to distillery is that there are such contrasts to be met. To move from automated Glen Rothes, part of the mighty Highland Distillers Group, to Glenfarclas, which was begun 150 years ago, but has belonged to one family, the Grants, since 1865 is to enter a very different world. Glenfarclas takes you back to the old tradition where the making of whisky was a part of the life of the land. In summer you grew and tended your crops, sheared the sheep, and, in general, were fully occupied on the land. In winter, what better occupation could you find than to turn to the warmth of the kiln and the still and set about turning your barley into drams?

The Glenfarclas story starts in 1836 when a tenant farmer decided that a still was indeed just the thing for a winter occupation, and so he continued in a small way until 1865 when John Grant bought the farm. He was a dealer in horses, sheep, and cattle who had recently married Barbara Grant of Blairfindy just

around the hill, and it was there he had hung his hat. He was looking for a staging post where he could keep his cattle on the drive from Blairfindy to market, and the distillery was simply thrown in as part of the deal. It was leased out for a while to a man from Glen Livet, but when he left John Grant decided to take it over for himself. An entry from his diary says a good deal about the relationship between farm and still.

> Thurs. June 9, 1870
> A fine soft day clipping sheep.
> 108 clipped.
> J. Ross in full for shearing – 16/-
> 6/- from Maggy on loan.
> Pumped first whisky at Glenfarclas.
> 2 backs mashed.

The whisky flowed and was carried around the country and sold along with the cattle and the sheep. In time, the importance of the whisky trade grew, but the Grants have never lost their contact with the land. Five generations later, they are still farming and they are as proud of their prize Angus herd as they are of their malt.

I met and talked to Mr George Grant who has officially handed over to son John but still pays his regular visits to keep an eye on things. His office speaks of continuity: on one side there is an ancient roll-topped desk that could easily have been there when Barnard came to Glenfarclas: on the other a photograph of grandson George, seven years old now, but expected one day to take over the family firm. Perhaps one cannot draw too many conclusions from a single visit but it seemed a friendly place. Certainly, I could not have asked for a warmer welcome, a view which I trust was not too coloured by the excellence of the fifteen-year-old malt. But, if I had to pick a spot where the essence as well as the reality of Highland whisky was distilled, then Glenfarclas would be that place. Here, on the flank of Ben Rinnes, the spring water flows down the open moorland to add that special, elusive ingredient which makes Scotch whisky unique. Nowhere else in the world could you produce a Glenfarclas whisky. This is the glory of the malt, the individuality that begins to develop as the western breezes pile the clouds on the hills, the rain seeps through the soil and the peat to re-emerge as springs and streams. This is not romantic fancy, this is fact. But, although we have seen all the processes of manufacture, we have still a long way to go before the liquor from the stills can be poured into the glass. And, because it is such a long process, we can while away the time by taking a look at how the modern industry is trying to pay its way, by making sure that nothing goes to waste.

I renewed my acquaintance with Mr Anderson of Daluaine who had promised to show me round the dark-grain-manufacturing plant. Distilleries provide two noxious waste products: pot ale, the liquor that does not go into the whisky but is still rich in sugar, and the driffs, the malt left behind after fermentation, and that is rich in proteins. You cannot dump them in the river as that would lead to dead fish, angry fishermen, and an end to a very lucrative local industry. So the distillers make a virtue out of necessity and the waste is converted into cattle feed. The liquid is concentrated by evaporation in a series of heat exchangers and finishes up as a thick, dark, evil-smelling syrup. The wet driff is squeezed dry, mixed with the syrup and the whole lot turned into pellets, over 200 tons of them a week. They are highly nutritious and quite fit for human consumption. There is, however, one small problem – they taste absolutely disgusting, though the cows do not seem to mind. After the noise of the dark-grain plant, I went up the hill behind the distillery hoping for Barnard's panoramic view of the Spey distilleries. I never found it so I settled for venison from the local dealer. This is not a place for the squeamish. We are used, these days, to meat cut, packaged, and laid out in cling-wrapped trays. Here it was animals on hooks, entrails on the floor, and a deal of gore. But my goodness, it tasted superb.

We had a cheery meal in the cottage that night and I could look across the river to the distillery and raise a glass in salutation. Poor Barnard was rushed away from Daluaine; '. . . we find our coachman impatient and anxious, so, after quaffing a drop of the nectar, for which the Distillery is famous, we trot merrily back to Craigellachie and arrive just in time to catch our train.' We had nowhere to rush off to, no coachman waiting, and could enjoy the peace of an evening with no noise but the birds and the splash of the burn. It was an evening to savour for we were near the end of

the journey and near the end of the whisky story.

The last journey followed the old railway line again, ending as I had begun the trips round the region with the old track beside the river. The railway has made a most successful walkway and, as at Tamdhu, Aberlour station has been renovated and is now the centrepiece of a riverside park. The scenery, as seems to be the case throughout the length of the Spey, is superb and, as you near Craigellachie, you get a glimpse of a fine old house on the opposite hillside with stepped gables and a small turret. That was my destination, but there was time still to enjoy the walk and the pleasures of the Spey. Where the water was at its busiest, boiling among the rocks, I watched grebes floating backwards with the current, then diving beneath the surface to reappear again many yards downstream. This is the sort of place that is an absolute treat simply to sit, watch and do absolutely nothing else whatsoever, but there was business to attend to and, if you are not going to be allowed to sit in peace by a river, it is some consolation to know that you are off to visit the home of The Macallan, one of the finest of all Highland malts.

The house I had seen was part of the Macallan empire, in the process of refurbishment as offices and as a delightful centre where visitors could be entertained. Barnard is rather short with Macallan, and locals who still know his work and have heard stories of his visits will tell you that the size of an entry in the great books was directly proportional to the size and number of the drams handed out by the proprietors. The Macallans of 100 years ago must have been a pretty parsimonious bunch for they won themselves a mere eight lines as against Glenlivet, for example, which was awarded three pages of text and two of pictures. This is all he had to say of the works: 'It was established in the year 1824, and its internal arrangements are similar to the other Speyside Distilleries.' And that is all I propose to say about the main works, not because the proprietors were ungenerous for they were not, but because I want to concentrate on the last, crucial stage of the making of a great whisky.

When you see the liquor emerging from the stills you see a colourless liquid; but when you have a bottle of Scotch, the liquid can be any-

Wooden casks in which the whisky will be matured for many years before it becomes a dram at the end of the day.

The sherry-cask Scotches were a very different matter, for something of the character of the sherry had permeated the whisky. A cask that had held dry sherry yielded a straw-coloured liquor with a delicate bouquet; a sweet sherry cask produced an altogether darker, stronger-smelling whisky. The experts said that they found an Oloroso to be a very happy compromise between the extremes. The directors of Macallan are determined to maintain their standards, so they have bought brand new casks and sent them to selected bodegas with strict instructions as to which sherry should be stored in them. In time, the casks will be returned and used to store whisky in the cool, quiet of the warehouses. Is it worth taking such trouble? No-one will know for certain for another ten years or so, but I have no doubt whatsoever that it is just that sort of care that makes malt whisky a drink of subtlety and refinement that can stand comparison with the finest cognacs.

The visit was over, the journeys were over. It had proved a remarkable experience following my travellers. I found that each one had in some hard-to-define way, influenced my journeyings. I had felt them at my elbow. As I cycled through Hampshire, I could sense Cobbett muttering about the social ills of the day; in Skye I was constantly trying to imagine the solid figure of that great man in such an unlikely environment. Celia Fiennes' avid curiosity helped to arouse my own. And so it went on. Now that it was all over, there was inevitably a slight feeling of sadness, but my last traveller knew what to do about that. He was not one to let a day's journey go by without acquiring his dram along the way and I had my own bottled souvenirs. Barnard, after a particularly satisfying visit, would end his description with a quotation in verse. I turned up the lines he quoted at the end of the visit to Glen Rothes. They seemed to carry the perfect message for a wistful ex-traveller.

> Gie him strong drink until he wink,
> That's sinking in despair;
> An' liquor guid to fire his bluid,
> That's prest wi' grief and care;
> Here let him bouse, an' deep carouse
> Wi' bumpers flowing o'er,
> Till he forgets his loves or debts,
> An' minds his griefs no more.

thing from a dark rich gold to the palest straw. What has happened between is maturation, the long years of storage in barrels. Traditionally, malt whisky has matured in sherry casks bought up from shippers in England but, in recent years, the Spanish have been bottling their own sherry and the casks no longer cross the sea. The whisky will mature in any cask, but are the results going to be the same? I had always thought that the sherry cask was simply a piece of colourful tradition, the sort of thing that would impress the overseas market. I now know that there is a huge difference between one cask and another.

I was taken up to the office where they have a series of labelled bottles, like chemists' samples. In the first was the raw, colourless liquid which had a sweet, rather sickly smell. I was then invited to take part in – not a tasting – but a sniffing. To do this you pour a little of the whisky into a glass and then waggle the glass vigorously backwards and forwards, do not swill it round in circles, to release the odour. Colour and smell, that is what you are after. Whisky matured in plain oak casks was pale, with a pleasing but not very distinctive smell.

INDEX

Numbers in *italics* refer to pages with illustrations

ACKNOWLEDGEMENTS

BBC Hulton Picture Library 112, 116, 117;

Bodleian Library 8 (Lane Poole 117), 51 (Gough Maps 5, Fol 33), 52-3 (Gough Maps 5 Fol 12b), 59 (210 b 252 p. 179), 82 (GA Gen Top b 33 Vol IV opp p. 15), 88 (210 c 27 p. 125), 90 (GA Gen Top b 33 Vol IV opp p. 42), 94-5 (GA Gen Top b 33 Vol IV opp p. 40), 104 (17016 d 65 p. 11), 110 (8 D 434 B 5 opp p. 176), 123 (Gough Adds Cornwall 8.5 opp p. 135), 132 (Gough Adds Gen Top 40 17 p. 168), 137 (Gough Adds Cornwall 8.5 opp. p. 189), 139 (Gough Adds Gen Top 40 17 p. 204), 145 (Gough Adds Wales 80 20 opp p. 206), 152-53 (Vet A. 5 d 39 opp p. 370), 156-57 (Vet A. 5 d 39 opp p. 297);

Burton, Anthony 12, 13, 18-19, 21, 22-3, 24-5, 27, 28, 29, 31, 38, 39, 42, 44, 47, 49, 52, 54, 55, 58, 60, 63, 64, 66, 68, 70 bottom, 72, 75 top and bottom, 76, 77, 84, 86-7, 89, 91, 98, 102, 105, 106, 107 bottom, 108, 111, 114, 115, 119, 124-25, 128, 129, 130, 134-35, 138, 148-49, 154, 158, 161, 163, 164-65, 168, 169, 172, 177, 180, 183, 184-85, 189;

Clwyd Record Office 159, 162;

Devon Record Office 37;

Hampshire Record Office 107 top, 109;

Her Majesty the Queen 10-11;

Leeds Central Library 69, 70-1, 74, 78, 79;

Moray District Council Libraries 174-75;

Museum of London, The 30-31, 32, 33;

National Portrait Gallery 56, 80, 99, 120, 143;

Royal Institution of Cornwall 131, 141;

Town & Country Books 40-1 (A Wheaton & Co Ltd);

Vale of the White Horse District Council 14-15 (photo: John Cornish).

Maps by David Hibberd.

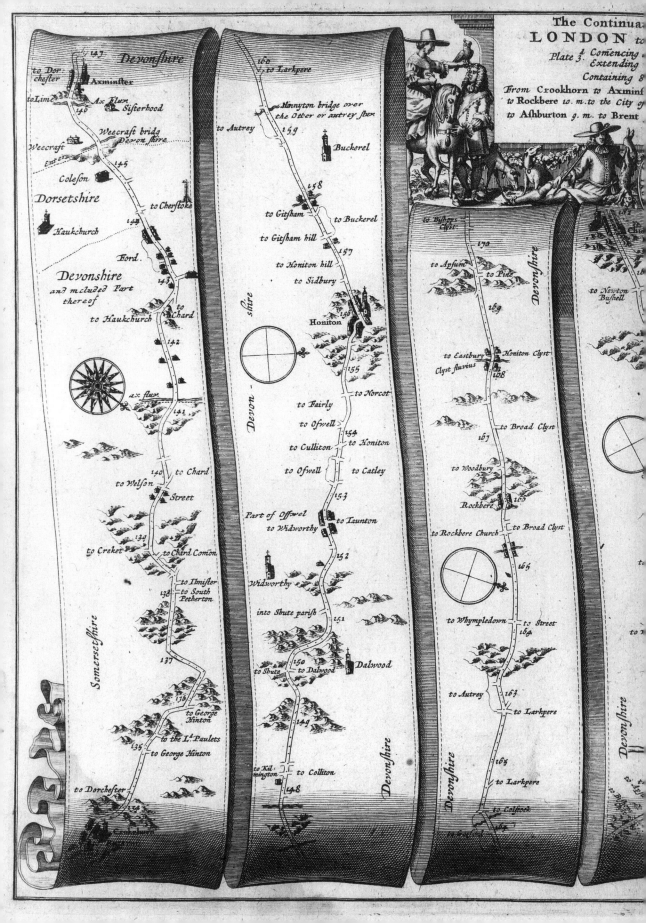

The Continua[tion]
LONDON to
Plate 3. Comencing
Extending
Containing 8
From Crookhorn to Axmin[ster]
to Rockbere 10. m. to the City of
to Aſhburton 9. m. to Brent

Strip 1 (left):

Devonſhire

147

to Dor-
cheſter . Axminſter

to Lime . Ax Flux
146 . Siſterhood

Weecraft bridg
Devonſhire

Weecraft
Ent 145

Coleſon

Dorſetſhire

144
Haukchurch . to Cherſtoke

Ford.

Devonſhire
and included Part
thereof

to Haukchurch 143 . to Chard

142

ax. flux.

141

to Welſon 140 . to Chard

Street

to Creket 139 . to Chard Comon

to Ilmiſter
138 . to South
Petherton

137

136

to George
Hinton
to the Ld. Paulets
135 . to George Hinton

to Dorcheſter

134

Strip 2:

160
to Larkpere

Minnyton bridge over
the Otter or autrey fluv.
159

to Autrey

Buckerel

158

to Gitſham . to Buckerel
to Gitſham hill
157
to Honiton hill
to Sidbury

156
Honiton

155

to Fairly . to Norcot
to Ofwell 154 . to Honiton
to Culliton
to Ofwell . to Catley

153

Part of Offwel
to Widworthy . to Taunton

152

Widworthy

into Shute pariſh 151

to Shute 150 . to Dalwood . Dalwood

149

to Kil-
mington . to Colliton
148

Devonſhire

Strip 3:

to Biſhops
Clyſt

170
to Apſum
to Pin . Devonſhire

169

to Eaſtbury . Honiton Clyſt
Clyſt fluvius
168

to Broad Clyſt
167
to Woodbury

Rockbere 166

to Rockbere Church . to Broad Clyſt

165

to Whympledown . to Street
164

to Autrey 164
to Larkpere

163

to Larkpere

to Colycock

Devonſhire

Strip 4 (right edge):

to Newton
Buſhell

Devonſhire